THE AUTHOR OF THE BOOK OF REVELATION
THE LORD JESUS CHRIST

THE
BOOK OF REVELATION

A Study of
The Last Prophetic Book
of Holy Scripture

By

CLARENCE LARKIN
Author of The Great Book on
"DISPENSATIONAL TRUTH"

Published by the
REV. CLARENCE LARKIN ESTATE
P. O. Box 334, Glenside, Pa. 19038
U. S. A.

ERWIN W. MOYER CO., PRINTERS
PHILADELPHIA, PA.

THIS BOOK IS
DEDICATED
TO THE AUTHOR OF THE
BOOK OF REVELATION
THE
LORD JESUS CHRIST
TRUSTING THAT ITS EXPOSITION
MAY MEET WITH HIS DIVINE
APPROVAL AND BLESSING

THE TABLE OF CONTENTS

CONTENTS.

ILLUSTRATIONS

FRONTISPIECE—THE PICTURE OF CHRIST
THE PATMOS VISION
THE BOOK OF REVELATION

CHARTS

MAPS

CONTENTS.

CUTS

FOREWORD

This work is the result of 25 years' study of the Book of Revelation. Twice within 6 years the writer gave a 4-months' course of Sunday morning sermons to his people on the Book. These lectures have also been given in Bible Institute Courses, illustrated with large, colored, wall charts.

The Book of Revelation is interpreted from the Futurist Standpoint. Chapters two and three cover the present Church Dispensation. From chapter four until the end of the Book all is future. The writer's purpose is to show that the Book of Revelation is to be taken literally, and that it is written in chronological order. The text of the Old Version is used and is printed at the top of each subject. The chapter and verse divisions are ignored. The text is emphasized by the use of capitals and black type. This helps to explain it and make it clear to the general reader. The descriptive matter of the book is emphasized in the same manner.

The book is also illustrated with over 30 charts, maps, and diagrams. Numerous cuts of symbols, beasts, etc., spoken of in the Book of Revelation are distributed through the book at the place where they are mentioned, and add greatly to its value by elucidating the text and saving much explanatory matter.

The make-up and printing of the book is unique. The writer has broken all rules of book-making in his desire to make the average reader see and grip the truth. This he has been able to do because of his skill as a draughtsman, and because the Printers of the book, who are lovers of the truth and like to see it "Rightly Divided," were in sympathy with the writer's purpose, and have done everything they could to make the "printer's art" express the writer's thought.

A book gotten up in this way is naturally more expensive to print than an ordinary book. The writer had to spend weeks and months in study and designing the charts, maps, diagrams, cuts, etc. These had to be inked in and lettered by hand. Then plates had to be made of the drawings, and electros of the plates. The emphasizing of the descriptive matter with black type costs extra, but all this trouble and expense makes the book doubly valuable. While there are but 210 pages in the book, the size of the type, and the enlarged page, 6 x 9 inches, make it equivalent to an ordinary book of 400 pages.

There is nothing fantastical in the book. It contains no speculative matter, nor opinions of the writer. The book is not a commentary made up of quotations from other writers. The writer is neither a copyist or compiler. The only Author the writer has sought to follow is the Author of the Book, the Lord Jesus Christ. Therefore the writer lays no claim to originality. All he has sought to do is to clearly present the **"MIND OF CHRIST"** as revealed in the Book, having in mind the **"CURSE"** to which every expositor of the Book subjects himself. "If any man shall **ADD** unto these things, God shall **ADD UNTO HIM** the 'PLAGUES' that are written in this Book, and if any man shall **TAKE AWAY** from the words of the 'Book of this Prophecy,' God shall **TAKE AWAY HIS PART OUT OF THE 'BOOK OF LIFE,' AND OUT OF THE HOLY CITY, AND FROM THE THINGS WHICH ARE WRITTEN IN THIS BOOK."** Rev. 22: 18-19.

The writer's aim has been to prepare a standard work on the Book of Revelation, from the Futurist Standpoint, that can be used as a text-book in Theological Seminaries and Bible Schools, and be of invaluable service to the busy pastor in his exposition of the Word of God. The book is sent out with the prayer that God will bless its testimony in these days when the prophetic utterances of the Book of Revelation are rapidly approaching their fulfilment.

CLARENCE LARKIN.

"Sunnyside"

THE BOOK OF REVELATION

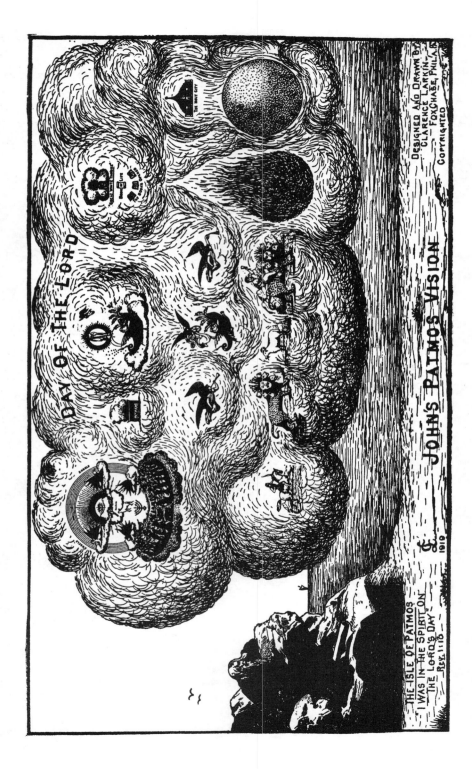

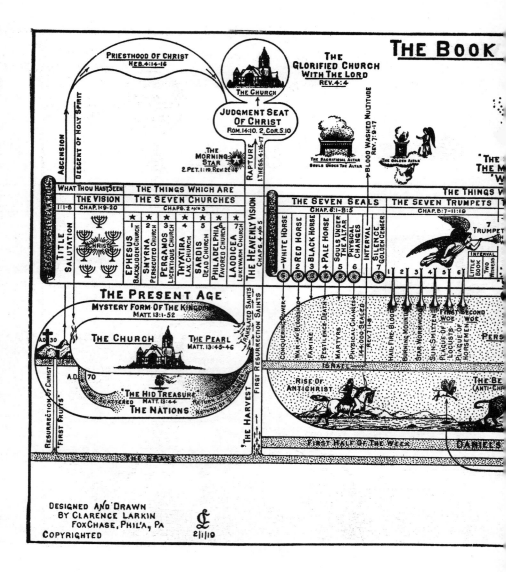

THE BOOK

PRIESTHOOD OF CHRIST
HEB.4:14-16

THE GLORIFIED CHURCH WITH THE LORD
REV.4:4

THE CHURCH

JUDGMENT SEAT OF CHRIST
ROM.14:10. 2.COR.5:10

THE MORNING STAR
2.PET.1:19.REV.22:16

BLOOD WASHED MULTITUDE
REV.7:9-17

THE SACRIFICIAL ALTAR
SOULS UNDER THE ALTAR

THE GOLDEN ALTAR

"THE
THE M
"W

ASCENSION
DESCENT OF HOLY SPIRIT

WHAT THOU HASTSEEN	THE THINGS WHICH ARE									THE THINGS V
THE VISION	THE SEVEN CHURCHES									THE SEVEN SEALS	THE SEVEN TRUMPETS
1:1-8 CHAP.1:9-20	CHAPS.2 AND 3									CHAP.6:1-8:5	CHAP.8:7-11:19

TITLE SALUTATION
CHRIST

★ EPHESUS BACKSLIDDEN CHURCH
★ 2 SMYRNA PERSECUTED CHURCH
★ 3 PERGAMOS LICENTIOUS CHURCH
+ 4 THYATIRA LAX CHURCH
5 SARDIS DEAD CHURCH
★ 6 PHILADELPHIA FAVORED CHURCH
7 LAODICEA LUKEWARM CHURCH

THE HEAVENLY VISION
CHAPS.4 AND 5

RAPTURE 1.THES.4:16-17

★ WHITE HORSE
② RED HORSE
3 BLACK HORSE
+ PALE HORSE
5 SOULS UNDER THE ALTAR
6 PHYSICAL CHANGES
INTERVAL
7 SILENCE GOLDEN CENSER

1 2 3 4 5 6 7 TRUMPET
INTERVAL LITTLE BOOK TWO WITNESS

THE PRESENT AGE
MYSTERY FORM OF THE KINGDOM
MATT.13:1-52

A.D. 30

THE CHURCH

THE PEARL
MATT.13:45-46

TRANSLATED SAINTS
FIRST RESURRECTION SAINTS

A.D. 70

THE HID TREASURE
MATT.13:44
SCATTERED RETURN
THE NATIONS

RESURRECTION OF CHRIST
"FIRST FRUITS"

"THE HARVEST"

CONQUERING POWER
WAR AND BLOODSHED
FAMINE
PESTILENCE DEATH
MARTYRS
PHYSICAL CHANGES
144,000 SEALED
REV.7:1-8

HAIL-FIRE-BLOOD
BURNING MOUNTAIN
STAR WORMWOOD
SUN-SMITTEN
PLAGUE OF LOCUSTS
PLAGUE OF HORSEMEN
FIRST WOE
SECOND WOE

ISRAEL

RISE OF ANTICHRIST

THE BE (ANTI-CHR

PERS

FIRST HALF OF THE WEEK

DANIELS

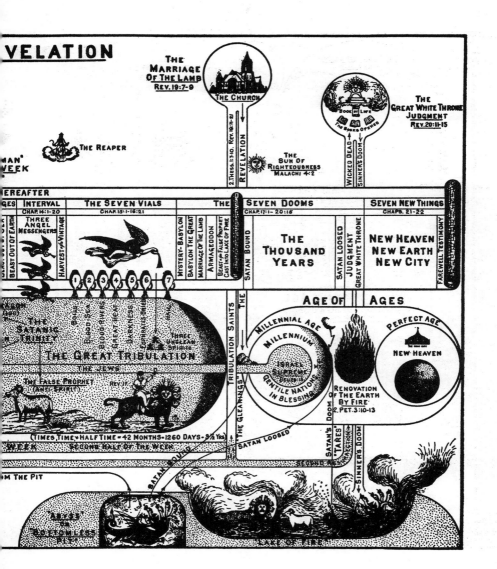

The Book of Revelation

THE TITLE.

"THE REVELATION OF

Jesus Christ,

WHICH GOD GAVE UNTO HIM, TO SHOW UNTO HIS
SERVANTS THINGS WHICH MUST SHORTLY
COME TO PASS;
AND HE SENT AND SIGNIFIED IT BY HIS
ANGEL UNTO HIS SERVANT

John:

WHO BARE RECORD OF THE WORD OF GOD,
AND OF THE TESTIMONY OF JESUS CHRIST,
AND OF ALL THINGS THAT HE SAW.

THE BLESSING.

BLESSED IS HE THAT 'READETH,'
AND THEY THAT 'HEAR' THE WORDS OF THIS
PROPHECY, AND 'KEEP' THOSE THINGS WHICH
ARE WRITTEN THEREIN:
FOR THE TIME IS AT HAND."
Rev. 1:1-3.

The "Title" of the Book describes its character. It is not **"The Revelation of St. John the Divine,"** as the heading in our Bibles would have us believe, but it is

"THE REVELATION OF JESUS CHRIST."

The word "Revelation" in the Greek is **"APOCALUPSIS."** Hence the title **"THE APOCALYPSE,"** by which it is often called. It is from the verb **"APOCALUPTO,"** to unveil; from **"APO,"** away from; and **"KALUMMA,"** a veil. Hence "Apocalupsis" means a taking away of a veil, as when a statue is unveiled, that what is behind the veil may be seen. It is not so much a revelation or unveiling of the Person of Christ, though it discloses His High Priestly and Kingly glory, as it is the unveiling of those events that shall precede and accompany His return to the earth. This is seen from the fact that what is revealed in the Book, was given unto Jesus Christ, by God the Father, to show unto His Servants the **"things which must shortly come to pass."**

When Jesus was asked just before His death, when the things that He had prophesied against Jerusalem should come to pass (Mark 13:1-31), He replied in verse 32, "But of that day and that hour knoweth no man, no, not the angels which are in Heaven, neither (NOT YET) the Son, but the FATHER." But after His Ascension He received from the Father the information that the Disciples asked for, and before the close of the first century, while at least one of those Disciples was still living, the beloved John, He sent an angel messenger to impart to him, and through him to the Churches, the information that is "unveiled" in this Book of Revelation. Thus we see that the canon of Scripture would be incomplete without this message from Jesus to His Church after His return to Heaven.

While the Apostle John is the writer of the Book he is not the author or composer. The Author was the Lord Jesus Himself. The Apostle was only a "scribe" or "amanuensis." Twice he declares that the contents of the Book were revealed to him by an angel. Rev. 1:1; 22:8. The fact that the style of the Book differs so strikingly from the other writings of John, as the Gospel and Epistles, is the strongest kind of evidence that John did not compose the Book, but that it was dictated or visualized to him. In its subject matter, and in the majesty and sublimity of its language, which is in harmony with its contents, the Book of Revelation differs from all other books, and is incomparably above them, thus revealing its Divine Authorship. In fact it is the only portion of the New Testament to which Jesus gives His endorsement, and affixes His signature, saying at its close—"I JESUS have sent Mine Angel to testify unto you these things in the Churches." Rev. 22:16.

The Book of Revelation then is not a compilation of Jewish "Apocalyptic Literature," intermixed with "Heathen Visions Christianized," thus being a "patchwork" of Jewish and Heathen Folklore, but it is the Revelation of Jesus Christ, which God gave unto Him, to show unto His servants things which must shortly come to pass. This He sent by His ANGEL. Who this Angel was we are not told, but when John fell down to worship him, he said, "See thou do it not: for I am thy fellowservant, and of thy brethren the prophets, and of them which keep the sayings of this book." Rev. 22:8-9. He must therefore have been one of the old prophets raised for the purpose.

The Book is a PROPHETIC Book. It is not a history. It does not record the past, but reveals the future. It makes this claim in the Title—"Blessed is he that readeth, and they that hear the words of THIS PROPHECY," Rev. 1:3; and four times in the concluding chapter. Rev. 22:7, 10, 18, 19. It is the summing up and consummation of all prophecy. In it all unfulfilled prophecy is fulfilled. It is the "finality" in prophecy until Jesus comes back. There has been no "new revelation" since it was written; and all those who claim to have received new and later "revelations" are impostors and false prophets. There is no place for "additions" or "subtractions" in the Book. It opens with a "blessing" promised the reader, and ends with a "curse" upon those who "ADD UNTO" or "TAKE FROM" it. Rev. 1:3; 22:18-19.

Nothing is said about understanding the Book, but blessed is he that "readeth," or if too illiterate to read, blessed are they that "hear," that is, listen to its reading. The reference here is doubtless to the "reader" and "hearers" of the Scripture as read in the Synagogue in the Apostle's day. That the Book should be shunned by many because of its mysterious character is no wonder. It is one of the "devices" of Satan to get people to neglect a Book that foretells his casting as "Prince of the Powers of the Air," and the "God of This Age," out of the Heavenlies; of his imprisonment in the "Bottomless Pit" for 1000 years; and his final casting into the Lake of Fire. While Satan hates all Scripture in general, he hates the books of Genesis and Revelation in particular. Therefore he attacks the authenticity of Genesis, and seeks to have Revelation neglected.

The Book is not only a "Prophetic" book, it is a "SYMBOLIC" book, that is, it is written largely in "symbolic" language, that is the meaning of the statement in the Title—"He sent and 'SIGNIFIED' it by His Angel unto His Servant John." The word "signified" means given in "signs" and "symbols" and should be pronounced "SIGN'-IFIED." There are more "signs" and "symbols" in the Book of Revelation than in any other book in the Bible, but they are either explained there or in some other part of the Scriptures. No one can understand the Book of Revelation who does not understand the Book of Daniel. The Prophet Daniel was told to "seal up" the words of his prophecy until the "Time of the End," not the "end of time," but the end of the "Times of the Gentiles." Dan. 12:4,9. But the writer of the Book of Revelation was told to "seal NOT" the sayings of the Book, for the TIME IS AT HAND. Rev. 22:10.

The symbolism of the Book of Revelation shows that it was written for a "special class," for those who are acquainted with the "Word of God," and who have "spiritual discernment," and not for the carnally minded reader. "The secret things belong unto the Lord our God, but those things which are REVEALED belong unto us and our children forever." Deu. 29:29. The Book of Revelation was written to reveal or disclose the purpose of God as to the earth and the nations, and we are not prying into God's secrets when we read and study it. It being the last prophecy, we naturally would expect it to sum up all previous prophecy, and as all previous prophecy had to do with the CHURCH, ISRAEL, and THE NATIONS, so we should expect this last prophecy to give us the final word as to them; and that is what it does. We find the CHURCH in the beginning, ISRAEL in the middle, and the saved NATIONS at the end. These three are also seen in the construction of the Holy City, New Jerusalem; where we have the CHURCH in the Foundation, represented by the names of the Twelve Apostles, and ISRAEL in the Gates, with the names of the Twelve Tribes of Israel written over them, and the saved NATIONS in the Streets, where they walk in the light of the City's Glory.

The Book is largely Jewish. This is seen in its "signs" and symbols, such as the Tabernacle, the Ark, the Altar, the Trumpets and Plagues, and the sealing of the 144,000 of Israel. It is Jewish because

God in it, after the Church is taken out, deals again with Israel, and in chapters 6 to 19 inclusive He reveals what shall take place during the last or "Seventieth Week" of Daniel's "Seventy Weeks."

It is the Book of "CONSUMMATION" and its proper place in the sacred canon is where it is placed, at the end of the Bible. The Book is full of ACTION. Earth and heaven are brought near together. The clouds roll away, thrones, elders, and angelic forms are seen; harps, trumpets, cries from disembodied souls and choruses of song are heard. Earth touches heaven, and alas it touches hell also. Good and evil meet. There is no blending, but sharp contrasts, and a long protracted conflict that ends in victory for the good, and the "BEAST," the "FALSE PROPHET," SATAN and his hosts, and "DEATH" and HADES find their place in the "Lake of Fire." It describes the culmination of the evils foreseen and described in I. Tim. 4:1; 2 Tim. 3:1-5; 2 Pet. 2:1-2; Jude 14-19, and declares the CONSUMMATION of that which the Prophets foretold, the creation of a

NEW HEAVEN AND A NEW EARTH

in which righteousness shall dwell. Isa. 65:17. At last the patience of the patriarchs and saints is rewarded; the longings of faith, and the hope of Israel and the Church fulfilled, and the glory of God shines unhindered on a scene of righteousness and peace. The Bible begins with Paradise LOST, and closes with Paradise REGAINED.

The Salutation.
Chap. 1:4-6.

"JOHN to the Seven Churches which are in Asia: Grace be unto you, and peace, from Him which Is, and which Was, and which IS TO COME; and from the 'Seven Spirits' which are before HIS Throne; and from Jesus Christ, who is the FAITHFUL WITNESS, and the FIRST BEGOTTEN OF THE DEAD, and the PRINCE OF THE KINGS OF THE EARTH. Unto Him that LOVED US and WASHED (Loosed) US from our sins in His own blood. And hath made us KINGS and PRIESTS unto God and His Father; to Him be glory and dominion for ever and ever. Amen."

The Salutation is addressed to the "Seven Churches Which Are In Asia." By Asia is not meant the great Continent of Asia, or even the whole of Asia Minor, but only the western end of Asia Minor bordering on the Aegean and Mediterranean Seas, and about the size of the State of Pennsylvania. Neither do these Seven Churches mean that there were only seven churches in that district, for there were at least three other churches, that of Colosse, Col. 1:2; Hierapolis, Col. 4:13; and Troas, Acts 20:6-7. These seven Churches then must be representative or typical churches, chosen for certain characteristics typical of the character of the Church of Christ, not only in that day, but on down the centuries until the Church shall be removed from the earth, and represent seven church periods clearly defined in Church History. This we shall see, in our study of chapters two and three, to be the case.

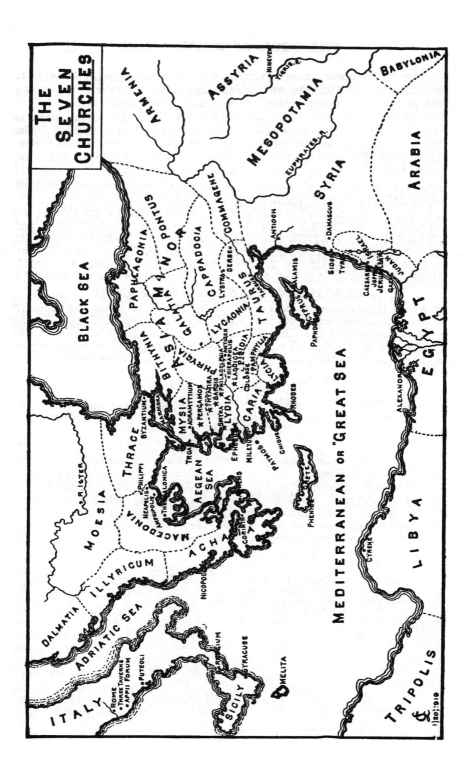

In the Benediction—"Grace be unto you, and peace, from Him which is, and which was, and which is to come; and from the Seven Spirits which are before His Throne; and from Jesus Christ, who is the Faithful Witness, etc.," we behold the Trinity. Here Jesus is distinguished from—"HIM (the Father) which Is, and which Was, and which Is To Come," but in verse 8, He claims the same Title, which only proves that Jesus was God manifest in the flesh, and that He and the Father are one.

It is also worthy of note that the "Threefold Office" of Jesus, as PROPHET, PRIEST, and KING is brought out in the Salutation. He is called the "Faithful Witness," as such he is a PROPHET. As the "First Begotten From The Dead," He carried His own blood into the Heavenly Tabernacle, and thus performed the work of a PRIEST. As the "Prince Of The Kings Of The Earth," as He will be when He takes the Throne, He will be a KING. As Prophet Jesus is God's WORD, as Priest He is God's LAMB, and as King He is God's LION.

John also emphasizes the fact that Jesus LOVED us before He WASHED (Loosed) us from our sins in His own blood, and that He has made us "Kings" and "Priests" unto God, and that we need no human Priest to stand between us and God.

The Announcement.

"Behold, He cometh with clouds; and every eye shall SEE HIM, and they also which PIERCED HIM: and all kindreds of the earth shall wail because of Him. Even so, Amen."
Rev. 1:7.

This refers to the Second Stage of Christ's Coming, the "Revelation" or "Appearing." The First Stage of His Coming, the "Rapture," is not mentioned in the Book. This will fulfil Zech. 12:10, "They (the Jews) shall look upon Me (Jesus) whom they have PIERCED." This is confirmatory of the view that the Book of Revelation deals mainly with the events that follow after the "Rapture" and precede and attend the "Revelation" or the coming to the earth of the Lord.

It is difficult to imagine the grief and remorse that will fill the hearts of those Jews who shall witness the return of the Lord to the Mount of Olives, when they shall see in His hands and feet the "PRINT OF THE NAILS," and He shall be revealed as the One they crucified. Like Thomas they will cry, "MY LORD AND MY GOD." John 20:24-29. The Prophet Zechariah (Zech. 12:9-14) describes it as a time of great "BITTERNESS" and a day of great mourning in Jerusalem, when families will separate themselves from their neighbors and mourn every family apart. And not only shall the Jews mourn because they rejected Him when He came the first time, but the nations of the earth will WAIL when they realize that He has come back, not as a Saviour, but a Judge to punish them for their iniquities.

I
The Things Which Thou Hast Seen

I. The Things Which Thou Hast Seen

THE VISION.

"I John, who also am your brother, and companion in tribulation, and in the Kingdom and patience of Jesus Christ, was in the Isle that is called Patmos, for the word of God, and for the testimony of Jesus Christ. I was in the SPIRIT on the LORD'S DAY, and heard behind me a great voice, as of a Trumpet, saying, I am ALPHA and OMEGA, the FIRST and the LAST: and, What thou SEEST, write in a book, and send it unto the Seven Churches which are in Asia; unto Ephesus, and unto Smyrna, and unto Pergamos, and unto Thyatira, and unto Sardis, and unto Philadelphia, and unto Laodicea. And I turned to to see the voice that spake with me. And being turned, I saw

SEVEN GOLDEN CANDLESTICKS;

and in the midst of the Seven Candlesticks one like unto the

SON OF MAN,

clothed with a garment down to the foot, and girt about the paps (breast) with a golden girdle. His Head and his Hairs were white like wool, as white as snow; and His Eyes were as a flame of fire; and His Feet like unto fine brass, as if they burned in a furnace; and His Voice as the sound of many waters. And He had in His Right Hand "Seven Stars"; and out of His Mouth went a sharp two edged Sword; and His Countenance was as the sun shineth in his strength. And when I saw Him, I fell at His feet as dead. And He laid His Right Hand upon me, saying unto me, "Fear not; I am the FIRST and the LAST: I am He that LIVETH, and WAS DEAD; and behold, I am ALIVE FOR EVERMORE, AMEN; and have the KEYS of HELL (Hades, the Underworld), and of DEATH (the Grave). Write the things which thou hast SEEN, and the things which ARE, and the things which shall be HEREAFTER (after these); the Mystery of the 'Seven Stars' which thou sawest in my right hand, and the 'Seven Golden Candlesticks.' The 'Seven Stars' are the ANGELS (Messengers) of the 'Seven Churches': and the 'Seven Candlesticks' which thou sawest are the SEVEN CHURCHES."

Rev. 1 : 9-20.

The Apostle John addresses the Churches as their brother and companion in TRIBULATION. This does not mean "The Great Tribulation," for that is not for the Church but for Israel, and is still future. When John wrote the Book of Revelation in A. D. 95-96 the Christians were undergoing a persecution under the Roman Emperor Domitian, and as a result of this persecution John had been banished to the Isle of Patmos, a small, rocky island in the Aegean Sea 30 miles off the west coast of Asia Minor, and opposite the city of Ephesus. John was pastor of the Church at Ephesus at the time of his banishment, and it was to that Church that the first Message to the Seven Churches was addressed. John was banished for "the Word of God, and his testimony to Jesus Christ."

He tells us that he was "in the Spirit on the LORD'S DAY." There has been much confusion as to what is meant here by the "Lord's Day" Some hold that the "First Day of the Week" or the Christian Sabbath is meant, others that John meant the "Day of the Lord."

Both the Old and the New Testament speak of the "Day of the Lord." Isa. 2 : 12, Joel 1 : 15, 2 : 1, 3 : 14, Ezek. 13 : 5, Malachi 4 : 5, Acts 2 : 20, 2. Cor. 1 : 14, 1. Thess. 5 : 2, 2. Pet. 3 : 10. The term applies to the "Day of the Lord's Return" and includes both the Tribulation and the Millennium. See the Chart on the Prophetic Days of Scripture. The Christian Sabbath was never called the "LORD'S DAY" until after the Book of Revelation was written and got its name from that source. It is always called in the Gospels and Epistles the "First Day of the Week."

It is hardly likely that John could have been caught up as Paul was into the Third Heaven and seen and heard all that he describes in the Book of Revelation on one Sabbath Day, and as the Book from chapter 5 is a description of the things that are to come to pass in the "DAY OF THE LORD," what better understanding of the "LORD'S DAY" can we have than that John was projected by the Holy Spirit across the centuries into the "DAY OF THE LORD" and had visualized to him the things that shall come to pass in that day. This is the rational solution of the question. See the Chart, John's Patmos Vision.

When John thus found himself in the "Day of the Lord" he heard behind him a great voice, as of a trumpet, which said—"I am Alpha and Omega, the First and the Last," and the repetition of the statement in verses 17 and 18, with the added words—"I am He that Liveth, and WAS DEAD; and behold, I am ALIVE FOR EVERMORE, AMEN; and have the keys of Hell (Hades, the Underworld), and of Death (the Grave)," identifies the speaker as the Lord Jesus Christ Himself. John had his back turned to the speaker, and when he turned around he saw one like unto the

SON OF MAN

standing in the midst of "Seven Candlesticks." "LAMPSTANDS" is a better translation and is so given in the margin of our Bibles. A candlestick requires a light such as a candle, which is self-consuming, while a "Lampstand" is for the support of a lamp whose wick instead of burning away is fed from the oil within. In the Scriptures oil is emblematic of the Holy Spirit, and as Jesus Himself interprets the "Lampstands" as meaning the Seven Churches to whom He was about to send messages, we see that Jesus looks upon the churches as not the LIGHT, but simply the "LIGHT HOLDER." From the fact that Jesus speaks of "Stars" and "Lampstands" it is clear that we are living in the NIGHT of this Dispensation, for "stars" and "lampstands" belong to the night.

THE VISION OF THE GLORIFIED SON OF MAN.

The Vision that John saw was that of the GLORIFIED "SON OF MAN." When Jesus ascended He took up with Him His HUMANITY, and we now have in the Glory the MAN Christ Jesus. 1. Tim. 2:5. When Jesus was on the earth He was, as the "Son of Man," a PROPHET, now as the "Son of Man" in Glory He is a Priest, and when He comes again it will be as the "Son of Man" to reign as KING.

While Jesus is now a High Priest in heaven, John did not see Him engaged in any High Priestly work. While He was clothed in a High Priestly robe, there was no mitre upon His head, nor

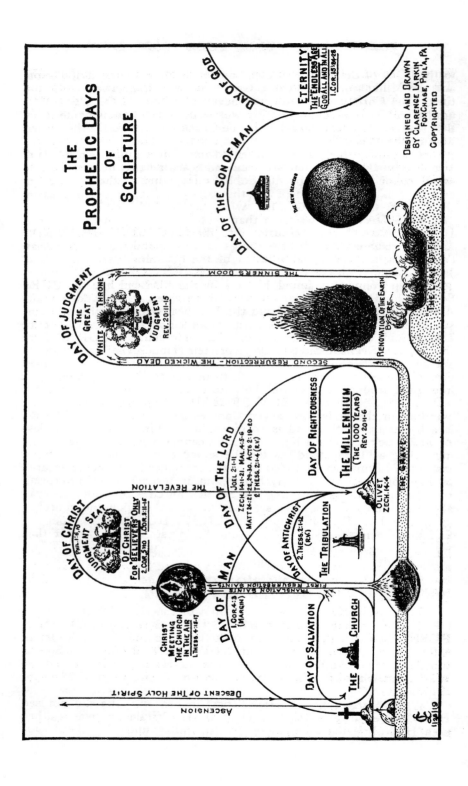

THE PROPHETIC DAYS OF SCRIPTURE

Designed and Drawn by Clarence Larkin, Fox Chase, Phila., Pa. Copyrighted

Kingly Crown. The description of Him is more that of a **JUDGE.**
This is confirmatory evidence that John was transported into the
"Day of the Lord," and that his vision of Christ is as Christ shall
appear after His High Priestly work is finished and before He
assumes His Kingly Office. This is seen in that He was girded
about the breasts, and not around the waist. The High Priest was
girded around the waist, signifying service, but a girdle or sash over
the shoulder and around the breasts is an insignia of the Magis-
terial Office. This is still further revealed when we study the

SEVENFOLD GLORY OF HIS PERSON.

1. HIS "HEAD AND HIS HAIR."

His "Head" and "Hair" were **"WHITE LIKE WOOL,"** as
"WHITE AS SNOW." Here there is a correspondence to the "Snow
White Wig" worn by English judges. This description of Christ
reminds us of Daniel's vision of the **"ANCIENT OF DAYS,"** "whose
garment was white as snow, and the hair of his head like the **PURE
WOOL."** Dan. 7:9. Daniel refers three times to the "Ancient Of
Days." In Chap. 7:13, he distinguishes between the "Son of Man"
and the "Ancient of Days," but in verses 9 and 22 he associates the
"Ancient of Days" with a "Throne of Judgment," and as God the
Father has committed all judgment to the Son (John 5:22), and the
Father and the Son are one, the title "Ancient Of Days" is used
interchangeably. And as the title "Ancient of Days" is applied to
the "Son of Man" (Christ) at the time He assumes the Judgeship
(Dan. 7:9-10), which is not until after the Rapture of the Church,
we have here additional corroborative proof that John's Vision
belongs to the "Day of the Lord." The "White Hair" of the Son
of Man refers to His **ANTIQUITY,** to His patriarchal dignity, not
that His hair was made white by age, for the Eternal never grows
old, but it bespeaks wisdom and experience, and the venerableness
of His character.

2. HIS EYES.

"His Eyes were a **FLAME OF FIRE.**" Those eyes that had
often been dimmed with human tears, and that wept at the grave of
Lazarus, are here pictured as burning with an **"OMNISCIENT
FLAME."** How often when on the earth those eyes read the inner-
most thoughts of men, and even soldiers quailed before His soul pene-
trating gaze, so when He sits as the Judge of men all things will be
NAKED and **OPEN** before Him.

3. HIS FEET.

"His Feet like unto fine **BRASS,** as if they **BURNED IN A
FURNACE.**" In that day those feet that trod the Via Dolorosa of
suffering will be like unto **INCANDESCENT BRASS,** that shall
tread and crush Antichrist and Satan when He comes to "Tread the
WINE-PRESS of the fierceness and wrath of Almighty God." Rev.
19:15.

4. HIS VOICE.

"His Voice as the **SOUND OF MANY WATERS.**" There is
nothing more melodious or musical than the babbling brook, or more

thunderous than the rush of the cataract over the falls, and there is nothing more fearful to the criminal than the words of the Judge as he passes sentence; but how terrifying will be the sentence when with a strong voice the Son of Man shall say in the Judgment Day, "Depart from me, ye cursed, into everlasting fire, prepared for the Devil and his angels." Matt. 25:41.

5. HIS HAND.

"In His Right Hand SEVEN STARS."

We are told in verse 20, that the "Seven Stars" stand for the "ANGELS" of the "Seven Churches." These "Angels" are not angelic beings but the Messengers or Ministers of the churches. What a beautiful and solemn lesson is taught here. It is that the ministers of Christ derive their power and office from Him, and that He holds them in His hand. If they are false to Him, no one can deliver them from His power, and if they are true and loyal, no one can touch or molest, or do them harm.

6. HIS MOUTH.

"Out of His Mouth went a SHARP TWO-EDGED SWORD." While the "Sword of the Spirit" is the "Word of God" (Eph. 6:17), and the "Word of God" is quick, and powerful, and sharper than any TWO-EDGED SWORD, piercing even to the dividing asunder of soul and spirit, and of the joints and marrow (the body), (Heb. 4:12), that is not the sword meant here.

The "Sword of the Spirit" is the Holy Spirit's SWORD, and He alone wields it. The sword meant here is the Sword of the Son of Man (Christ), and it is the "SWORD OF JUSTICE," for the Son of Man, out of whose mouth this sword comes, is the "White Horse Rider" of Rev. 19:11-15, "out of whose mouth goeth a SHARP SWORD, that with it He should smite the nations." And that sword, like the "Sword of the Spirit" will be TWO-EDGED also, for the protection of His people, and the destruction of His enemies. This is still further proof that John's vision of Christ was as He shall appear in the "DAY OF THE LORD."

7. HIS COUNTENANCE.

"His Countenance was as the SUN SHINETH IN HIS STRENGTH." This recalls to our memory His appearance on the Mount of Transfiguration when "His Face did shine AS THE SUN," Matt. 17:2. And we read of the New Jerusalem that the inhabitants thereof have no need of the SUN, for the LAMB is the Light thereof. Rev. 21:23. And when we recall that the Prophet Malachi tells us that when Jesus comes back He will be the SUN OF RIGHTEOUSNESS (Malachi 4:2), we see that John's vision of the Son of Man was as He shall appear at the Second Stage of His Return, the "Revelation." Thus we have in John's "Seven-Fold" description of the person of the "Glorified Son of Man" circumstantial or indirect evidence that John saw his vision of the Son of Man, not on a Sabbath Day (or the "Lord's Day" as we now call it), but was projected by the Holy Spirit forward into the "Day of the Lord" and saw Him as He will appear then as the Judge, and the coming "SUN OF RIGHTEOUSNESS."

The "Key" to the Book.

The "Key" to the Book is its
"THREE-FOLD DIVISION."
Rev. 1:19

1. The Things Which Thou Hast "SEEN."
2. The Things Which "ARE."
3. The Things Which "SHALL BE HEREAFTER."

This is the only book in the Bible where the Divisions are given, and they are here given by Christ Himself.

1. The Things Which Thou Hast "SEEN."

The Vision of the Son of Man in the midst of the "Seven Lampstands." Rev. 1:10-20.

2. The Things Which "ARE."

The Messages to the Seven Churches, Rev. 2:1-3; 22. As these Messages were to seven churches that were in existence in John's day, and to whom he personally wrote, the advocates of the theory that John was in the Spirit on a certain Sabbath or "Lord's Day," naturally claim that John at that time could not have been transported into the "Day of the Lord." But that does not necessarily follow. As we now know (see exposition of chapters 2 and 3) those Churches were REPRESENTATIVE CHURCHES, and were typical of seven well defined periods in Church History, that could not be so understood until the history of the Christian Church would be complete, and that will not be until the "Day of the Lord," so John could have been projected in vision by the Spirit into the "Day of the Lord," and after his Vision of the Glorified Son of Man, the "Messages to the Seven Churches" were dictated to him by the Son of Man Himself, that John when he recovered from his vision and found himself back on the Isle of Patmos could send them to the churches.

3. The Things Which "SHALL BE HEREAFTER."

Literally—"after these." In other words the "Things" which shall come to pass after the "Church Period" ends.

The Book naturally divides into

Seven Sevens.

I. THE SEVEN CHURCHES. Rev. 2:1-3:22.
II. THE SEVEN SEALS. Rev. 6:1-8:5.
III. THE SEVEN TRUMPETS. Rev. 8:7-11:19.
IV. THE SEVEN PERSONAGES. Rev. 12:1-13:18.
V. THE SEVEN VIALS. Rev. 15:1-16:21.
VI. THE SEVEN DOOMS. Rev. 17:1-20:15.
VII. THE SEVEN NEW THINGS. Rev. 21:1-22:5.

Between these series of "Sevens," and between some of the parts of a series there are Parenthetical Statements and Episodes or Intervals, as seen in the following Table of Contents.

Table of Contents

Daniel's Seventieth Week

The Angel Warning
"Three Woes" Announced. Rev. 8:13.

FIFTH TRUMPET.
FIRST WOE—Plague of Locusts. Rev. 9:1-12.

SIXTH TRUMPET.
SECOND WOE— Plague of Horseman. Rev. 9:13-21.

INTERVAL
Between The Sixth And Seventh Trumpets
(1) Little Book. Rev. 10:1-11.
(2) Two Witnesses. Rev. 11:1-14.

SEVENTH TRUMPET.
THIRD WOE—Cover Remainder of the Week.
And Includes the "Seven Personages"
The "Seven Vials" and "Four Dooms."
Rev. 11:15-20:10.

THE MIDDLE OF THE WEEK.

3. THE SEVEN PERSONAGES.

FIRST PER. The Sun-Clothed Women. Rev. 12:1-2.
SECOND PER. The Dragon. Rev. 12:3-4.
THIRD PER. The Man-Child. Rev. 12:5-6.
FOURTH PER. The Archangel. Rev. 12:7-12.
FIFTH PER. The Jewish Remnant. Rev. 12:13-17.
SIXTH PER. The Beast Out of the Sea. Rev. 13:1-10.
SEVEN PER. The Beast Out of the Earth. Rev. 13:11-18.

INTERVAL
Between The "Seven Personages"
And The "Seven Vials."
(1). The Lamb On Mt. Zion. Rev. 14:1-5.
(2). The Three Angel Messengers. Rev. 14:6-7.
(3). The Blessed Dead. Rev. 14:12-13.
(4). The Harvest And Vintage. Rev. 14:14–20.

---

4. THE SEVEN VIALS.

Prelude. Rev. 15:1.
(1). The Sea Of Glass. Rev. 15:2-4.
(2.) The Tabernacle Of Testimony. Rev. 15:5-8.

THE THINGS WHICH THOU HAST SEEN.

FIRST VIAL. Boils. Rev. 16:1-2.
SECOND VIAL. Blood On The Sea. Rev. 16:3.
THIRD VIAL. Blood On The Rivers. Rev. 16:4-7.
FOURTH VIAL. Great Heat. Rev. 16:8-9.
FIFTH VIAL. Darkness. Rev. 16:10-11.
SIXTH VIAL. Euphrates Dried Up. Rev. 16:12.

INTERVAL
Between The Sixth And Seventh Vials
Three Unclean Spirits. Rev. 16:13-16.

SEVENTH VIAL. Great Hail. Rev. 16:17-21.

5. THE SEVEN DOOMS.

FIRST DOOM—Ecclesiastical Babylon. Rev. 17:1-18.
SECOND DOOM—Commercial Babylon. Rev. 18:1-24.

INTERVAL
Between The Second And Third Dooms.
(1). The Hallelujah Chorus. Rev. 19:1-7.
(2). The Marriage Of The Lamb. Rev. 19:8-10.
(3). The Battle Of Armageddon. Rev. 19:11-21.

THIRD DOOM—The Antichrist And The False Prophet.
Rev. 19:20.
FOURTH DOOM—The Antichristian Nations. Rev. 19:21.

INTERVAL
Between The Fourth And Fifth Dooms
(1). Satan Bound. Rev. 20:1-3.
(2). First Resurrection. Rev. 20:4-5.
(3). The Millennium. Rev. 20:6.
(4). Satan Loosed. Rev. 20:7.

FIFTH DOOM—Gog and Magog. Rev. 20:8-9.
SIXTH DOOM—Satan. Rev. 20:10.
SEVENTH DOOM—The Wicked Dead. Rev. 20:11-15.

6. THE SEVEN NEW THINGS.

FIRST NEW THING—The New Heaven. Rev. 21:1.
SECOND NEW THING—The New Earth. Rev. 21:2-8.
THIRD NEW THING—The New City. Rev. 21:9-23.
FOURTH NEW THING—The New Nations. Rev. 21:24-27.
FIFTH NEW THING—The New River. Rev. 22:1.
SIXTH NEW THING—The New Tree. Rev. 22:2.
SEVENTH NEW THING—The New Throne. Rev. 22:3-5.

The Final Testimony And Warnings. Rev. 22:6-21.

II
The Things Which Are

II. The Things Which Are

THE MESSAGES TO THE SEVEN CHURCHES.

It is worthy of note that the "Messages to the Seven Churches" are inserted between **Two Visions,** the **"Vision of Christ"** in the midst of the "Seven Lampstands" in chapter one and the **"Vision of the Four and Twenty Elders"** round about the Throne, in chapter four.

As chapter four is a vision of the **"Glorified Church"** with the Lord, after it has been caught out (1 Thess. 4: 13-17), then the Second Division of the Book—

"The Things Which Are,"

and which includes chapters two and three, must be a description or prophetic outline of the "Spiritual History" of the Church from the time when John wrote the Book in A. D. 96, down to the taking out of the Church, or else we have no "prophetic view" of the Church during that period, for she disappears from the earth at the close of chapter three, and is not seen again until she reappears with her Lord in chapter nineteen. This we shall find to be the case. See Chart of the Book of Revelation.

This interpretation of the "Messages to the Seven Churches" was hidden to the early Church, ·because time was required for Church History to develop and be written, so a comparison could be made to reveal the correspondence. If it had been clearly revealed that the Seven Churches stood for "Seven Church Periods" that would have to elapse before Christ could come back, the incentive to watch would have been absent.

While the character of these Seven Churches is descriptive of the Church during seven periods of her history, we must not forget that the condition of those churches, as described, were their exact condition in John's day. So we see that at the close of the First Century the leaven of "False Doctrine" was at work in the Churches. The churches are given in the order named, because the peculiar characteristic of that Church applied to the period of Church History to which it is assigned. It also must not be forgotten, that, that which is a distinctive characteristic of each Church Period, does not disappear with that Period, but continues on down through the next Period, and so on until the end, thus increasing the imperfections of the visible Church, until it ends in an open Apostasy, as shown on the chart— "The Messages to the Seven Churches Compared with Church History."

It is noteworthy that the "Salutation" to each Church contains a reference to some characteristic of the Son of Man as described in chapter one. We will now consider each message separately.

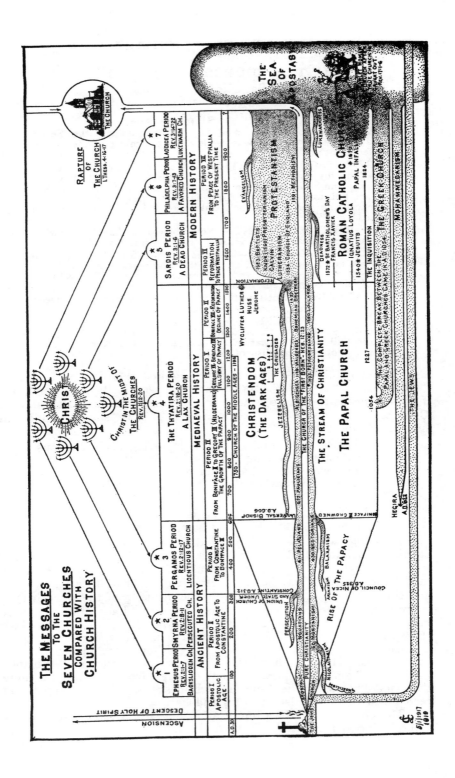

THE MESSAGES
TO THE
SEVEN CHURCHES
COMPARED WITH
CHURCH HISTORY

I. THE CHURCH AT EPHESUS.
(A Backslidden Church.)
Rev. 2: 1-7.

1. **THE SALUTATION**—"Unto the Angel of the Church of Ephesus write; these things saith He that **holdeth the 'Seven Stars' in His right hand, who walketh in the midst of the 'Seven Golden Candlesticks'."**

2. **THE COMMENDATION**—"I know thy **works,** and thy **labor,** and thy **patience,** and how thou canst not bear them which are evil; and thou hast tried them which say they are Apostles, and are not, and hast found them liars; and hast borne, and hast patience, and for **My Name's Sake** hast labored, and hast not fainted."

3. **THE COMPLAINT**—"Nevertheless I have somewhat against thee, because thou **Hast Left Thy First Love."**

4. **THE WARNING**—"Remember therefore **from whence thou art fallen, and repent, and do the first works;** or else I will come unto thee quickly, and will **remove thy CANDLESTICK out of his place,** except thou repent."

5. **PRAISE**—"But this thou hast, that thou **hatest** the deeds of the Nicolaitanes, which **I also hate."**

6. **THE PROMISE**—"He that hath an ear, let him hear what the **SPIRIT saith unto the Churches:** To him that **overcometh** will I give to **eat of the TREE OF LIFE,** which is in the midst of the Paradise of God."

The complaint that Christ makes against this Church is that it **"had left its First Love."** Its character is seen in its very name, for Ephesus means to "let go," "to relax." It had become a **Backslidden Church.** Paul, who founded it, warned it of what should happen, in his parting message.

"I know this, that after my departing shall grievous 'wolves' enter in among you, not sparing the flock. Also of your own selves shall men arise, 'speaking perverse things,' to draw away disciples after them." Acts 20: 29, 30.

The significance of this warning is seen in the commendation of the Message, vs. 6—"But this thou hast, that thou 'hatest' the deeds of the Nicolaitanes which I also hate." Here Paul's "wolves" are called Nicolaitanes. They were not a sect, but a party in the Church who were trying to establish a "Priestly Order." Probably trying to model the Church after the Old Testament order of Priests, Levites, and common people. This is seen in the meaning of the word, which is from "Niko" to conquer, to overthrow, and "Laos" the people or laity. The object was to establish a "Holy Order of Men," and place them over the laity, which was foreign to the New Testament plan, and call them not pastors, but—Clergy, Bishops, Archbishops, Cardinals, Popes. Here we have the origin of the dogma of "Apostolic Succession," and the separation of the Clergy from the Laity, a thing that God "hates." The Church at Ephesus was not deceived, but recognized them as false apostles and liars.

The character of the Church at Ephesus is a fair outline of the Church Period from A. D. 70 to A. D. 170.

II. THE CHURCH AT SMYRNA.
(A Persecuted Church.)
Rev. 2:8-11.

1. THE SALUTATION—"And unto the Angel of the Church in Smyrna write; These things saith the First and the Last, who was dead, and is alive."

2. THE PERSECUTION—"I know thy works, and TRIBULATION, and poverty, (but thou art rich), and I know the blasphemy of them which say, they are Jews, and are not, but are the 'Synagogue of Satan'."

3. THE EXHORTATION—"Fear none of those things which thou shalt suffer: behold the Devil shall cast some of you into prison, that ye may be tried; and ye shall have TRIBULATION ten days: be thou faithful UNTO death, and I will give thee a CROWN OF LIFE."

4. THE PROMISE—"He that hath an ear, let him hear what the Spirit saith unto the Churches: He that overcometh shall not be hurt of the SECOND DEATH."

The Church in its "Ephesian Period" having lost its "First Love," the Lord is now about to "chastise" it, so as to cause it to return to Him. Smyrna has for its root meaning "bitterness," and means "Myrrh," an ointment associated with death, and we see in the meaning of the word a prophecy of the persecution and death which was to befall the members of the Smyrna Church. They were told not to "fear" the things that they should be called on to suffer, but to be faithful "unto" death, not "until" death. That is, not until the end of their "natural" life. They were not to "recant" when called upon to face a Martyr's death, but remain faithful until death relieved them of their suffering. The reward would be a "Crown of Life." This is the Martyr's crown.

They were told that the "author" of their suffering would be the Devil, and its duration would be "ten days," which was doubtless a prophetic reference to the "Ten Great Persecutions" under the Roman Emperors, beginning with Nero, A. D. 64, and ending with Diocletian in A. D. 310. Seven of these "Great Persecutions" occurred during this "Smyrna Period" of Church History. Or it may refer to the 10 years of the last and fiercest persecution under Diocletian. This Period extended from A. D. 170 to Constantine A. D. 312.

See the Judgment of Reward Chart.

III. THE CHURCH AT PERGAMOS.
(A Licentious Church.)
Rev. 2:12-17.

1. THE SALUTATION—"And to the Angel of the Church in Pergamos write: These things saith He which hath the Sharp Sword with two edges.

2. THE COMMENDATION—"I know thy works, and where thou dwellest, even where SATAN'S SEAT IS: and thou holdest fast My Name, and hast not denied My Faith, even in those days wherein Antipas was My faithful martyr, who was slain among you, where Satan dwelleth.

3. THE COMPLAINT—"But I have a few things against thee, because thou hast there them that hold the DOCTRINE

OF BALAAM, who taught Balak to cast a stumbling block before the Children of Israel, to **eat things sacrificed unto idols,** and to **commit fornication.** So hast thou also them that hold the **DOCTRINE OF THE NICOLAITANES,** which thing I hate.

4. **THE WARNING**—"Repent! or else I will come unto thee quickly, and will fight against them with the **SWORD OF MY MOUTH.**

5. **THE PROMISE**—"He that hath an ear, let him hear what the Spirit saith unto the Churches; To him that overcometh will I give to **eat of the HIDDEN MANNA,** and will give him a **WHITE STONE,** and in the stone a **NEW NAME** written,** which no man knoweth saving he that receiveth it."

In this Message Pergamos is spoken of as "Satan's Seat." When Attalus III, the Priest-King of the Chaldean Hierarchy, fled before the conquering Persians to Pergamos, and settled there, Satan shifted his capital from Babylon to Pergamos. At first he persecuted the followers of Christ, and Antipas was one of the martyrs. But soon he changed his tactics and began to exalt the Church, and through Constantine united the Church and State, and offered all kinds of inducements for worldly people to come into the Church. Constantine's motive was more political than religious. He wished to weld his Christian and Pagan subjects into one people, and so consolidate his Empire. The result of this union was that two false and pernicious doctrines crept into the Church. The first was the "Doctrine of Balaam," and the second the "Doctrine of the Nicolaitanes." The latter we have already considered under the Message to the Church at Ephesus. And the foothold it had secured in the Church was seen in the First Great Council of the Church held at Nicaea, in A. D. 325. The Council was composed of about 1500 delegates, the laymen outnumbering the Bishops 5 to 1. It was a stormy council, full of intrigue and political methods, and from the supremacy of the "Clergy" over the "Laity" it was evident that the "Doctrine of the Nicolaitanes" had secured a strong and permanent foothold.

The "Doctrine of Balaam" is disclosed in the story of Balaam found in the Book of Numbers, chapters 22 to 25 inclusive. When the Children of Israel on their way to Canaan had reached the land of Moab, Balak the king of Moab sent for Balaam the Son of Beor, who lived at Pethor on the river Euphrates, to come and curse them. When the Lord would not permit Balaam to curse Israel, he suggested to Balak that he invite them to the licentious feasts of "Baal-Peor," and thus cause Israel to fall into a snare that would so anger the Lord that he would Himself destroy them. This Balak did, and the result was that when the men of Israel went to those sensual feasts and saw the "daughters of Moab" they committed whoredoms with them, which so kindled God's anger that He sent a plague that destroyed 42,000 of them. Now the word "Pergamos" means "Marriage," and when the Church entered into a union with the State it was guilty of "Spiritual Fornication" or "Balaamism."

The "Balaam Method" that Constantine employed was to give to the Bishops of the Church a number of imposing buildings called Basilicas for conversion into churches, for whose decoration he was lavish in the gift of money. He also supplied superb vestments for the clergy, and soon the Bishop found himself clad in costly vestments, seated on a lofty throne in the apse of the Basilica, with a marble altar, adorned with gold and gems, on a lower level in front of him. A sensuous form of worship was introduced, the character of the preaching was changed, and the great "Pagan Festivals" were adopted, with but little alteration, to please the Pagan members of the church, and attract Pagans to the church. For illustration, as the Winter Solstice falls on the 21st day of December, which is the shortest day in the year, and it is not until the 25th that the day begins to lengthen, which day was regarded throughout the Heathen world as the "birthday" of the "Sun-God," and was a high festival, which was celebrated at Rome by the "Great Games" of the Circus, it was found advisable to change the Birthday of the Son of God, from April, at which time He was probably born, to December 25th, because as He was the "Sun of Righteousness," what more appropriate birthday could He have than the birthday of the Pagan "Sun-God"?

It was at this time that

"Post-Millennial Views"

had their origin. As the Church had become rich and powerful, it was suggested that by the union of Church and State a condition of affairs would develop that would usher in the Millennium without the return of Christ, and since some scriptural support was needed for such a doctrine, it was claimed that the Jews had been cast off "forever," and that all the prophecies of Israel's future glory were intended for the Church. This "Period" extends from the accession of Constantine A. D. 312 to A. D. 606, when Boniface III was crowned "Universal Bishop."

IV. THE CHURCH AT THYATIRA.
(A Lax Church.)
Rev. 2:18-29.

1. **THE SALUTATION**—"And unto the Angel of the Church in Thyatira write: These things saith the Son of God, who hath His eyes like unto a **flame of fire,** and His feet are like **fine brass.**

2. **THE COMMENDATION**—"I know thy **works,** and **charity,** and **service,** and **faith,** and thy **patience,** and thy **works;** and the last to be more than the first.

3. **THE COMPLAINT**—"Notwithstanding I have a few things against thee, **because thou sufferest that woman JEZEBEL,** which calleth herself a **Prophetess,** to **teach** and to **seduce** my servants to **commit fornication,** and to **eat things sacrificed unto idols.** And I gave her space to repent of her fornication: and she repented not. Behold, I will cast her into a bed, and them that commit adultery with her into great tribulation, except they repent of their deeds. And I will kill her children with death; and all the churches shall know that I am He which searcheth the reins and hearts: and I will give unto every one of you according to your works."

4. **THE PROMISE**—"But unto you I say, and unto the rest in Thyatira, as many as have not this doctrine, and which have not known the depths of Satan, as they speak; I will put upon you none other burden. But that which ye have already,

hold fast till I come. And he that overcometh, and keepeth my works unto the end, to him will I give power over the nations: and he shall rule them with a rod of iron; as the vessels of a potter shall they be broken to shivers: even as I received of My Father. And I will give him the MORNING STAR. He that hath an ear, let him hear what the Spirit saith unto the Churches."

In His commendation of this Church, Christ lays the emphasis on their "works," as if they depended on them, and claimed they deserved merit for "works" of "Supererogation." But He had a complaint to make against them that was terrible in its awfulness. He charges them not merely with permitting a bad woman, Jezebel, who called herself a "Prophetess," to remain in the Church, but with permitting her to "teach" her pernicious doctrines, and to "seduce" the servants to "commit fornication," and to "eat things sacrificed to idols."

Who this woman was is a question. She was a "pretender," and called herself a "prophetess." Probably she was of noble lineage. She certainly was a woman of commanding influence. Whether her real name was Jezebel or not, she was so like her prototype in the Old Testament, Jezebel the wife of Ahab, that Christ called her by that name. Jezebel, the wife of Ahab, was not by birth a daughter of Abraham, but a princess of idolatrous Tyre, at a time, too, when its royal family was famed for cruel savagery and intense devotion to Baal and Astarte. Her father, Eth-baal, a priest of the latter deity, murdered the reigning monarch Phales, and succeeded him. Ahab, king of Israel, to strengthen his kingdom, married Jezebel, and she, aided and abetted by Ahab, introduced the licentious worship of Baal into Israel, and killed all the prophets of the Lord she could lay her hands on. And this influence she exercised, not only while her husband was alive, but also during the reign of her two sons, Ahaziah and Jehoram. Moreover, the marriage of her daughter Athaliah to Jehoram, son of Jehoshaphat, king of Judah, introduced idolatrous worship into Judah, and it was not long before there was a house of Baal built in Jerusalem, and so Jezebel caused all Israel to sin after the sin of Jeroboam the son of Nebat. 1 Kings 16:29-33.

There is no question that, whether Jezebel was a real person or not, she typified a "System" and that "System" was the "Papal Church." When the "Papal Church" introduced images and pictures into its churches for the people to bow down to it became idolatrous. And when it set up its claim that the teaching of the Church is superior to the Word of God, it assumed the role of "Prophetess." A careful study of the "Papal System" from A. D. 606 to the Reformation A. D. 1520, with its institution of the "Sacrifice of the Mass" and other Pagan rites, reveals in it the sway of "Jezebelism." It was also a period of "Jezebelistic Persecution," as seen in the wars of the Crusades, and the rise of the Inquisition. A careful comparison of this "Message" with the Parable of "The Leaven" will reveal the wonderful correspondence between the two, the "Jezebel" of the Church of Thyatira, being the "Woman" of the Parable, who inserted the "Leaven" of "False Doctrine" into the Meal of the Gospel. This Period extended from A. D. 606 to the Reformation A. D. 1520.

V. THE CHURCH AT SARDIS.
(A Dead Church.)
Rev. 3 . 1-6.

1. THE SALUTATION—"And unto the Angel of the Church in Sardis write: these things saith He that hath the Seven Spirits of God, and the Seven Stars.

2. THE CONDEMNATION—I know thy works, that thou hast a name that thou livest, and ART DEAD.

3. THE COUNSEL—Be watchful, and strengthen the things which remain, that are ready to die: for I have not found thy works perfect before God. Remember therefore how thou hast received and heard, and hold fast, and repent.

4. THE WARNING—If therefore thou shalt not watch, I will come on thee as a thief, and thou shalt not know what hour I will come upon thee.

5. THE PROMISE—Thou hast a few names even in Sardis which have not defiled their garments; and they shall walk with me in white: for they are worthy. He that overcometh, the same shall be clothed in WHITE RAIMENT; and I will not blot out his name out of the Book of Life, but I will confess his name before My Father, and before His angels. He that hath an ear, let him hear what the Spirit saith unto the Churches."

The Church at Sardis was called a "Dead Church" though it had a name to live. That is, it was a "Formalistic Church," a church given over to "formal" or "ritualistic" worship. It had the "Form of Godliness without the power." The meaning of the word "Sardis" is the "escaping one," or those who "come out" and so it is an excellent type of the Church of the

Reformation Period.

By the Reformation we mean that period in the history of the Christian Church when Martin Luther and a number of other reformers protested against the false teaching, tyranny and claims of the Papal Church.

This Period began about A. D. 1500. The condition of affairs in the realm dominated by the Papal Church became intolerable, and came to a crisis when Martin Luther, on October 31, 1517 A. D., nailed his 95 Theses on the church door at Wittenberg, Germany. From that date the Reformation set in. But it was more a struggle for political liberty than a purely Christian or religious movement.

It had the advantage of encouraging and aiding the circulation of the Holy Scriptures, that had hitherto been a sealed book, the revival of the Doctrine of "Justification by Faith," and a reversion to more simple modes of worship, but the multiplication of sects only led to bitter controversial contentions, that, while they threw much light on the Word of God, interfered greatly with the spiritual state of the Church, until it could truthfully be said, "That she had a name to live and was dead."

While the reformers swept away much ritualistic and doctrinal rubbish they failed to recover the promise of the Second Advent. They turned to God from idols, but not to "wait for His Son from the Heavens." The "Sardis Period" extended from A. D. 1520 to about A. D. 1750.

VI. THE CHURCH AT PHILADELPHIA.
(A Favored Church.)
Rev. 3:7-13.

1. THE SALUTATION—"And to the Angel of the Church in Philadelphia write: These things saith He that is **Holy,** He that is **True,** He that hath the **Key of David,** He that **openeth;** and no man shutteth; and **shutteth,** and no man openeth.

2. COMMENDATION—I know thy **works:** behold I have set before thee an **OPEN DOOR,** and no **man** can **shut it:** for thou hast a little **strength,** and hast kept My word, and hast not denied My name.

3. THE PROMISE—Behold, I will make them of the Synagogue of Satan, which say they are Jews, and are not, but do lie; behold, I will make them to come and worship before thy feet, and to know that I have loved thee. Because thou hast kept the word of **My Patience,** I also will keep thee from the **HOUR OF TRIBULATION,** which shall come upon **all the world,** to try them that dwell upon the earth. Behold, I come quickly: hold that fast which thou hast, that no man take thy **CROWN.** Him that overcometh will I make a **PILLAR** in the Temple of My God, and he shall go no more out: and I will write upon him the **NAME** of **My God,** and the name of the **CITY of My God,** which is **NEW JERUSALEM,** which cometh down out of Heaven from My God: and I will write upon him My **NEW NAME.** He that hath an ear, let him hear what the Spirit saith unto the Churches."

There is no question about the meaning of the word Philadelphia. It means "Brotherly Love," and well describes the charity and brotherly fellowship that dissipated the bitter personal animosities that characterized the theological disputants of the "Sardis Period," and made possible the evangelistic and missionary labors of the past 150 years. Three things are said of this Church:

1. It had a "little strength." It was like a person coming back to life who was still very weak. It was the "dead" Sardis Church "revived," and Revivals have been characteristic of the Philadelphia Period. These Revivals began with George Whitefield in A. D. 1739, followed by John Wesley, Charles G. Finney and D. L. Moody.

2. It had set before it an "open door," that no "man" could shut. Note that this promise was made by Him, who "hath the 'Key of David,' He that 'openeth' and no man shutteth; and 'shutteth' and no man openeth." In 1793 William Carey sailed for India, where he found an "open door," and since then the Lord has opened the door into China, Japan, Korea, India, Africa and the isles of the sea, until there is not a country in the world where the missionary cannot go.

3. It was to be kept from the **"Hour of Temptation"** (TRIBULATION), that shall come upon **ALL THE WORLD,** and as there has never as yet been a **WORLDWIDE** Tribulation, this **"Hour of Tribulation"** must still be future and refers doubtless to the "Great Tribulation" that is to come upon the "whole world," just before the return of the Lord to set up His Millennial Kingdom, and as the promise is that the "Philadelphia Church" shall **not pass through the Tribulation,** is not this additional proof that the Church shall be "caught out" before the Tribulation?

The Philadelphia Period covers the time between A. D. 1750 and A. D. 1900. We must not forget that the characteristics of all these Periods continue on in the Church down to the end. This is true of the Evangelistic and Missionary movements of the "Philadelphia Period," but they are now more mechanical and based on business methods, and there is less spiritual power, and this will continue until Christ returns.

VII. THE CHURCH AT LAODICEA.
(A Lukewarm Church.)
Rev. 3 : 14-22.

1. **THE SALUTATION**—"And unto the Angel of the Church of the Laodiceans write: These things saith the **Amen, the Faithful and True Witness,** the beginning of the creation of God.

2. **THE COMPLAINT**—I know thy **works,** that thou art neither hot nor cold: I would thou wert **cold** or **hot.** So then because thou art lukewarm, and neither cold or hot, I will **spue thee out of my mouth.** Because thou sayest, I am **rich** and **increased with goods,** and have need of **nothing,** and knowest not that thou are **wretched,** and **miserable,** and **poor,** and **blind,** and **naked.**

3. **THE COUNSEL**—I counsel thee to buy of Me **gold tried in the fire,** that thou mayest be rich; and **white raiment,** that thou mayest be clothed, and that the shame of thy nakedness do not appear; and **anoint thine eyes with eyesalve,** that thou mayest see.

4. **THE CHASTENING**—As many as I love, I **rebuke** and **chasten:** be zealous therefore, and repent.

5. **THE PROMISE**—Behold I stand at the door, and knock: if **any man** hear My voice, and **open the door,** I will come in to him, and will **sup with him,** and he with me. To him that overcometh will I grant to sit with me in **My Throne,** even as I also overcame, and am set down with My Father in His Throne. He that hath an ear, let him hear what the Spirit saith unto the Churches."

Christ has no "commendation" for this Church, but much to complain of. He says—

"I know thy works, that thou art **neither cold or hot;** I would thou wert **cold** or **hot.** So then, because thou art **lukewarm, and** neither cold or hot, I will **spue thee out of my mouth."**

There is nothing more disgusting or nauseating than "tepid" water. So there is nothing more repugnant to Christ than a "tepid" church. He would rather have a church "frozen" or "boiling." It was the "chilly spiritual atmosphere" of the Church of England that drove John Wesley to start those outside meetings which became so noted for their "religious fervor," and it was the same "chilly atmosphere" of the Methodist Church that drove William Booth in turn to become a "Red-hot" Salvationist.

Our churches today are largely in this "lukewarm" condition. There is very little of warm-hearted spirituality. There is much going on in them, but it is largely mechanical and of a social character. Committees, societies, and clubs are multiplied, but there is an absence of "spiritual heat." Revival meetings are held, but instead of waiting on the Lord for power, evangelists and paid singers are hired and soul winning is made a business. The cause of this "luke-warmness" is the same as that of the Church of Laodicea—**Self-Deception.**

"Because thou sayest I am rich, and increased with goods, and have need of nothing; and knowest not that thou art wretched, and miserable, and poor, and blind and naked."

They thought they were rich, and outwardly they were, but Christ saw the poverty of their heart. There are many such churches in the world today. More so than in any other period in the history of the church. Many of these churches have Cathedral-like buildings, stained glass windows, eloquent preachers, paid singers, large congregations. Some of them have large landed interests and are well endowed, and yet they are poor. Many of the members, if not the majority, are worldly, card playing, dancing, and theatre going Christians. The poor and the saintly are not wanted in such churches because their presence is a rebuke. These churches do not see that they are **wretched, miserable, poor, blind, and naked.**

If we were to visit such churches they would take pride in showing us the building, they would praise the preaching and singing, they would boast of the character of their congregations, the exclusiveness of their membership, and the attractiveness of all their services, but if we suggested a series of meetings for the "deepening of the **Spiritual Life,**" or the "**conversion of the unsaved,**" they would say—"Oh, no, we do not want such meetings, we have **need of nothing.**" The Church at Laodicea was not burdened with debt, but it was burdened with **WEALTH.**

The trouble with the church today is that it thinks that nothing can be done without **money,** and that if we only had the money the world would be converted in this generation. The world is not to be converted by money, but by the **Spirit of God.**

The trouble with the Church of Laodicea was that its "Gold" was not of the right kind, and so it was counseled to buy of the Lord "**gold tried in the fire.**" What kind of gold is that? It is gold that has no **taint** upon it. Gold that is not **cankered,** or secured by fraud, or the withholding of a just wage. What a description we have of these Laodicean days in James 5: 1-4.

But the Church of Laodicea was not only poor, though rich, it was **blind.** Or to put it more accurately—"Near-Sighted." They could see their worldly prosperity, but were "Short-Sighted" as to heavenly things, so the Lord counseled them to anoint their eyes with "**Eye-Salve.**" Their merchants dealt in ointments and herbs of a high degree of healing virtue, but they possessed no salve that would restore **impaired Spiritual Vision,** only the **Unction of the Holy One** could do that.

But the Church was not only poor, and blind, it was **naked.** Their outward garments were doubtless of the finest material and the latest fashionable cut, but not such as should adorn the person of a Child of God. So they were counseled to purchase of Christ "**White Raiment,**" in exchange for the "raven black woolen" garments for which the garment makers of Laodicea were famous.

Then a most startling revelation was made to the Church of Laodicea, Christ said—

"Behold, I Stand at the Door and Knock."

These words are generally quoted as an appeal to sinners, but they are not, they are addressed to a Church, and to a Church in whose midst Christ had once stood, but now found Himself **excluded** and standing outside knocking for admittance.

This is the most startling thing recorded in the New Testament, that it is possible for a church to be outwardly prosperous and yet have no Christ in its midst, and be unconscious of the fact. This is a description of a **Christless Church.** Oh, the

EXCLUDED CHRIST.

Excluded from His own nation, for they **Rejected Him**; excluded from the world, for it **Crucified Him**; excluded from His Church, for He stands outside its door **Knocking for Entrance.**

How did Christ come to be outside the Church? He had been **within** it once or there never would have been a Church. How did He come to leave? It is clear that they had not **thrust** Him out, for they do not seem to have missed His presence. They continued to worship Him, to sing His praises, and engage in all manner of Christian service, yet He had withdrawn. Why? The reason is summed up in one word—**Worldliness.**

But how is Christ to get back into His Church? Does it require the unanimous vote or invitation of the membership? No. "If any man hear my voice, and open the door, I will come in to him, and will sup with him, and he with Me." That is the way to revive a lukewarm church is for the individual members to open their hearts and let Christ **re-enter, and thus open the door** for His reappearance.

The character of the Church today is Laodicean, and as the Laodicean Period is to continue until the Church of the "New-Born" is taken out, we cannot hope for any great change until the Lord comes back.

What do these "Messages to the Churches" teach us? They clearly teach the **DECLINE OF THE CHURCH.** That the professing Church instead of increasing in spiritual and world converting power will become lukewarm, faithless, and **CHRISTLESS.**

In Paul's Parable of the "Two Olive Trees" (Rom. 11:15-27), he shows how the "natural branches" of the "Good Olive Tree," (Israel) were broken off because of **UNBELIEF,** that the "Wild Olive Tree" of the Church might be "grafted in," which in turn, because of **UNBELIEF,** would be displaced that the "**Natural branches**" might be "grafted back again," thus showing that the Church does not take the place of Israel permanently, but simply fills up the "Gap" between Israel's "casting off" and "restoration to Divine favor." As the Laodicean Period closes the "Church Age," the Church disappears at the end of Chapter Three, and Israel comes again into view. See the Chart on the next page.

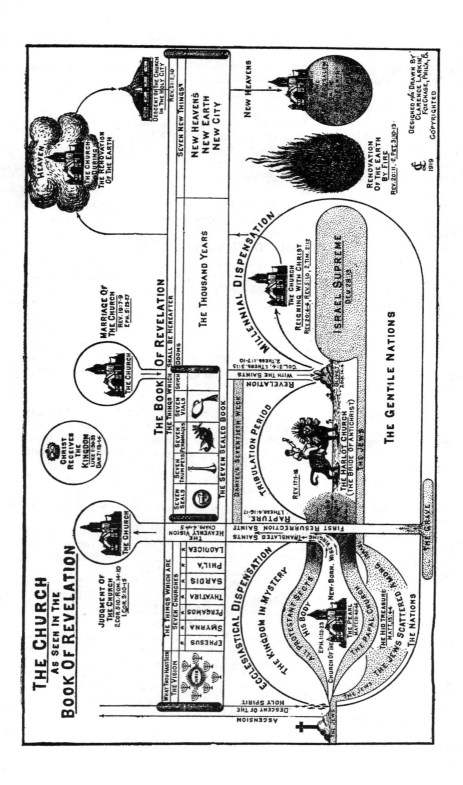

III
The Things Which Shall Be Hereafter

III. The Things Which Shall Be Hereafter

We have now come to the Third Division of the Book. The Three Divisions of the Book do not overlap nor are they concurrent. The word translated "hereafter," would be better translated "after these things." The word "hereafter" permits a "time space," while the words "after these things" refer to the things that shall immediately follow the completion of the "Church Age," as prefigured in the Messages to the Seven Churches. The Church disappears from view with the close of the third chapter and is not heard of again until the nineteenth chapter, where her marriage to the Lamb is announced. Rev. 19:7-9. The removal of the Church at the end of the third chapter opens the way for God to renew His dealings with Israel, and take up the broken thread of Jewish History. That the portion of the Book from chapter three to the end of chapter nineteen is largely made up of symbols taken from the Old Testament, as the Tabernacle, Ark of the Covenant, Altar, Censer, Elders, Cherubim, Seals, Trumpets, Plagues, etc., is conclusive evidence that we are here back on Jewish ground, and that the Parenthetical Dispensation of the Church is complete, and that the last or "Seventieth Week" of Daniel's "Seventy Weeks" is in course of fulfilment. It is clear therefore that we must look for the explanation of these symbols to the Old Testament.

Chapters four and five are introductory and preparatory to the "Prophetic Action" of the "Seals," "Trumpets" and "Vials," and must be considered first.

1. THE HEAVENLY DOOR.

Rev. 4:1.

"AFTER THIS I looked, and, behold, a **DOOR WAS OPENED IN HEAVEN:** and the first voice which I heard was as it were a **trumpet** talking with me; which said, Come up hither, and I will shew thee things which must be hereafter" (after these).

The scene now changes from earth (Patmos) to Heaven. John tells us that **After This,** after his Vision of Christ in the midst of the "Seven Candlesticks," and his foreview of the history of the Christian Church, as reviewed in the Messages to the Seven Churches, which carried him down to the end of the Church Age, he looked, and behold a **DOOR WAS OPENED IN HEAVEN**, and the same voice that spoke to him from the midst of the "Seven Golden Candlesticks," which was the voice of Christ (Rev. 1:10-13), said with the clearness and sweetness of a **trumpet**—

"COME UP HITHER
AND I WILL SHOW THEE THINGS WHICH MUST BE HEREAFTER."

And John adds

"IMMEDIATELY I WAS IN THE SPIRIT:

and, behold, a Throne was set in Heaven, and ONE sat on the Throne."

The experience of John was similar to that of Paul, who was caught up into Paradise. Whether in the body or out of the body they are uncertain, at least Paul was. 2. Cor. 12:2-4. The difference between them however was, that, while Paul heard words that he was forbidden to speak, John was told to **"WRITE IN A BOOK"** the things he saw and heard, and send them to the Seven Churches in Asia.

In this "Rapture" of John we have a type of the
RAPTURE OF THE CHURCH,
and it is at this place in the Book that the "RAPTURE" of the Church takes place.

After the confession of Peter at Caesarea Philippi, that Jesus was the Christ, the Son of the living God (Matt. 16:13-28), and Jesus had said that upon the rock of that confession He would build His Church, He said to His Disciples—"Verily I say unto you, there be some standing here **which shall not taste of death,** till they see the Son of Man **COMING IN HIS KINGDOM."** And then we read in the next chapter (and there should be no chapter division), "And after six days Jesus taketh Peter, James and John his brother, and bringeth them up into an high mountain apart, and was **TRANSFIGURED BEFORE THEM."** Matt. 17:1-9. Now this "Transfiguration Scene" is a type of the Second Coming of Christ, Moses being a type of the "Resurrected Saints," and Elijah of the "Translated Saints."

As the promise of Christ to His Disciples that some of them should not "taste of death" until they saw in vision a rehearsal of the manner of His Second Coming, was fulfilled in the "Transfiguration Scene," so the statement made to Peter as to John, "If I will that he **TARRY TILL I COME"** (John 21:20-23), finds its fulfilment in John's being caught up in vision and beholding **before his death,** what he would have witnessed and experienced if his life had been prolonged until Jesus came back. Thus John was permitted to live, until, in vision, he saw the Return of the Lord.

The "Rapture" of the Church is described in 1. Thess. 4:16-17. "For the Lord **HIMSELF** shall descend from Heaven with a **SHOUT,** with the **VOICE OF THE ARCHANGEL,** and with the **TRUMP OF GOD;** and the **DEAD IN CHRIST** shall rise first: then we **WHICH ARE ALIVE** and **REMAIN** shall be **CAUGHT UP TOGETHER WITH THEM** in the clouds, to meet the Lord **IN THE AIR:** and so shall we ever be with the Lord." Note how John's taking up corresponds with this. He was summoned by the **"VOICE OF CHRIST,"** and it will be the **"SHOUT of Christ"** that shall summon the saints at the Rapture. It was with a **"LOUD VOICE"** that Jesus called Lazarus from the tomb. John 11:43. And as it was a **Trumpet Like Voice** that summoned John, so it will be a **TRUMPET CALL** that will summon the Saints at the Rapture.

As confirmatory proof that the Church is "caught out" at this time and place, we have in the description of the Throne, the statement that the Holy Spirit in the Seven-fold plentitude of His power, is **BACK IN HEAVEN.** In none of the Epistles is the Holy Spirit invoked along with the Father and the Son, except in 2. Cor. 13:14, because He is viewed as abiding on the earth with the Church, convicting of sin, comforting believers, and gathering out the elect, but here He is no longer on the earth but back in Heaven, and before the Throne. This is the strongest kind of evidence that the Church at this time has been "caught out" and is no longer on the earth, for when the Holy Spirit goes back to Heaven He will take the Church WITH HIM. And the presence of the Holy Spirit in Heaven is conclusive evidence that the events that follow are to take place after the Church has been caught out, and therefore the Church is not to pass through the Tribulation.

2. THE HEAVENLY THRONE.
Rev. 4:2-3, 5-6.

"And immediately I was in the SPIRIT: and, behold, a THRONE was set in Heaven, and ONE sat on the THRONE. And HE that sat was to look upon like a Jasper and a Sardius stone: and there was a Rainbow round about the THRONE, in sight like unto an Emerald. . . . And out of the THRONE proceeded Lightnings and Thunderings and Voices; and there were Seven Lamps of Fire burning before the THRONE, which are the SEVEN SPIRITS OF GOD. And before the THRONE there was a Sea of Glass like unto crystal."

The first thing John saw in Heaven was a THRONE. The Throne was not vacant, but One sat upon it, upon whom to look was like looking at glistening gems, such as Jasper and Sardius. The occupant of the Throne was no other than God Himself. In Rev. 21:10-11, John in describing the New Jerusalem says, that its light is the "GLORY OF GOD." A light like unto a stone most precious, even like a JASPER stone, clear as crystal. This corresponds with John's declaration in 1. John 1:5, that "GOD IS LIGHT."

Ezekiel in describing his vision of the "Throne of God" says—"Above the Firmament that was over their heads was the likeness of a Throne, as the appearance of a Sapphire Stone: and upon the likeness of the Throne was the likeness as the appearance of a MAN above upon it. And I saw as the color of Amber, as the appearance of fire round about within it, from the appearance of His loins even upward, and from the appearance of His loins even downward, I saw as it were the appearance of fire, and it had brightness round about. As the appearance of the Bow that is in the cloud in the day of rain, so was the appearance of the brightness round about. This was the appearance of the likeness of the GLORY OF THE LORD." Ez. 1:26-28.

Now there are two things in Ezekiel's Vision that correspond with John's Vision of the "THRONE OF GOD." First that the form of the one who sat on the Throne could not be clearly distinguished or described, but that it was RESPLENDENT WITH LIGHT, which veiled the form or person; and secondly, that there was a RAINBOW ROUND ABOUT THE THRONE. The person of God then, as He sits upon His Throne, is veiled in a Glory that can only be compared to the shining of some beautiful gem. But one of the remarkable things about the Throne of God is, that it is surrounded by a "RAINBOW" that is emerald in color. The first mention we have in the Bible of a Rainbow is in Gen. 9:13-17. "I do set My BOW in the cloud, and it shall be for a token of a COVENANT between Me and the Earth." A Covenant that God would not destroy this earth again by a Flood. But that Rainbow was only SEMI-CIRCULAR, such as we see in the heavens in summer after a shower; but the Rainbow Ezekiel and John saw around the Throne of God was CIRCULAR. In this world we only see half a Rainbow, or the half of things, in Heaven we shall see the whole of things. The Rainbow is the sign of a Covenant based on an accepted Sacrifice, the Sacrifice of Noah (Gen. 8:20-22), and the Rainbow about the Throne of God is the sign of a Covenant based on the accepted Sacrifice of Christ on the Cross. The difference between Noah's Rainbow and the one around the Throne of God is, that Noah's is composed of the seven primary colors, Red, Orange, Yellow, Green, Blue, Indigo, and Violet, while the one around the Throne of God is EMERALD. What does this "CIRCULAR GREEN RAINBOW" about the Throne of God signify? It signifies that God is a Covenant keeping God, that His promises as to this earth shall be fulfilled. Even though He is about to bring great judgments upon it, He will not destroy it, but it shall pass through those judgments safely. He will redeem it, and bless it, until its hills, and valleys, and plains, shall teem with the green verdure, fruitful orchards, and bountiful vineyards of the long Millennial Day that is to follow those judgments. If the Rainbow did not encircle the Throne as a "Halo," it might by its reflection in the "Sea of Glass" appear to John to be round.

The "Throne" was not the "Throne of Grace" for out of it proceeded lightnings and thunderings and voices, that remind us of Mt. Sinai, and proclaim it to be the

"THRONE OF JUDGMENT."

Before the Throne was a "SEA OF GLASS." This "Sea of Glass" was unoccupied, but later is seen mixed with fire (Rev. 15:2-3), and occupied by martyrs of the Tribulation Period who get the victory over the Beast, and who have harps, and sing the Song of MOSES AND THE LAMB. This "Glassy Sea" reminds us of the "Brazen Sea" that stood before Solomon's Temple (1. Kings 7:23-45), and thus was in front of the Ark of the Covenant, the "Mercy Seat" of which was the earthly Throne of God in Old Testament days.

Right here it might be well for us to remember that the earthly Tabernacle erected by Moses, with all its vessels and instruments of service and mode of worship, was patterned after the "Heavenly Tabernacle." Heb. 9:23.

A knowledge then of the Tabernacle and its various parts and vessels of service, will help us to understand John's Vision of the "Heavenly Tabernacle." Like John, Paul was "caught up" into Heaven, and saw the "Heavenly Tabernacle," and he most beautifully and clearly makes a comparison between it and the "Mosaic Tabernacle" in his Letter to the Hebrews.

The "Throne" that John saw in Heaven corresponds with the "Mercy Seat" of the Ark of the Covenant. The "Four Beasts (Living

Ones)" with the "Cherubim" that guarded the "Mercy Seat." The "Four and Twenty Elders" with the "Priestly Courses" that officiated in the Tabernacle. The "Seven Lamps (Spirits)" before the "Throne," with the "Seven Branched Candlestick" of the Holy Place of the Tabernacle. The "Sea of Glass" with the "Brazen Laver" for cleansing, that stood in front of the Tabernacle. The "Altar" under which John saw the "soul of Martyrs" with the "Altar of Burnt Offering." If the "Throne" section of the "Heavenly Tabernacle" corresponds with the "Most Holy Place" of the "Mosaic Tabernacle," and the "Four and Twenty Elder" section with the "Altar of Incense" and "Seven Lamps of Fire" corresponds with the "Holy Place," then the "Sea of Glass" and the "Altar" should correspond with the "Court" of the Tabernacle. This will help us to relatively locate what John saw in the Heavenly Tabernacle.

It is also profitable and instructive to compare the "Heavenly" and "Earthly" Tabernacles with the "Tabernacle of Man." See the Chart of "The Three Tabernacles." Here we see that the "Spirit"

THE HEAVENLY TABERNACLE

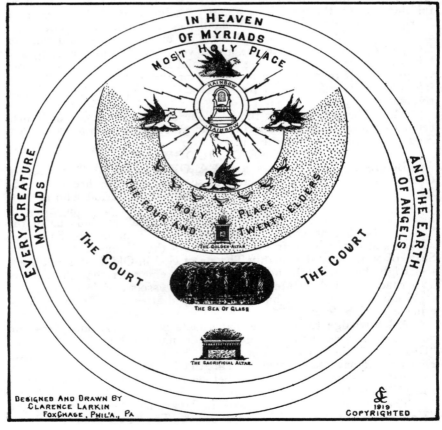

IN HEAVEN
OF MYRIADS
MOST HOLY PLACE
RAINBOW
RAINBOW
EVERY CREATURE
MYRIADS
THE FOUR AND TWENTY ELDERS
HOLY PLACE
THE GOLDEN ALTAR
AND THE EARTH
OF ANGELS
THE COURT
THE COURT
THE SEA OF GLASS
THE SACRIFICIAL ALTAR.

DESIGNED AND DRAWN BY
CLARENCE LARKIN
FOXCHASE, PHIL'A., PA

1919
COPYRIGHTED

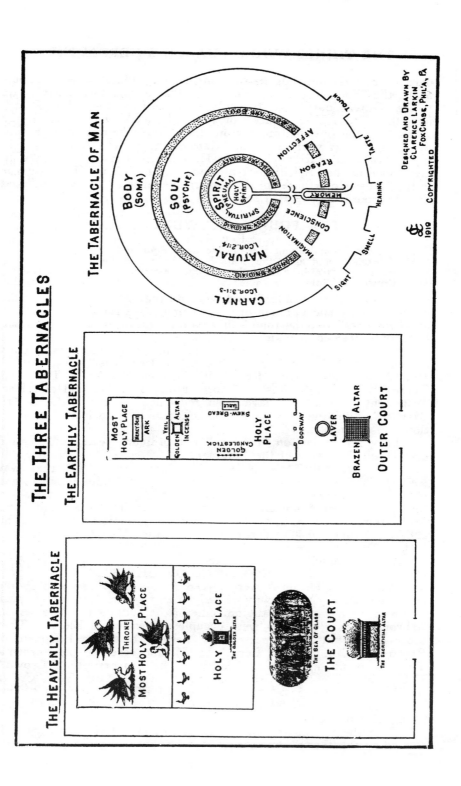

The Three Tabernacles

The Heavenly Tabernacle

MOST HOLY PLACE

THRONE

HOLY PLACE

The Golden Altar

The Sea of Glass

THE COURT

The Sacrificial Altar

The Earthly Tabernacle

MOST HOLY PLACE

MERCY SEAT
ARK

A VEIL

GOLDEN ALTAR
INCENSE

SHEW-BREAD
TABLE

GOLDEN CANDLESTICK

HOLY PLACE

DOORWAY

LAVER

BRAZEN ALTAR

OUTER COURT

The Tabernacle of Man

BODY
(SOMA)

SOUL
(PSYCHE)

SPIRIT
(PNEUMA)

HOLY
SPIRIT

SPIRITUAL
BODY & SOUL SPIRIT

SPIRITUAL SOMA
MEMORY SOMA

NATURAL
1 COR. 2:14

CARNAL
1 COR. 3:1-3

IMAGINATION

CONSCIENCE

MEMORY

REASON

AFFECTION

SIGHT

SMELL

HEARING

TASTE

TOUCH

Designed And Drawn By
Clarence Larkin
Fox Chase, Phila., Pa.
Copyrighted

1919

part of man corresponds to the "Most Holy Place" of the Tabernacle, the "Soulish" part to the "Holy Place," and the "Body" part to the "Outer Court." As the only entrance from the "Holy Place" into the "Most Holy Place" of the Tabernacle was through the "Veil," so the only entrance from the "Soulish" part of man into the "Spirit" part is through the "Gate of the Will." And it is only when the "Will" surrenders to the Holy Spirit that God can take up His abode in the "Spirit" part of man, as He took up His residence in the "Most Holy Place" of the Tabernacle on the "Mercy Seat," and man become a regenerated soul.

3. THE FOUR AND TWENTY ELDERS.
Rev. 4:4.

"And round about the Throne were **Four and Twenty Seats** (Thrones): and upon the Seats I saw **Four and Twenty Elders** sitting, **clothed in white raiment**; and they had on their heads **Crowns of Gold.**"

Who are these "**Elders**" and what do they represent? They are not a heavenly and unfallen order of beings, like the angels or "Living Creatures" that surround the Throne, they are the representatives of **redeemed mankind.** The name Elder is never applied to angels, neither do angels have "**crowns**" and sit on "**thrones.**" Only **redeemed MEN** are promised "**Thrones**" and **Crowns.**" Matt. 19:28. Rev. 3:21. Rev. 20:4. Rev. 2.10. 1. Pet. 5:2-4. 2. Tim. 4:8. These "**Elders**" then must be representatives of the Old and New Testament Saints, that have been redeemed by the **BLOOD OF CHRIST.** This will be made more clear as we consider their position, dress, and song.

They are seated on "**thrones,**" not ordinary seats, and remind us of Daniel's Vision of the Judgment.

"I beheld till **THRONES** were placed and **ONE** that was **ANCIENT OF DAYS** did sit; His raiment was white as snow, and the hair of His head like **pure wool**; His Throne was **fiery flames,** the wheels thereof **burning fire.** A **fiery stream** issued and came forth from before Him, thousand thousands ministered unto Him, and **10,000** times **10,000** stood before Him; the **JUDGMENT** was set, and the 'Books' were opened." Dan. 7:9-10 R. V.

This is Daniel's foreview of the

"JUDGMENT SEAT OF CHRIST."

While the "Thrones" were **placed** (ready for those who should be found worthy to occupy them) they were as yet unoccupied. Their occupancy awaited the outcome of the Judgment. Now as the "Thrones" that John saw were occupied by **crowned** Elders. Then those Elders must have passed the "**fiery test**" of the Judgment of Reward (2. Cor. 5:10, 1. Cor. 3:11-15), and received their **crowns.** Those Crowns are five in number. The "Incorruptible Crown." 1. Cor. 9:25-27. The "Crown of Life." Rev. 2:10. The "Crown of Glory." 1. Pet. 5:2-4. The "Crown of Righteousness." 2. Tim. 4:8. The "Crown of Rejoicing." 1. Thess. 2:19-20. See the Chart— "Judgment of Reward."

That these "**Elders**" were **REDEEMED MEN** is further evidenced by the "**Song**" they sung.

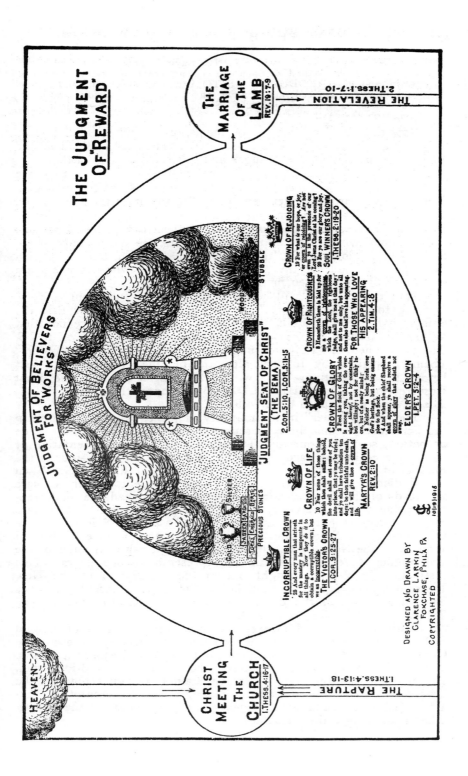

THE JUDGMENT OF "REWARD"

JUDGMENT OF BELIEVERS FOR "WORKS"

THE MARRIAGE OF THE LAMB
REV.19:7-9

THE REVELATION 2.THESS.1:7-10

HEAVEN

CHRIST MEETING THE CHURCH
1.THESS.4:16-17

THE RAPTURE 1.THESS.4:13-18

"JUDGMENT SEAT OF CHRIST"
(THE BEMA)
2.COR.5:10. 1.COR.3:11-15

GOLD — Silver
PRECIOUS STONES
WOOD — HAY — STUBBLE

INCORRUPTIBLE CROWN
25 And every man that striveth for the mastery is temperate in all things. Now they do it to obtain a corruptible crown; but we an incorruptible.
THE VICTOR'S CROWN
1.COR.9:25-27

CROWN OF LIFE
10 Fear none of those things which thou shalt suffer: behold, the devil shall cast some of you into prison, that ye may be tried; and ye shall have tribulation ten days: be thou faithful unto death, and I will give thee a crown of life.
MARTYR'S CROWN
REV.2:10

CROWN OF GLORY
2 Feed the flock of God which is among you, taking the oversight thereof, not by constraint, but willingly; not for filthy lucre, but of a ready mind;
3 Neither as being lords over God's heritage, but being ensamples to the flock.
4 And when the chief Shepherd shall appear, ye shall receive a crown of glory that fadeth not away.
ELDER'S CROWN
1.PET.5:2-4

CROWN OF RIGHTEOUSNESS
8 Henceforth there is laid up for me a crown of righteousness, which the Lord, the righteous judge, shall give me at that day: and not to me only, but unto all them also that love his appearing.
FOR THOSE WHO LOVE HIS APPEARING
2.TIM.4:8

CROWN OF REJOICING
19 For what is our hope, or joy, or crown of rejoicing? Are not even ye in the presence of our Lord Jesus Christ at his coming?
20 For ye are our glory and joy.
SOUL WINNER'S CROWN
1.THESS.2:19-20

DESIGNED AND DRAWN BY
CLARENCE LARKIN
FOXCHASE, PHILA. PA.
COPYRIGHTED

"And they sung a **NEW SONG,** Saying, Thou art worthy to take the Book, and to open the Seals thereof, for thou wast slain, and hast **REDEEMED US TO GOD BY THY BLOOD,** out of every **kindred,** and **tongue,** and **people,** and **nation;** and hast made us unto our God **KINGS** and **PRIESTS;** and we shall **reign on the earth."** Rev. 5: 9-10.

Now this could not be said of angels, or any other created heavenly beings, for they have not been redeemed by the Blood of the Lamb, nor are they to be "Kings" and "Priests" on the earth.

While the "Elders" sit on Thrones and wear Crowns, they are not dressed in royal robes but in "white raiment," the garment of a Priest. They are the members of a **"ROYAL PRIESTHOOD."** 1. Pet. 2:9. That the time has not yet come for them to reign is clear, for they are engaged in Priestly duties, having "Golden Vials full of odors, which are the **prayers of saints,"** in their hands. Rev. 5:8. These saints are not the saints of the Church, but the Jewish saints on earth during the "Tribulation Period," whose prayers are so beautifully prewritten in the Psalms.

That the "Elders" will be given the right of Judgment is clear. Writing to the Corinthians Paul says—"Do ye not know that the Saints shall **JUDGE THE WORLD.** . . . Know ye not that **We** shall **JUDGE ANGELS."** (The Fallen Angels.) 1. Cor. 6:2-3. The time when this right of Judgment is conferred on the "Elders" (Saints) is given by John as **after** the binding of Satan, and just before the Millennium—"I saw **THRONES,** and they (the First Resurrection Saints—**THE ELDERS**) sat upon them, and **JUDGMENT** was given unto them." Rev. 20:4.

The word "Elder" in the majority of places where it is used in the Scriptures means the **representative head** of a city, family, tribe or nation, so the "Four and Twenty Elders" are representative of the redeemed human race. But why **24 Elders?** Twenty-four is the number of the Priestly Courses as given in 1. Chron. 24: 1-19. When David distributed the Priests into "Courses" he found there were **24 Heads** of the Priestly families, and these 24 Heads he made **representative** of the **WHOLE PRIESTHOOD.** As the "Elders" are representative of both the Old and New Testament Saints, and the Old Testament Saints are represented by the Twelve Tribes of Israel, and the New Testament Saints by the Twelve Apostles of the Lamb, they together make up 24 representative characters. This distinction is clearly brought out in the description of the New Jerusalem, where the 12 Foundation Stones are named after the Twelve Apostles of the Lamb, and the 12 Gates after the Twelve Tribes of Israel. Rev. 21: 10-14.

While the Four and Twenty Elders are representative of the Old and New Testament Saints, they do not, as a whole, represent the Church, for the Church is composed only of New Testament Saints. The Old Testament saints are merely the Friends of the Bridegroom. But the fact that the New Testament Saints, as represented by the Twelve Apostles, are required to make up the 24 representative characters (Elders), is additional evidence that the Rapture of the Church takes place before the Tribulation.

4. THE FOUR BEASTS.
Rev. 4:6-11.

"In the midst of the Throne, and round about the Throne, were FOUR BEASTS full of eyes before and behind. And the First Beast was like a LION, and the Second Beast like a CALF, and the Third Beast had a face as a MAN, and the Fourth Beast was like a FLYING EAGLE. And the four Beasts had each of them six wings about him; and they were full of eyes within; and they rest not day or night, saying, HOLY, HOLY, HOLY, LORD GOD ALMIGHTY, WHICH WAS, AND IS, AND IS TO COME."

The word translated "Beasts" should be translated "LIVING CREATURES," as in the Revised Version. The word here translated "beast" (Zoon), is not the same as the one translated "beast" (Therion) in chapters eleven, thirteen, and seventeen. The word here used means a "living being" or "creature," while the word used in chapters eleven, thirteen, and seventeen, means a wild, untamed animal. They are not angelic beings, for they are distinguished from the angels, who are mentioned as a class by themselves in Rev. 5:11. Neither are they representative of redeemed human beings, for they do not join in the Redemption Song. Rev. 5:8-10. The word "they" in this passage does not refer to the "Four Living Creatures," but to the "Four and Twenty Elders."

The "Four Living Creatures" are not in the same class with the "Elders," for they have no "thrones" or "crowns" or "harps" or "golden vials." They are the "Guardians" of the Throne of God, and accompany it wherever it goes. Ez. 1:24-28. They are four in number, which is the "earth number," and therefore have something to do with the earth. That is, they are interested in the "re-genesis" of the earth to its former glory before the Fall. They have eyes before and behind and within, which reveals their intelligence and spiritual insight of things past, present, and to come, and they are tireless in their service, for they rest not day nor night, saying, "Holy, Holy, Holy, Lord God Almighty, which was, and is, and is to come."

The first time these "Living Creatures" are mentioned in the Bible is in Gen. 3:24, where they are called "CHERUBIM," but are not described. They were placed at the entrance to the "Garden of Eden" to prevent the re-entrance of Adam and Eve, and to keep the way of the "Tree of Life." It would appear as if at the place where they were stationed there was a Tabernacle, a place of worship to which Cain and Abel resorted to make their offerings, and that it was from there that Cain went out from the "PRESENCE OF THE LORD." Gen. 4:16.

When Moses was given on the Holy Mount the pattern of the Tabernacle, he was instructed to make the "Ark of the Covenant" with two Cherubim upon it. Ex. 25:10-22. These Cherubim were guardians of the "Mercy Seat," or the place of God's PRESENCE when He in His "Shekinah Glory" visited the Tabernacle. But it is not until Ezekiel had his vision of the Cherubim (Ez. 1:1-28; 10:1-22), that we have a description of what they are like. See the Chart on the Cherubim the next page.

THE CHERUBIM

JOHN'S LIVING CREATURES
REV. 4:6-11

EZEKIEL'S CHERUBIM
EZEK. 1:4-28   EZEK. 10:1-22

N

 THE EAGLE

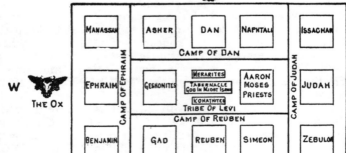

MANASSAH	ASHER	DAN	NAPHTALI		ISSACHAR
		CAMP OF DAN			
EPHRAIM	GERSHONITES	MERARITES / TABERNACLE GOD IN MIDST ISRAEL / KOHATHITES	AARON MOSES PRIESTS		JUDAH
		TRIBE OF LEVI			
		CAMP OF REUBEN			
BENJAMIN	GAD	REUBEN	SIMEON		ZEBULON

W   THE OX   CAMP OF EPHRAIM   CAMP OF JUDAH   THE LION   E

THE CAMP
NUM. 2:1-3:39

THE   MAN

S

Ezekiel describes them as having the likeness of a man, with 4 faces, and 4 wings, and feet like a calf's foot, and hands like a man's hand under their wings on their 4 sides. Their 4 faces were different. The front face was that of a MAN, the right side face was that of a LION, the left side face was that of an OX, and the rear face was that of an EAGLE, and their whole body, back, hands, and wings, were full of eyes round about. Ez. 10:12. In John's Vision of the "Cherubim" or "Living Creatures" they are described as like animals, the first was like a LION, the second like a CALF, or a young Ox, the third had the face of a MAN, and the fourth was like a FLYING EAGLE. John's "Living Creatures" had 6 wings, while Ezekiel's "Cherubim" had only 4. In Ezekiel's vision, the "Cherubim," or "Living Creatures," were accompanied by the Holy Spirit (Ez. 1:12) and traveled on wheels, which shows that they were on some tour or mission, attended by the Lord, who sat on His Throne over their heads (Ez. 1:25-28), but the wheels are absent in John's vision, for the scene is in Heaven, the permanent home of the Throne of God.

In the camping and marching order of Israel in the Wilderness, there was a fixed relation of the Twelve Tribes to the Tabernacle. In camp the Tabernacle rested in the middle. The Camp of Judah, composed of 3 Tribes, rested on the East, with its Standard bearing the figure of a LION. The Camp of Ephraim, composed of 3 Tribes, rested on the West, with its Standard bearing the figure of an OX. The Camp of Reuben, composed of 3 Tribes, rested on the South, with its Standard bearing the figure of a MAN. The Camp of Dan, composed of 3 Tribes, rested on the North, with its Standard bearing the figure of an EAGLE. Thus the Tabernacle in the centre of the Camp, the place of God's Presence, was surrounded and protected by Standards that bore the figures of Ezekiel's and John's "Living Creatures."

The dissimilarity between Ezekiel's "Living Creatures," and John's "Living Creatures" can only be explained on the supposition that there are different orders of "Living Creatures" or "Cherubim," each adapted to the service he is created to perform. In Isaiah's Vision in the Temple of the Lord seated on His Throne, he saw a heavenly order of beings that he called the "Seraphim." They had 6 wings, like John's "Living Creatures," and cried "Holy, Holy, Holy, is the Lord of Hosts: the whole earth is full of His Glory" (Isa. 6:1-4), but they stood above the Throne, while Ezekiel's Cherubim supported the Throne, and John's "Living Creatures" were in the midst or around the Throne. Whatever significances there may be in the different forms the "Cherubim" or "Living Creatures" took, it is clear that they do not represent the Church, but are attendants or officials attached to the Throne of God, for they summon the four Horsemen to appear (Rev. 6:1-8), and one of them hands to the "Seven Vial Angels," the "Golden Vials" filled with the "Wrath of God." Rev. 15:7. And when they give glory and honor and thanks to Him that sits upon the Throne, who liveth forever and ever, the "Four and Twenty Elders" fall down before Him that sits upon the Throne, and worship Him . . . and cast their crowns before the Throne, saying, "Thou art worthy, O Lord, to receive glory and honor and power; for Thou hast created all things, and for Thy pleasure they are and were created." Rev. 4:9-11.

5. THE SEVEN-SEALED BOOK.
Rev. 5:1-14.

"And I saw in the right hand of Him that sat on the Throne a Book written **within** and on the **back, sealed with SEVEN SEALS.** And I saw a strong angel proclaiming with a loud voice, Who is worthy to open the Book, and to loose the **SEALS** thereof? And no **man** in heaven, nor in earth, neither under the earth, was able to open the Book, neither to look thereon. And one of the Elders saith unto me, Weep not: behold, the **LION OF THE TRIBE OF JUDA**, the **ROOT OF DAVID**, hath prevailed to open the Book, and to loose the **SEVEN SEALS** thereof. And I beheld, and, lo, in the **midst** of the Throne, and of the Four Beasts, and in the midst of the Elders, stood a **LAMB as it had been slain**, having **SEVEN HORNS** and **SEVEN EYES**, which are the **SEVEN SPIRTS OF GOD** sent forth into all the earth. And **HE** came and took the Book out of the right hand of Him that sat upon the Throne."

What is this "SEVEN SEALED BOOK"? Writing to the Ephesians (Eph. 1:13-14), Paul said—"Ye were **SEALED** with the Holy Spirit of promise, which is the **earnest** of our inheritance until the **REDEMPTION** of the **PURCHASED POSSESSION**." Then there is a **POSSESSION** that is to be **REDEEMED**. What this is, Paul tells us in Rom. 8:22-23. "We know that the **WHOLE CREATION GROANETH AND TRAVAILETH IN PAIN TOGETHER UNTIL NOW.** And not only they (all earthly created things), but ourselves also, which have the "First fruits of the Spirit," even we ourselves groan within ourselves, waiting for the **adoption,** to wit, the **REDEMPTION OF OUR BODY.**" (This will take place at the First Resurrection).

We see from these references that there is something that was lost to mankind and the earth that is to be redeemed, and we do not have to go far to find out what it was. It is the inheritance of the **earth** and of **immortal life** given to Adam and Eve, and that was lost in the Fall of Eden. When Adam sinned he lost his inheritance of the earth, and it passed out of his hands into the possession of Satan, to the disinheritance of all of Adam's seed. The forfeited Title Deed is now in God's hands and is awaiting redemption. Its redemption means the **legal repossession** of all that Adam lost by the Fall. Adam was impotent to redeem the lost possession, but the law provides (Lev. 25:23-34) that a **kinsman** may redeem a lost possession. That **KINSMAN** has been provided in the person of **JESUS CHRIST.**

To become a **kinsman** He had to be born into the human race. This the Virgin Birth accomplished. Jesus paid the **REDEMPTIVE PRICE**, which was His own **BLOOD**, on the Cross (1. Pet. 1 : 18-20), but He has not as yet claimed that which He then purchased. When the time comes for the **Redemption** of the **PURCHASED POSSESSION** Jesus will do so. That time and the act is described in the scripture we are now considering. The **"SEVEN SEALED BOOK"** is the **"TITLE DEED"** to the redeemed inheritance. In Old Testament days when a kinsman desired to redeem a property he took his position, with ten men (Elders) as witnesses, in the gate of the city and advertised his purpose. This is beautifully illustrated in the story of Boaz and Ruth. Ruth 4 : 1-12. The kinsman who redeemed the property was called the "Goel" or **REDEEMER**.

When the "strong angel" proclaimed with a loud voice—**"WHO** is worthy to open the Book, and to loose the **Seals** thereof ?" that was the advertisement for the **"KINSMAN REDEEMER"** to appear. But, said John, there was no **MAN** (redeemed man) in Heaven, nor in Earth, neither under the Earth, who was able to open the Book, neither to look thereon. It was not a question of the worthiness of some angelic being, as Michael or Gabriel, to open the Book, but of a **MAN**. When John saw that there was no one worthy to open the Book he wept. Some say he wept because he was disappointed that he could not satisfy his curiosity as to the contents of the Book, but such a statement is puerile. A man under the influence of the Holy Spirit would not be so foolish. John wept because he knew what the Book was, and that if there was no one to open that **"BOOK OF REDEMPTION,"** that all hope of the redemption of the earth and of man was gone. But John's sorrow was of short duration, for one of the Elders said—"Weep not: behold, the **LION OF THE TRIBE OF JUDAH,** the **ROOT OF DAVID,** hath prevailed to open the Book, and to loose the 'Seven Seals' thereof." And John saw, what he had not noticed before a **LAMB, as it had been slain,** standing in the midst of the Throne, and of the "Four Living Creatures." John had not seen the Lamb before, because it (He) had been seated on the Throne with the Father, and advanced out of the Glory of the Throne as the Elder spoke.

John looked for a **"Lion"** and saw a **LAMB.** But the Elder was right in calling it a **"Lion,"** for Jesus was about to assume His Title as the **LION OF THE TRIBE OF JUDAH,** and reign and rule with **KINGLY POWER.** That the Lamb was not an animal is clear from verse seven, where it says—"And **HE** (the Lamb) came and took the Book out of the right hand of Him that sat upon the Throne." This is the sublimest individual act recorded in the Scriptures. On it the redemption of the whole creation of God depends. It is still future and takes place after the Church has been "caught out" and Judged, and before the Tribulation Period begins, and you and I, if we are redeemed by the Blood of the Lamb, will witness the scene, and take part in the "Song of Redemption" that follows. Rev. 5 : 8-10.

THE "SEVEN-HORNED" LAMB.

This is the **"DUE TIME,"** when the **"MAN" CHRIST JESUS,** who gave Himself as a **"RANSOM"** (on the Cross) for the redemption of the lost inheritance, will be **TESTIFIED TO** before the Throne of God, by redeemed mankind, angels, and every creature in Heaven and Earth, and under the Earth. 1. Tim. 2:5-6; Rev. 5:8-14.

When the Lamb leaves the Throne to take the Book, His Mediatorial Work ceases, and His **REDEMPTIVE WORK** begins. When our **"KINSMAN REDEEMER"** is handed the "Book," the **"TITLE DEED"** to the "Purchased Possession," He has the right to break its **SEALS,** and claim the "Inheritance," and **DISPOSSESS** the present claimant **SATAN.** This He will immediately proceed to do, as He breaks the **SEALS.** Satan is not evicted at once. He contests the claim and it is only after a prolonged conflict that he is finally dispossessed and cast into the Lake of Fire.

In the Gospels four titles are given to Jesus. He is the Son of David; the Son of Abraham; the Son of Man; and the Son of God.

1. As the Son of David, He has title to the Throne of David.

2. As the Son of Abraham, He has title to the Land of Palestine, and all included in the Royal Grant to Abraham. See Map of The Royal Grant.

3. As the Son of Man, He has title to the Earth and the World.

4. As the Son of God, He is the Heir of All Things.

The manner of redemption of a lost inheritance is beautifully set forth in the Old Testament. A property could not be alienated from the original owner or his heirs for a longer period than 50 years, at which time it reverted to the original owner. If however for some reason the owner was forced to sell it, it could be redeemed by the next of kin on the payment of the proportionate amount of its value due until the next "Year of Jubilee." Lev. 25:8-17. Two illustrations of this method of redeeming a forfeited possession are given in the Old Testament; one in Ruth 4:1-12, where Boaz redeems the possession of Elimelech, the other in Jer. 32:6-12, where the Prophet Jeremiah purchased the possession of his cousin Hanameel. The "Deed" was written on a parchment roll, and when the inside was filled, the outside was used, but enough space was left to not show the writing when the parchment was rolled up and sealed, and on the outside of the roll that showed, the Title of the Deed, and the names

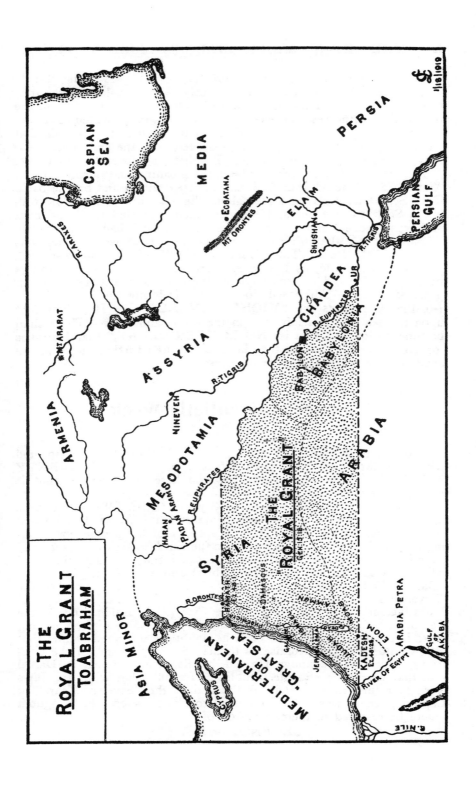

THE
ROYAL GRANT
TO ABRAHAM

of the subscribing witnesses were written. Two copies of the "Deed" were made. One was sealed, and the other left unsealed for the purpose of reference. These deeds were handed to the purchaser in the presence of witnesses, and either kept by him, or intrusted to a custodian, or placed, as in the case of Jeremiah, in an earthen vessel, that would neither rot nor rust, to be preserved until the end of the Seventy Years of Captivity that the Prophet had foretold was to be. This method of taking title, explains the meaning and purpose of the "Seven Sealed Book" that John saw written **within** and on the **back.** The "Seals" were not in a row along the edge of the Book or Roll, but a Seal was broken and the parchment unrolled until the next seal was reached, and so on until all the "Seals" had been broken. We are not told that what happened as the "Seals" were broken was read out of the Book. The contents of the "Book" are not disclosed. We are simply told, as the "Seals" are broken, that certain things happened. They doubtless were preliminary to the Lamb's taking possession of the Purchased Possession. It is not until chapter 10: 1-6, that Christ, as the "MIGHTY ANGEL," puts His right foot upon the sea, and His left foot on the earth, and cries—"There shall be time no longer," that is "NO LONGER DELAY," that He takes formal possession, but as the claim is disputed further steps, as we shall see, are necessary to secure possession.

Daniel's Seventieth Week
Daniel 9: 1-27.

As the events recorded in Rev. 6: 1 to Rev. 19: 21, are connected with the last, or "Seventieth Week," of Daniel's "SEVENTY WEEKS," it is necessary that we stop here and explain what is meant by Daniel's "Seventieth Week."

The Prophet Daniel had been 68 years (B. C. 538) in Babylon, and by a study of the Prophecy of Jeremiah (Jer. 25: 11), he discovered that the "Seventy Years" Captivity of his people was nearing its end, and so he set his face unto the Lord, to seek by prayer and supplication (Dan. 9: 3) to know the exact time of its ending, and while he was praying the Angel Gabriel appeared to enlighten him. (Dan. 9: 20-23.) Daniel was concerned about the expiration of the "Seventy Years" of the Captivity, and the restoration of his people to Palestine, and the rebuilding of the City of Jerusalem and of the Temple. But the Angel Gabriel came to disclose to him something more important than that. While he doubtless informed Daniel that God would fulfil His promise as to the "Seventy Years" of the Captivity, which, as we know, He did, he also made known to Daniel that that would **not end** the troubles of Israel. That while the Jews were to return to Jerusalem at the end of the "Seventy Years" of Captivity, there was a **longer period** to elapse before the Kingdom would be restored to them, a period of

"SEVENTY WEEKS."

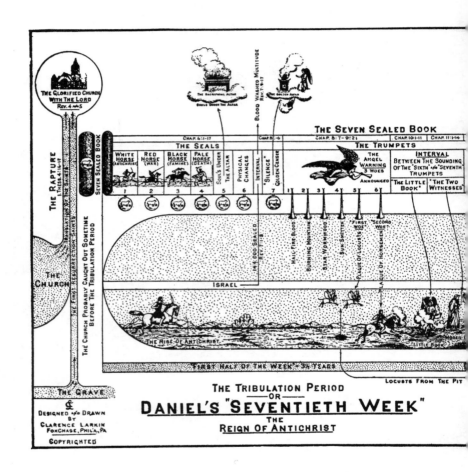

THE SEVEN SEALED BOOK

THE SEALS

THE TRUMPETS

INTERVAL
BETWEEN THE SOUNDING
OF THE "SIXTH" AND "SEVENTH"
TRUMPETS

THE LITTLE BOOK | THE TWO WITNESSES

THE GLORIFIED CHURCH WITH THE LORD
Rev. 4 AND 5

THE RAPTURE
I. Thess. 4:16-17

SEVEN SEALED BOOK

WHITE HORSE (ANTICHRIST) | RED HORSE (WAR) | BLACK HORSE (FAMINE) | PALE HORSE (DEATH) | SOUL'S UNDER THE ALTAR | PHYSICAL CHANGES | INTERVAL | "SILENCE" GOLDEN CENSER

THE ANGEL WARNING 3 WOES ANNOUNCED

THE CHURCH

THE CHURCH PROBABLY CAUGHT OUT SOMETIME BEFORE THE TRIBULATION PERIOD

THE FIRST RESURRECTION SAINTS

ISRAEL

144,000 SEALED
REV. 7:1-8

HAIL-FIRE-BLOOD

BURNING MOUNTAIN

STAR WORMWOOD

SUN SMITTEN

PLAGUE OF LOCUSTS

FIRST "WOE"

SECOND "WOE"

PLAGUE OF HORSEMEN

THE RISE OF ANTICHRIST

LITTLE BOOK

FIRST HALF OF THE WEEK - 3½ YEARS

LOCUSTS FROM THE PIT

THE GRAVE

DESIGNED AND DRAWN BY
CLARENCE LARKIN
FOXCHASE, PHILA., PA
COPYRIGHTED

THE TRIBULATION PERIOD
—OR—
DANIEL'S "SEVENTIETH WEEK"
THE
REIGN OF ANTICHRIST

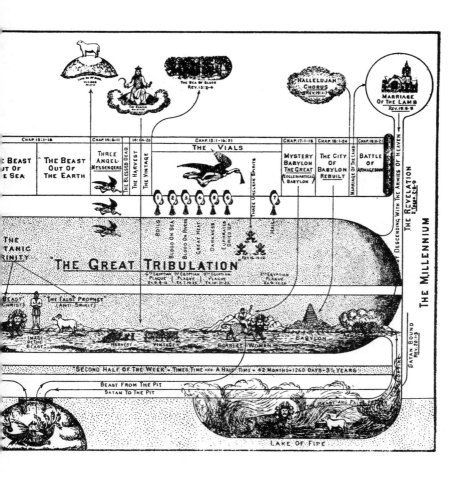

"SEVENTY WEEKS are determined upon Thy People (Daniel's people the Jews) and upon the Holy City (Jerusalem), to finish the transgression, and to make an end of sins, and to make reconciliation for iniquity, and to bring in everlasting righteousness, and to seal up the vision and prophecy, and to anoint the most Holy. Know therefore and understand, that from the going forth of the commandment to restore and to build Jerusalem unto the 'MESSIAH THE PRINCE' shall be SEVEN WEEKS, and THREESCORE AND TWO WEEKS: the street shall be built again, and the wall, even in troublous times. And after THREESCORE AND TWO WEEKS shall MESSIAH BE CUT OFF, but not for Himself: and the people (Roman) of the PRINCE THAT SHALL COME (Antichrist) shall destroy the City and the Sanctuary; and the end thereof shall be with a flood, and unto the end of the war desolations are determined. And he (Antichrist) shall confirm the Covenant with many for ONE WEEK (the last or Seventieth Week): and in the midst of THE WEEK he (Antichrist) shall cause the Sacrifice and the oblations to cease, and for the overspreading of abominations (the Abomination of Desolation spoken of by Christ. Matt. 24:15) he shall make it desolate, even until the consummation, and that determined shall be poured upon the desolate." Dan. 9:24-27.

This Vision of the "SEVENTY WEEKS" is the most important revelation, in many ways, made in the Scriptures. We are here told that this Period of "SEVENTY WEEKS" was determined upon Daniel's PEOPLE (the Jews), and upon the HOLY CITY (Jerusalem). This is very important. It discloses the fact that the "SEVENTY WEEKS" have nothing to do with the Gentiles, or the Church, but only with the JEWS and JERUSALEM. It also discloses another important fact that the "SEVENTY WEEKS" only cover the period when the Jews are DWELLING IN THEIR OWN LAND, and does not cover the present period of their Dispersion. We are told in verse 24 that these "SEVENTY WEEKS" were determined for a SIX-FOLD purpose.

1. TO FINISH THE TRANSGRESSION.

It is the transgression of ISRAEL that is here referred to, and the finishing of it will be the turning away of UNGODLINESS FROM JACOB. Rom. 11:26-27. The transgression of Israel has not yet come to an end, and will not until they as a Nation shall be converted.

2. TO MAKE AN END OF SINS.

The margin reads to "seal up" sins. The sins of ISRAEL. This may refer to the author of Israel's sins—Satan, who shall at that time be "sealed up" in the Pit. Rev. 20:1-3.

3. TO MAKE RECONCILIATION FOR INIQUITY.

This refers to ISRAEL'S iniquity in the rejection of their Messiah. While atonement was made for their sin on the Cross, its application to Israel as a Nation awaits the day when they shall look on Him whom they pierced (Zech. 12:10), and a fountain shall be opened to the "House of David," and the inhabitants of Jerusalem for sin and uncleanliness, Zech. 13:1, and a nation, the Jewish Nation, shall be "born again" in a day. Isa. 66:8.

4. TO BRING IN EVERLASTING RIGHTEOUSNESS.

When the "Transgression of ISRAEL" has come to an end, and her sins are "sealed up," then everlasting righteousness shall be brought in.   The King will come, and the Kingdom be restored to Israel, and the Millennium will be here, and the "Knowledge of the Lord" shall cover the earth, as the waters cover the sea.   Hab. 2:14.

5. TO SEAL UP THE VISION AND PROPHECY.

When the "Transgression of ISRAEL" has ceased and they have uninterrupted communion with God, there will no longer be any need for "Vision" or "Prophet."   It is a noteworthy fact that "Vision" and "Prophecy" has been confined to the Jewish race.

6. TO ANOINT THE MOST HOLY.

This probably refers to the anointing of the "Most Holy Place," or the "Holy of Holies" of the MILLENNIAL TEMPLE, described by Ezekiel.   Ezek. 41.   There is great significance in this announcement; for, although the Tabernacle of Moses was anointed (Lev. 8:10), there is no mention of such a ceremony in the Consecration of either Solomon's Temple, or the Temple of Zerubbabel, for those buildings were considered merely as continuations of the Mosaic Tabernacle.   But when the King comes back and sits upon the Throne of His father David, there is to be a magnificent Temple erected, the like of which has never as yet been seen on this planet of ours.   There will be no "Ark of the Covenant" with its "Mercy Seat," in the "Most Holy Place" of the Millennial Temple (Jer. 3:16), but in its place will stand the ROYAL THRONE on which the "BRANCH," the Messiah shall sit as a KING-PRIEST (Zech. 6:12-13), and whose anointing is here referred to.

Now as the fulfilment of this "Six-Fold" purpose of the "SEVENTY WEEKS" synchronizes with the things that shall happen at the close of this Dispensation, and that are described in Rev. 6:1; 19:21, it is clear that the last, or "SEVENTIETH WEEK" of Daniel's "Seventy Weeks," covers the "TIME PERIOD" of Rev. 6:1; 19:21, and confirms the claim that that "Period" is Jewish and has nothing to do with the Church.   To prove this it is only necessary to outline Daniel's "Seventy Weeks."

The "Seventy Weeks" are divided into "THREE PERIODS" of 7 Weeks, and 62 Weeks, and 1 Week.   They cover the time from the going forth of the commandment to restore and to build Jerusalem, which was the 14th day of the month Nisan (March) B. C. 445, to the Second Stage (The Revelation) of the Second Coming of Christ.   The "First Period," 7 WEEKS, refers to the time required to rebuild the walls of Jerusalem, which was 49 years, thus giving us the "Key" to the meaning of the word "WEEK," for if 7 WEEKS are equal to 49 YEARS, then 1 WEEK is equal to 7 YEARS.   Now we are told that from the going forth of the commandment to restore and rebuild Jerusalem (B. C. 445) unto the "MESSIAH THE

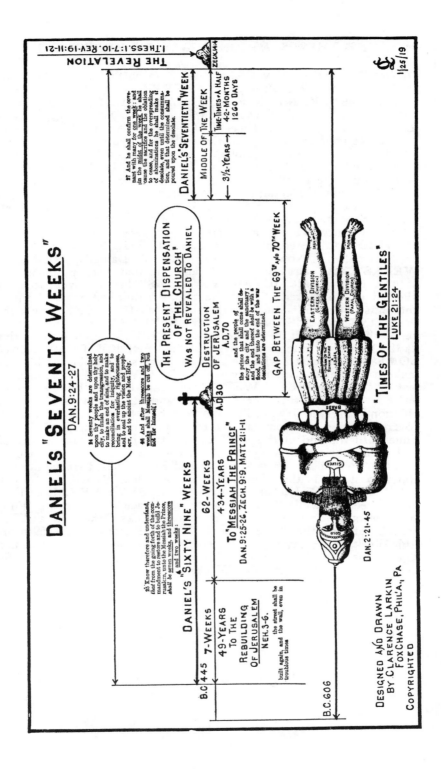

PRINCE," shall be 7 WEEKS, and THREESCORE AND TWO WEEKS, or 69 WEEKS, or, if 1 WEEK is equal to 7 YEARS, 7 x 69 or 483 YEARS. Now Jesus, as "MESSIAH THE PRINCE," rode in triumph into Jerusalem on Palm Sunday, April 2, A. D. 30. The difference in time between B. C. 445 and A. D. 30 is 475 years, but, as we have seen, 69 WEEKS equal 483 years, a difference of 8 years. How are we to explain this difference?

The 475 years between B. C. 445 and A. D. 30, are Julian or Astronomical years of 365¼ days each, but when we reduce them to Calendar years of 360 days each, the year used in the Scriptures, we find that we have exactly 483 years of 360 days each. This proves that there was no break between the "First" and "Second" Periods of the "Seventy Weeks," and that the prophecy that there should be 69 WEEKS to the coming of "MESSIAH THE PRINCE" was literally fulfilled. Now as 69 WEEKS of Daniel's "SEVENTY WEEKS" have already expired, and all that was prophesied to occur during those "SEVENTY WEEKS" has not yet been fulfilled, it stands to reason that the things unfulfilled are still future, and must be fulfilled in the remaining "ONE WEEK," and that that "ONE WEEK" shall be "SEVEN YEARS" long, for it must be of the same length as the other "WEEKS." This then gives us the length of time of the reign of the "PRINCE THAT SHALL COME" (Antichrist), who we are told in verse 27 (Dan. 9:27) shall make a Covenant with the Jews for "ONE WEEK" (7 years), the last or "SEVENTIETH WEEK," and that in the "Middle" of the WEEK he shall break the Covenant and cause the "sacrifice and oblation" that the Jews will have restored, to cease, and then the "overspreading of abominations that maketh desolate," shall continue until the end of the WEEK. As this is just what is foretold will occur during the reign of Antichrist (2. Thess. 2:3-4) we see that the "Period" between Rev. 6:1 and Rev. 19:21, that we are now about to study, is the "Third Period" of ONE WEEK, of Daniel's "SEVENTY WEEKS" and that it is to last SEVEN YEARS. From this we see that while there was no "Time Space" between the "First" and "Second" Periods of the "Seventy Weeks," there is a "Time Space" between the "Second" and "Third" Periods or the 69th and 70th Week, of already (A. D. 1919) 1889 years, or the present Church Age. This was hidden so the Church should not fail to watch. See the Chart, "Daniel's Seventy Weeks."

The Seven Seals

FIRST SEAL.
(A White Horse.)
Rev. 6:1-2.

"And I saw when the **LAMB** opened one of the **SEALS, and** I heard, as it were the noise of thunder, one of the 'Four Beasts' saying, **Come and see.** And I saw, and behold a **WHITE HORSE**: and he that sat on him had a **bow**; and a **crown was given unto him**: and he went forth **conquering, and to conquer.**"

When the **LAMB** broke the "First Seal," the first, or "Lion-like Living Creature" cried with a voice of thunder—"**COME.**" The words "and see" are omitted in many manuscripts, and in the Revised Version. John had no need to "come" for he was already there. The command then of "Come" was to the "**Rider**" of the White Horse. When he appeared, John says—"And I saw, and behold a **WHITE HORSE**; and he that sat on him had a **bow**; and a **crown was given unto him**: and he went forth **conquering, and to conquer.**"

Who is the "**Rider**" upon this White Horse? He is not Christ, as some claim, for Christ, as the **LAMB**, is holding the "Seven Sealed Book" and breaking its "Seals." Christ does not appear as a White Horse Rider until chapter 19:11-16, when He comes with the armies of Heaven to engage in the Battle of Armageddon. Then He is called "Faithful and True," and on His head there is a many "Diademed Crown," and He is clothed in a vesture dipped in blood, and His name is called the "**WORD OF GOD,**" and there is no weapon of warfare in His hand, but a **sharp sword** comes out of His **mouth,** and the effect upon His enemies will be swift and terrible.

This "Rider" has a "**bow,**" no arrow is mentioned, and he is not crowned at first, but a crown will be given to him later, the "Stephanos" or "Victor's Crown," as a reward for his victories which are prolonged and bloodless. This is the picture of a brilliant, strategical, and irresistible conqueror, whose victories will dazzle the world, and elevate him to a leadership that will place him at the Head of the

Ten Federated Kingdoms of the revived Roman Empire. As a subaltern, like Napoleon I, he will rise from the ranks until a crown will be given him. His triumphs will be due to his skilful diplomacy. Like Antiochus Epiphanes, his prototype, he "will come in **peaceably,** and obtain the Kingdom by **flatteries."** Dan. 11:21. As the "Tool of Satan" he will be endowed with wonder working powers, and when he comes, he will find the world ready to receive him, for God will send upon its inhabitants a "**strong delusion**" that they will believe a **LIE,** or "**THE LIE,**" for that is what he will be. 2. Thess. 2:9-11.

In other words this White Horse Rider is the **ANTICHRIST.** He is the "**PRINCE WHO IS TO COME**" of Daniel's Vision of the "Seventy Weeks," and who will confirm the Covenant for "**ONE WEEK,**" the last or "Seventieth Week," with Daniel's people the Jews. Dan. 9:27. This Covenant will probably be the privilege to return to Palestine and rebuild the Temple and re-establish their sacrificial form of worship, and national existence, in exchange for the financial assistance of the Jewish bankers of the world in his schemes of establishing world wide commerce, and the formation of a gigantic corporation, with its commercial centre in the rebuilt city of Babylon, so that no one can buy or sell unless they have his "**MARK,**" (the "Mark of the Beast," Rev. 13:16-17), for we are told in Dan. 8:23-25, that "through his policy also he shall cause **CRAFT** (manufactories) to prosper in his hand."

The rise of this White Horse Rider necessarily antedates the beginning of the "Seventieth Week," or the "**SEVEN YEARS**" of his reign, for he must have reached a position of power to make a Covenant with the Jews at the beginning of the "**WEEK,**" but he does not become "**THE BEAST,**" as described in chapter 13:1-8, until the "Middle" of the WEEK, that is, until after Satan is cast out of the Heavenlies and incarnates himself in him. His rise to power and the rebuilding of Babylon will take time, so the Rapture of the Church will doubtless antedate the **beginning** of the WEEK by some years.

But while the establishment of the Antichrist's power will be comparatively peaceful, that peace will be shortlived as is evident from the breaking of the "Second Seal."

This "White Horse Rider" will be Satan's "**SUPERMAN.**" The Scriptures clearly teach that there is some day to arise a human being who shall be the embodiment of all Satanic power. He **will** be known as the "**WILFUL KING**" because he shall do according to his own will. He will be the Czar of Czars. He will have no respect for sacred things or places. He will cause a throne to be erected in the Most Holy Place of a Temple that the Jews will build at Jerusalem, and, seating himself upon it, he will proclaim himself God, and men will be commanded to worship him; and Satan will give unto him his **power** and his **seat** (Throne) and great authority. All this will be fully brought out under the "Sixth Personage," the "Beast Out of the Sea," Page 103.

SECOND SEAL.
(A Red Horse.)
Rev. 6: 3-4.

"And when He had opened the 'SECOND SEAL,' I heard
the 'Second Beast' say, **Come.** And there went out another Horse
that was **RED**: and power was given to him that sat thereon to
take peace from the earth, and that they should kill one another:
and there was given unto him a **GREAT SWORD.**"

There is no need to tarry long with this **SEAL.** When it was
broken John heard the second, or "Calf-like Living Creature" say,
"Come," and a "RED HORSE" appeared and went forth, whose
Rider was given a "GREAT SWORD," and who had power to take
peace from the earth, and cause men to kill one another. The symbolism is very clear. **Red,** the color of the Horse, is a symbol of
BLOOD, and the **Sword** is a symbol of **WAR.** The time is clearly
that prophesied by Christ—"And ye shall hear of wars and rumors of
wars . . . for nation shall rise against nation, and kingdom
against kingdom." Matt. 24:6-7. This seems to imply that the Antichrist will not have everything his own way, and that his Autocratic
methods will lead to insubordination and civil wars among the nations
under some great leader represented by the Rider of the Red Horse,
whose "Great Sword" is symbolical of the awful destruction of
human life that will follow.

This is a fulfillment of 1. Thess. 5:3. "When they shall say
PEACE and **SAFETY**; then sudden destruction cometh upon them,
as travail upon a woman with child; and they shall not escape." We
learn from this "Seal" that wars are likely to break out at any time
and that there will be no peace on the earth until the return of the
"Prince of Peace."

THIRD SEAL.
(A Black Horse.)
Rev. 6:5-6.

"And when He opened the 'THIRD SEAL,' I heard the 'Third Beast' say, **Come.** And I beheld, and lo a **BLACK HORSE:** and he that sat on him had a **pair of balances in his hand.** And I heard a voice in the midst of the Four Beasts say, **A measure of wheat for a penny,** and **three measures of barley for a penny:** and see thou hurt not the oil and the wine."

When the "THIRD SEAL" was broken John heard the third or "Man-like Living Creature" say—"Come," and a "BLACK HORSE" appeared and went forth, whose Rider held in his hand a "pair of balances," and John heard the voice of an invisible person in the midst of the "Four Living Creatures" say—"A measure of wheat for a penny, and three measures of barley for a penny, and see thou hurt not the oil and the wine." The "BLACK HORSE" signifies famine, and the Rider the "Conserver of Food." When all able bodied men are drafted for war, and no one left to sow and harvest the crops, then famine is sure to follow. So great will be the famine, that it will take a "denarius" a day's wages, to buy a "choenix" (2 pints) of wheat," the daily ration of a slave. What is meant by not hurting the oil and wine, may be, that as the Olive tree and grapevine do not bear their fruit until some months after the wheat and barley harvest, and grow without much attention, their crops would not be so much affected by war, and therefore the Olive trees and grapevines were not to be ruthlessly destroyed by invaders for they were needed for medicinal purposes.

FOURTH SEAL.
(A Pale Horse.)
Rev. 6:7-8.

"And when He had opened the 'FOURTH SEAL,' I heard the voice of the 'Fourth Beast' say, **Come.** And I looked, and behold a **PALE HORSE:** and his name that sat on him was **DEATH,** and **HELL (Hades)** followed with him. And power was given unto them over the' **fourth part of the earth, to kill** with **SWORD,** and with **HUNGER,** and with **DEATH,** and with the **BEASTS OF THE EARTH.**"

When the "FOURTH SEAL" was broken John heard the fourth, or "Eagle-like Living Creature" say—"Come," and a "PALE HORSE" appeared and went forth. Note the "corpse-like" color of the Horse. We are not surprised then when the Rider upon the "PALE HORSE" is called "DEATH," and that "HADES," the "Grave," not "Hell," follows after "Death" like a great "Voracious Monster" to swallow up the victims of "DEATH." It is worthy of note that the Riders of the first three Horses are not named, but it will be very clear when the events they chronicle occur, who and what is meant. Here however the Rider is **personified** and called "DEATH," and his consort is called "HADES," they are inseparable companions. The reference here is clearly to some great **PESTILENCE** that shall come upon the earth. After a devastating war, followed by famine, during which the dead are left unburied, a **PESTILENCE** is sure to follow. The "fourth part of the earth" over which the Pestilence shall sweep will probably be that part of the Eastern Hemisphere covered by the revived Roman Empire. See Map of the Old Roman Empire. So great will be the destruction of human life in the days of the "Fourth Seal" that **HADES** will have to **enlarge herself** and **open her mouth** without measure, as foretold in Isa. 5:13-16. The means of destruction mentioned—the **SWORD, HUNGER, DEATH,** and the **BEASTS OF THE EARTH,** are the "FOUR SORE JUDGMENTS" of Ez. 14:21, that are to fall upon JERUSALEM—"For thus saith the Lord God: How much more when I send my 'FOUR SORE JUDGMENTS' upon JERUSALEM, the SWORD, and the FAMINE, and the NOISOME BEAST, and the PESTILENCE, to cut off from it man and beast." Those will be awful times to those who must pass through them. But the Church will not be in them having been "caught out" before as promised. But awful as those days will be, they will be only the "BEGINNING OF SORROWS" for those who are left. Matt. 24: 6-8. And the worst thing about them will be that they are "Hardening Judgments," and instead of the people repenting and calling upon God, they will call on the mountains and rocks to hide them from the face of Him that sitteth on the Throne. Rev. 6: 15-17.

FIFTH SEAL.
(The Souls of Martyrs.)
Rev. 6: 9-11.

THE SACRIFICIAL ALTAR
(Souls Under the Altar.)

"And when He had opened the 'FIFTH SEAL,' I saw under the 'Altar' the SOULS of them that were slain for the Word of God, and for the testimony which they held: and they cried with a loud voice, saying, How long, O Lord, Holy and True, dost Thou not judge and avenge our BLOOD on them that dwell on the earth? And white robes were given unto every one of them: and it was said unto them, that they should rest yet for a 'little season,' until their fellow servants also and their brethren, that should be killed as they were, should be fulfilled."

When the Lamb had opened the "FIFTH SEAL," John saw under the "Sacrificial Altar," corresponding to the "Burnt Offering Altar," the "SOULS" of them that were slain for the "Word of God" and for the "testimony they held." The fact that their "SOULS" were under the "Sacrificial Altar" is proof that they had been offered as a "Sacrifice," that is that they were MARTYRS. But they were not the Martyrs of the Christian Church, for they had been resurrected and taken up with the Church. These Martyrs are those who will be killed for the "Word of **God**" and their "testimony" **after** the Church is caught out.

According to Christ (Matt. 24:9-14), a persecution will be brought about by the preaching of the "**GOSPEL OF THE KINGDOM.**" When the Church is caught out the preaching of the "**GOSPEL OF THE GRACE OF GOD**" (Acts 20:24), which is being preached now, will cease, and the preaching of the "**GOSPEL OF THE KINGDOM**" will be revived. It is the Gospel that John the Baptist preached, "Repent ye: for the Kingdom of Heaven is at hand." Matt. 3:1-2, and that Elijah the Prophet when he returns will preach. Malachi 4:5-6. It is to be preached in all the world for a **witness**; and then shall the "**End**," the End of this Dispensation, come. It will be preached by the Jews, and will be the announcement that Christ is coming back to set up His Earthly Kingdom, and rule over the affairs of men. This will be exceedingly distasteful to the Kings of the Earth, particularly to Antichrist and the Kings of the Ten Federated Kingdoms, and the outcome will be a "Great Persecution" of those who preach and accept such a Gospel, and the "**SOULS**" that John saw under the "Sacrificial Altar," are the souls of those who shall perish during that time of persecution. That there is no such thing as "Soul Sleep," and that disembodied **SOULS** are conscious and can speak and cry, is clear from what John saw and heard, for these "**SOULS**" cried with a loud voice—"How long, O Lord, Holy and True, dost Thou not judge and avenge our **BLOOD** on them that dwell on the earth?" The character of their cry is further proof that they are not the Martyrs of the Christian Church, for they would not cry to be avenged, but like Stephen would say—"Lord, lay not this sin to their charge." Acts 7:60. Their cry is that of the Imprecatory Psalms (Psa. 35, 55, 59, 94, etc.) and indicates that these Martyrs whose **SOULS** are seen are mainly **JEWS**. This is still more likely when we consider that the "Gospel of the Kingdom" is to be preached to the **NATIONS**, and Israel has never been numbered among the Nations. Num. 23:9.

To these martyred "**SOULS**" white robes were given. This does not mean that they were resurrected, that is, given glorified **BODIES**, and then robed, but that they in their "Soulish" or "**PSYCHICAL**" bodies were given white robes, for while the "Spirit" of man loses its earthly, or **FLESHY** body, at death, it still has a body, its **SOULISH** body, that can see, hear, speak, etc., for how could a **SOUL** "cry" if it did not have a form and physical senses. For a full exposition of this see the Author's Book on "Dispensational Truth," the Chapter on the "Spirit World."

These martyred **SOULS** were comforted, and told that they should rest for a "**little season**," about 3½ years, until their fellow servants also, and their brethren (Jews) that should be killed, **as they were**, should be fulfilled. This promise is fulfilled in Rev. 20:4-6. These are the Saints of the Most High that Daniel foresaw would receive the Kingdom. Dan. 7:27.

SIXTH SEAL.
(Physical Changes.)
Rev. 6: 12-17.

"And I beheld when He had opened the 'SIXTH SEAL,' and, lo, there was an **earthquake**: and the sun became **black as sackcloth of hair**, and the moon **became as blood**: and the stars of heaven fell unto the earth, even as a fig tree casteth her untimely figs, when she is shaken of a mighty wind. And the heaven departed as a scroll when it is rolled together; and every mountain and island were moved out of their places. And the **kings of the earth**, and the **great men**, and the **rich men**, and the **chief captains**, and the **mighty men**, and every **bond man**, and every **free man** hid themselves in the dens and in the rocks of the mountains; and said to the mountains and rocks, **FALL ON US**, and **HIDE US** from the face of Him that sitteth on the Throne, and from the **WRATH OF THE LAMB**: for the great day of **HIS WRATH** is come; and who shall be able to stand?"

When the "SIXTH SEAL" was broken John tells us that there was a "GREAT EARTHQUAKE," and the "SUN BECAME BLACK AS SACKCLOTH OF HAIR," and the "MOON BECAME AS BLOOD," and the "STARS OF HEAVEN FELL TO THE EARTH," and the "HEAVEN DEPARTED AS A SCROLL," and "EVERY MOUNTAIN AND ISLAND WERE MOVED OUT OF THEIR PLACE." It will not do to say that these things prefigure and symbolize the overthrow of the Powers of the Earth by great social and political convulsions. These are nothing more or less than great **physical convulsions** that shall shake the earth, and that have been foretold by the Prophets and by Christ Himself. Such physical phenomena and changes have happened before. We must not forget the "GREAT DARKNESS" that for 3 days overspread Egypt in the days before the Exodus (Ex. 10: 21-23), nor the "DARKNESS" that settled over Jerusalem and Calvary on the day of the Crucifixion of Christ. Matt. 27: 45.

The Prophet Zachariah speaks of a day that shall not be "clear" or "dark," and he associates it with an earthquake at the time of the return of the Lord. Zech. 14: 1-7. On May 19, 1780, there was in New England what is called in history the "Dark Day." It was not an eclipse of the sun, and yet it was dark enough to make the stars visible, and the chickens went to roost. The cause of that darkness has never been explained. In the prophecy of Joel we read—"I will shew wonders in the heavens, and in the earth, blood, and fire, and pillars of smoke. The sun shall be TURNED INTO DARKNESS, and the moon into BLOOD, before THE GREAT AND TERRIBLE DAY OF THE LORD COME." Joel 2: 30-31. In Isa. 13: 9-10, we read—"Behold the 'DAY OF THE LORD' cometh, cruel both with wrath and fierce anger, to lay the land desolate, and He shall destroy the sinners thereof out of it. For the stars of heaven and the constellations thereof shall NOT GIVE THEIR LIGHT, the sun shall be DARKENED in his going forth, and the moon shall not CAUSE HER LIGHT TO SHINE." In Isa. 34: 4 we read—"All the host of heaven (the stars) shall be dissolved and the heavens shall be rolled together as a scroll: and all their host shall fall down, as the leaf falleth from the vine, and as falling fig from the figtree." This corresponds to the "stars of heaven" of this "SEAL," and probably refers not to the constellations and heavenly bodies (stars), they are too far away to be affected by judgments on the earth, but to our own atmosphere, and to "meteors" and "shooting stars," similar to the "shooting stars" of November 13th, 1833, when they fell for 3 hours during the evening, and so terrified the people that they thought the end of the world had come. These physical convulsions will be the earth's "TRAVAIL PAINS" as she labors to bring forth the NEW CREATION of the Millennial Age. Christ refers to this period in Matt. 24:29, where He says—"In those days shall the SUN BE DARKENED (that is, its light obscured), and the MOON SHALL NOT GIVE HER LIGHT, and the STARS SHALL FALL FROM HEAVEN, and the POWERS OF THE HEAVENS (the Principalities and Powers of the Heavenly Places (Eph. 6:12), not the Powers and Kingdoms of the Earth), SHALL BE SHAKEN." All these startling physical changes and convulsions will cause a great fear to fall upon all classes and conditions of men (7 classes are named), who will no longer attribute such changes merely to natural law, but will see the "HAND OF THE ALMIGHTY" in it all. To them the "DAY OF JUDGMENT" will become a reality, and in their fear and terror they will hide themselves in the dens and in the rocks of the mountains, and say to them—"FALL ON US, AND HIDE US FROM THE FACE OF HIM THAT SITTETH ON THE THRONE, AND FROM THE 'WRATH OF THE LAMB,' FOR THE GREAT DAY OF HIS WRATH IS COME, AND WHO SHALL BE ABLE TO STAND?" What a prayer? Instead of repenting and crying for Salvation, they will call on the mountains and rocks to bury them from the sight of the Almighty.

At this point it will be interesting to compare, as on the next three pages, Christ's "Olivet Discourse" (Matt. 24:1-30), with the "Six Seals" of Rev. 6:1-17. The similarity between them is most striking, and proves that the author of the "Olivet Discourse" foreknew, in the "Days of His Flesh," in their exact order, the things that shall come to pass in the "Day of the Lord." This is indisputable evidence of the Deity of Jesus.

COMPARISON OF CHRIST'S "OLIVET DISCOURSE" AND "REVELATION SIX"

MATT. 24:1-3

TUESDAY AFTERNOON APRIL 4: A.D. 30

AND Jesus went out, and departed from the temple: and his disciples came to *him* for to shew him the buildings of the temple.

2 And Jesus said unto them, See ye not all these things? verily I say unto you, There shall not be left here one stone upon another, that shall not be thrown down.

TUESDAY EVENING

3 ¶ And as he sat upon the mount of Olives, the disciples came unto him privately, saying, Tell us, when shall these things be? and what *shall be* the sign of thy coming, and of the end of the world?

THE THREE-FOLD QUESTION

1- WHEN SHALL THESE THINGS BE?
2- WHAT SHALL BE THE SIGN OF THY COMING?
3- AND OF THE END OF THE WORLD (AGE)?

ANSWER TO FIRST QUESTION

MATT. 24:4-5

4 And Jesus answered and said unto them, Take heed that no man deceive you.
5 For many shall come in my name, saying, I am Christ; and shall deceive many.

**1-SEAL
FALSE CHRIST'S**

REV. 6:1-2

AND I saw when the Lamb opened one of the seals, and I heard, as it were the noise of thunder, one of the four beasts saying, Come and see.
2 And I saw, and behold a white horse: and he that sat on him had a bow; and a crown was given unto him: and he went forth conquering, and to conquer.

MATT. 24:6-7

6 And ye shall hear of wars and rumours of wars: see that ye be not troubled: for all *these things* must come to pass, but the end is not yet.
7 For nation shall rise against nation, and kingdom against kingdom:

**2-SEAL
WARS**

REV. 6:3-4

3 And when he had opened the second seal, I heard the second beast say, Come and see.
4 And there went out another horse *that was* red: and *power* was given to him that sat thereon to take peace from the earth, and that they should kill one another: and there was given unto him a great sword.

MATT 24:7

and there shall be famines,

3-SEAL
FAMINES

REV. 6:5-6

5 And when he had opened the third seal, I heard the third beast say, Come and see. And I beheld, and lo a black horse; and he that sat on him had a pair of balances in his hand.

6 And I heard a voice in the midst of the four beasts say, A measure of wheat for a penny, and three measures of barley for a penny; and *see* thou hurt not the oil and the wine.

MATT. 24:7-8

and pestilences, and earthquakes, in divers places.

8 All these *are* the beginning of sorrows.

4-SEAL
PESTILENCE
AND
DEATH

REV. 6:7-8

7 And when he had opened the fourth seal, I heard the voice of the fourth beast say, Come and see.

8 And I looked, and behold a pale horse: and his name that sat on him was Death, and Hell followed with him. And power was given unto them over the fourth part of the earth, to kill with sword, and with hunger, and with death, and with the beasts of the earth.

MATT. 24:9-13

9 Then shall they deliver you up to be afflicted, and shall kill you: and ye shall be hated of all nations for my name's sake.

10 And then shall many be offended, and shall betray one another, and shall hate one another.

11 And many false prophets shall rise, and shall deceive many.

12 And because iniquity shall abound, the love of many shall wax cold.

13 But he that shall endure unto the end, the same shall be saved.

5-SEAL
MARTYRDOMS

REV. 6:9-11

9 And when he had opened the fifth seal, I saw under the altar the souls of them that were slain for the word of God, and for the testimony which they held:

10 And they cried with a loud voice, saying, How long, O Lord, holy and true, dost thou not judge and avenge our blood on them that dwell on the earth?

11 And white robes were given unto every one of them; and it was said unto them, that they should rest yet for a little season, until their fellow servants also and their brethren, that should be killed as they *were*, should be fulfilled.

MATT. 24:14

14 And this gospel of the kingdom shall be preached in all the world for a witness unto all nations; and then shall the end come.

THE GOSPEL NOW BEING PREACHED, IS THE "GOSPEL OF THE GRACE OF GOD". ACTS 20:24.

ANSWER TO SECOND QUESTION

MATT. 24:15

15 When ye therefore shall see the abomination of desolation, spoken of by Daniel the prophet, stand in the holy place, (whoso readeth, let him understand,)

"THE SIGN" OF THE "DESOLATOR"
DAN. 9:27

MATT. 24:16-22

16 Then let them which be in Judea flee into the mountains:

17 Let him which is on the housetop not come down to take any thing out of his house:

18 Neither let him which is in the field return back to take his clothes.

19 And woe unto them that are with child, and to them that give suck in those days!

20 But pray ye that your flight be not in the winter, neither on the sabbath day:

21 For then shall be great tribulation, such as was not since the beginning of the world to this time, no, nor ever shall be.

22 And except those days should be shortened, there should no flesh be saved: but for the elect's sake those days shall be shortened.

) THE "GREAT TRIBULATION"

ANSWER TO THIRD QUESTION

MATT. 24:29-30

29 ¶ Immediately after the tribulation of those days shall the sun be darkened, and the moon shall not give her light, and the stars shall fall from heaven, and the powers of the heavens shall be shaken:

30 And then shall appear the sign of the Son of man in heaven: and then shall all the tribes of the earth mourn, and they shall see the Son of man coming in the clouds of heaven with power and great glory.

6-SEAL PHYSICAL CHANGES

REV. 6:12-17

12 And I beheld when he had opened the sixth seal, and, lo, there was a great earthquake; and the sun became black as sackcloth of hair, and the moon became as blood;

13 And the stars of heaven fell unto the earth, even as a fig tree casteth her untimely figs, when she is shaken of a mighty wind.

14 And the heaven departed as a scroll when it is rolled together; and every mountain and island were moved out of their places.

15 And the kings of the earth, and the great men, and the rich men, and the chief captains, and the mighty men, and every bond man, and every free man, hid themselves in the dens and in the rocks of the mountains;

16 And said to the mountains and rocks, Fall on us, and hide us from the face of him that sitteth on the throne, and from the wrath of the Lamb:

17 For the great day of his wrath is come; and who shall be able to stand?

THE "FIG-TREE" SIGN

MATT. 24:32-35

32 Now learn a parable of the fig tree; When his branch is yet tender, and putteth forth leaves, ye know that summer is nigh:

33 So likewise ye, when ye shall see all these things, know that it is near, even at the doors.

34 Verily I say unto you, This generation shall not pass, till all these things be fulfilled.

35 Heaven and earth shall pass away, but my words shall not pass away.

) JEWISH RACE

The Interval Between the Sixth and Seventh Seals

1. THE SEALING OF THE 144,000.
Rev. 7: 1-8.

"And after these things I saw four angels standing on the four corners of the earth, holding the four winds of the earth, that the wind should not blow on the earth, nor on the sea, nor on any tree. And I saw another angel ascending from the East, having the 'SEAL OF THE LIVING GOD': and he cried with a loud voice to the four angels, to whom it was given to hurt the earth and the sea, Saying, Hurt not the earth, neither the sea, nor the trees, till we have SEALED THE SERVANTS OF OUR GOD IN THEIR FOREHEADS. And I heard the number of them which were SEALED: and there were SEALED A HUNDRED AND FORTY AND FOUR THOUSAND OF ALL THE TRIBES OF ISRAEL."

Here we have a respite in the breaking of the "Seals" that God's "elect of Israel" may be "SEALED." As God reserved 7000 in the days of Ahab who did not bow the knee to Baal (1. Kings 19: 18), so there will be a "remnant according to the election of grace" (Rom. 11: 4-6), and God will reserve 144,000 of Israel who during the period of the Tribulation will not bow the knee to **Antichrist.** This **SEAL-ING** is not the Sealing of the Holy Spirit, by whom the Believer is sealed (Eph. 1: 13-14), but it is a "sealing" at the hand of **Angels.** Christ refers to it in Matt. 24: 31. What this **SEALING** is we are told in Rev. 14: 1. The "FATHER'S NAME" is to be written on their foreheads. They were "Sealed" on their **FOREHEADS** where others could see it. Theirs was no secret discipleship. In the same public manner the followers of Antichrist will be "Sealed" in their **Foreheads** or on their **RIGHT HAND,** with the "MARK OF THE BEAST" which is the **NUMBER OF HIS NAME,** or 666. Rev. 13: 16-18.

The 144,000, 12,000 from each Tribe, will be of the earthly Israel, the literal seed of Abraham, living at that time, and not of a mystical or spiritual Israel. Though the "Twelve Tribes" were long ago lost among the nations, their whereabouts is not unknown to God. And though they may have lost their genealogical books and records, so as not to be able to trace their Tribal descent, God knows **where** they are, and **who is who,** and in that day the angels, with **omniscient precision,** will seal them according to their Tribes, 12,000 from each Tribe. The Angel who has charge of the **SEALING** comes from **the EAST.** This is significant. It intimates that the "Sealed Ones" have their gaze directed toward the "SUN-RISING," as if looking for the fulfilment of the promise in Malachi, "Unto you that **fear My name** shall the 'SUN OF RIGHTEOUSNESS' arise with healing in His wings." Mal. 4: 2. The "Elect" then of Israel will be those who **"fear Christ's name,"** and who, like as Simon and Anna watched for His First Coming, will be looking for the coming of their Messiah.

There is a remarkable difference in the names of the Tribes as here recorded and the names of the original Twelve Tribes. Here the names of Dan and Ephraim are omitted, and the names of Joseph and Levi are substituted. Why is this? The reason is plain. In Deu. 29: 18-21, we read that the man, or woman, or family, or **TRIBE,** that should introduce **idolatry** into Israel, should have their or its name "blotted out" from under heaven, and be **separated** out of the Tribes of Israel. This is just what the Tribes of Dan and Ephraim were guilty of when they permitted Jeroboam to set up "**Golden Calves**" to be worshipped, one at Dan in the "Tribe of Dan," and the other at Bethel in the "Tribe of Ephraim." 1. Kings 12: 25-30. This is the reason why the Tribes of Dan and Ephraim are omitted from the list in this chapter, and the names of Joseph and Levi substituted. But as the Tribes of Dan and Ephraim are in the list of the Twelve Tribes that shall occupy the Holy Land during the Millennium (Ez. 48: 1-7, 23-29), it is evident that the **SEALING** of the Tribes in this chapter is more for **HEAVENLY PRESERVATION,** than to keep them for an **earthly inheritance,** and this view is confirmed by the fact that they are later seen with the Lamb on the Heavenly Mount Zion. Rev. 14: 1-5. The omission of their names in this list of these "**SEALED ONES**" is to show that the Tribes of Dan and Ephraim must pass through the Great Tribulation **unprotected by sealing.**

2. THE BLOOD WASHED MULTITUDE.
Rev. 7: 9-17.

"After this I beheld, and, lo, a **great multitude,** which no man could number, of ALL nations, and kindreds, and people, and tongues, stood before the Throne, and before the Lamb, **clothed in white robes,** and **palms in their hands;** and cried with a loud voice, SALVATION TO OUR GOD WHICH SITTETH UPON THE THRONE, AND UNTO THE LAMB. And all the angels stood round about the Throne, and about the Elders and the Four Beasts, and fell before the Throne on their faces, and worshipped God, saying, AMEN: BLESSING, AND GLORY, AND WISDOM, AND THANKSGIVING, AND HONOR, AND POWER, AND MIGHT, BE UNTO OUR GOD FOR EVER AND EVER. AMEN.

And one of the Elders answered, saying unto me, **What are these which are arrayed in White robes? and whence came they?** And I said unto him, Sir, thou knowest. And he said to me, These are they which came out of great tribulation, and have washed their robes, and made them white in the BLOOD OF THE LAMB. Therefore are they before the Throne of God, and serve Him day and night in His Temple: and He that sitteth on the Throne shall dwell among them. They shall **hunger no more,** neither thirst any more: neither shall the sun light on them, nor any heat. For the Lamb which is in the midst of the Throne shall **feed them,** and shall **lead them unto living fountains of water:** and God shall **wipe away all tears from their eyes.**"

This "Blood Washed Multitude" introduces us to another class of the saved of the "End-time." They do not represent the Church, for the Church has already been taken out. They differ from the Elders, who represent the Church, in that they **stand,** and have **"palms"** in their hands, while the Elders have **"crowns,"** and **"sit on thrones,"** and have **"harps,"** and **"golden vials"** in their hands. They are an "elect body" of Gentiles gathered out from **all nations, and kindreds, and people, and tongues.** The statement that they "**came out of great tribulation**" does not necessarily imply that it was "**The Great Tribulation**" that they came out of, for that covers only the "last half" of the Week, and they are seen by John in the middle of the "first half" of the Week. The Revised Version uses the word "come" instead of "came," and some versions the words "coming out." It does not say that they came out of "**THE Great Tribulation,**" but simply that they came out of "**great tribulation,**" and as the whole of the Week is a period of **tribulation** they could come out of **tribulation** any time during the Week. They are a vast multitude saved by the preaching of the "Gospel of the Kingdom." While the Holy Spirit went back with the Church to escort the "Bride to be" home, it does not follow that He remained there. For in Old Testament times, and during the earthly ministry of Jesus, He was active in the conversion of men, and so it will be after the Church is caught out. Those who are converted during the Tribulation period will be converted by the Holy Spirit.

The claim has been made that this "Blood Washed Multitude" represent the Gentiles who shall pass safely through "The Great Tribulation," and who cry "**SALVATION**" because they have been saved from martyrdom and death during the Tribulation, and that they serve God day and night in the new "Millennial Temple" on the earth because there is no day or night or Temple in Heaven. While that is true of the Holy City, New Jerusalem (Rev. 21:22-25), it is not true of Heaven, for they are not the same. The New Jerusalem is the place (City) that Jesus went to prepare for His Bride, the Church (John 14:2), and John declares that he saw it coming down "**out of**" Heaven. Rev. 21:2. Therefore the New Jerusalem is not Heaven. That there **is a "TEMPLE" in Heaven** we are told in chapters 11:19, 15:5-8, and 16:1. And the statement "That they shall **hunger no more, neither thirst any more; neither shall the sun light on them, nor any heat,** for the **LAMB** which is in the **MIDST OF THE THRONE** shall feed them, and shall lead them unto **living fountains of waters: and GOD** shall wipe away **all tears from their eyes,**" is not Millennial but Heavenly in character. And further this "Blood Washed Multitude, **being Gentiles,** could not serve in an earthly Jewish Temple."

The sight of this "Blood Washed Multitude" will so thrill and rejoice the Angelic Hosts that they will fall upon their faces and worship God, saying, "**AMEN: BLESSING, AND GLORY, AND WISDOM, AND THANKSGIVING, AND HONOR, AND POWER, AND MIGHT, BE UNTO OUR GOD FOR EVER AND EVER. AMEN.**"

SEVENTH SEAL
(Silence.)
Rev. 8:1.

"And when He had opened the 'SEVENTH SEAL,' there was SILENCE IN HEAVEN ABOUT THE SPACE OF HALF AN HOUR."

We must not forget that the "SEVENTH SEAL" includes all that happens during the sounding of the "Trumpets," and the pouring out of the "Vials," and so extends down to the ushering in of the Millennium. To illustrate, a rocket fired into the air may burst into "seven stars," and one of these stars into "seven other stars," and one of the second group of stars into a third group of "seven stars." So the "Seventh" Seal includes the "Seven Trumpets," and the "Seventh" Trumpet includes the "Seven Vials."

The "SILENCE" that followed the breaking of the "Seventh Seal" was preparatory to what was to follow during the sounding of the "Trumpets," and the pouring out of the "Vials." This "SILENCE" was something remarkable. The Four and Twenty Elders ceased their harp-playing; the angels hushed their voices, and the Cherubim and Seraphim and all the host of Heaven were silent, and so great was the silence that all Heaven was awed by it; and to add to the noticeableness of it, John added that it lasted for "HALF AN HOUR." Now a "half an hour" is not long when engaged in some pleasant employment, but it causes a nerve breaking tension when we do not know what is going to happen, and when a life is at stake a minute, or even a few seconds, seem to be hours. The suspense of the half hour of SILENCE in Heaven was intense. But why that half hour of silence? What did it portend? It was the period of silent preparation for the awful judgments that were to burst forth in the earth under the "Trumpets" and "Vials."

THE GOLDEN CENSER.
Rev. 8:2-5.

"And I saw the SEVEN ANGELS which stood before God; and to them were given SEVEN TRUMPETS. And ANOTHER ANGEL came and stood at the ALTAR (The Golden Incense Altar), having a GOLDEN CENSER; and there was given unto him much Incense, that he should offer it with the prayers of all saints upon the GOLDEN ALTAR which was before the Throne. And the smoke of the Incense, which came with the prayers of the saints, ascended up before God out of the Angel's hand. And the Angel took the CENSER and FILLED IT WITH FIRE OF THE ALTAR, and cast it INTO THE EARTH; and there were VOICES, and THUNDERINGS, and LIGHTNINGS, and an EARTHQUAKE."

THE GOLDEN ALTAR

Following the **SILENCE** in Heaven John saw **"SEVEN ANGELS"** of official importance, for they stand in the presence of God, to whom **"SEVEN TRUMPETS"** were given. Trumpets are used to call to war, to worship, for the convocation of the people, to proclaim Festivals, as the Year of Jubilee, the Feast of Tabernacles, and for Judgments. Ex. 19:16. Amos 3:6. Joshua 6:13-16. Zeph. 1:14-16. These "Seven Angels" **prepared** themselves to sound. That is, they took the Trumpets that were handed them and took up their positions where they could in turn sound their Trumpets. But before the Trumpets were sounded John saw **ANOTHER ANGEL** with a **"GOLDEN CENSER"** in his hand come and stand before the "Golden Incense Altar." The name of this "Angel Priest" is not given, and it is useless to speculate as to who he was. Some claim it was Christ, because He is our "Great High Priest," but that is immaterial. We are told that he was given much incense, and that he offered with it the prayers of the **"ALL SAINTS."** These Saints were the Saints of the Tribulation period, and their prayers were for deliverance from their enemies. This will account for the remarkable act of the "Angel Priest" of filling the Censer with **FIRE FROM OFF THE ALTAR,** and casting it **on to the earth,** the effect of which was seen in the **VOICES** and **THUNDERINGS,** that broke the **SILENCE** of Heaven, and the **LIGHTNINGS** and **EARTHQUAKE** on the Earth. As the same four things happen when the "Seventh Trumpet" sounds (Rev. 11:19), and the "Seventh Vial" is poured out, it is clear that the "Seventh Seal," the "Seventh Trumpet," and the "Seventh Vial," all end alike, and synchronize as to their ending, that is, all end at the **same time,** the **"end of the Week."** The Judgments that follow on the Earth as the Trumpets sound, and the Vials are poured out, are the answers to the prayers of the Saints for vengeance on their enemies.

The Seven Trumpets

FIRST TRUMPET.
(Hail—Fire—Blood.)
Rev. 8:6-7.

"And the 'SEVEN ANGELS' which had the 'SEVEN TRUM-PETS' prepared themselves to sound. The 'First Angel' sounded, and there followed HAIL and FIRE mingled with BLOOD, and they were cast **upon the Earth: and the third part of trees was burnt up, and all green grass was burnt up.**"

There is no need to spiritualize this. It means just what it says. These things have happened before why not again? It is the ful-filment of Joel 2:30-31, where the Lord says that in the "latter days" He will—"Shew wonders in the heavens and in the earth, **BLOOD**, and **FIRE**, and **PILLARS OF SMOKE**. The sun shall be turned into **DARKNESS**, and the Moon into **BLOOD, before** the **GREAT AND THE TERRIBLE DAY OF THE LORD COME."** The **DAY** when He shall come to take **VENGEANCE ON HIS ENEMIES.** The Lord is going to repeat the "**PLAGUES OF EGYPT.**" They were literal, why not the "Trumpet" and "Vial" Judgments? The literalness of these Judgments give us the "**key**" to the **LITERAL-NESS** of the Book of Revelation. No less than 5 of the 9 Plagues of Egypt are to be repeated during the Tribulation Period. This Plague is the same as the "**SEVENTH EGYPTIAN PLAGUE.**" "And the Lord said unto Moses, Stretch forth thine hand toward heaven, that there may be **HAIL** in all the Land of Egypt, upon **man,** and upon **beast,** and upon every **herb of the field,** throughout the Land of Egypt." And Moses stretched forth his "**rod**" toward heaven: and the Lord sent **THUNDER** and **HAIL,** and the **FIRE ran along upon the ground;** and the Lord rained **HAIL** upon the Land of Egypt. So there was **HAIL,** and **FIRE mingled with the HAIL,** very grievous, such as there was **none like it** in all the Land of Egypt since it became a nation. And the **HAIL** smote throughout all the Land of Egypt all that was in the **field,** both **man and beast; and the HAIL** smote every **herb of the field,** and **brake every tree**

of the field. ONLY IN THE LAND OF GOSHEN, WHERE THE CHILDREN OF ISRAEL WERE, WAS THERE NO HAIL." Ex. 9:22-26. The difference between this Egyptian Plague, and the Plague of the First Trumpet, is, that the situation will be **reversed.** Then the **"CHILDREN OF ISRAEL"** escaped, now they will suffer. The Judgments of Egypt were directed against Pharoah, the Judgments of the Tribulation Period will be directed against Israel.

The Egyptian "Plague of Hail" was clearly a great **"ELECTRICAL STORM"** that did not touch the Land of Goshen where the Children of Israel dwelt. The **FIRE** that **"ran along the ground"** was lightning. The difference between the Egyptian Plague and the one John describes is, that in Egypt **man** and **beast** suffered **with the vegetation,** while only the **trees** and the **green grass** will suffer when the First Trumpet sounds, and the **HAIL** and **FIRE** will be **MINGLED WITH BLOOD.** In Egypt the "Hail" smote **every herb of the field,** and **broke every tree,** but under the First Trumpet only **one-third** of the trees and grass will be burnt up.

SECOND TRUMPET.
(The Burning Mountain.)
Rev. 8:8-9.

"And the 'SECOND ANGEL' sounded, and as it were a 'GREAT MOUNTAIN' burning with fire was cast into the sea: and the third part of the sea BECAME BLOOD; and the third part of the creatures which were in the sea, and had life, DIED; and the third part of the ships were DESTROYED."

As this **"MOUNTAIN"** is to fall on the **sea,** and the Judgments poured forth by the "Trumpets" and "Vials" are to fall mainly on that part of the world bordering on the Mediterranean Sea, it is highly probable that the **"SEA"** here mentioned is the Mediterranean Sea. Notice that John does not say that it **was** a "Mountain" that he saw cast into the sea, but that it **appeared like a mountain,** not a burning volcano, but an **immense meteoric mass ablaze with fire.** That was as near as John could describe it. The effect of this "burning mass" on the sea, into which it fell, was to turn a **third part of the sea** into **BLOOD.** If any are disposed to doubt the possibility of such a thing let them turn to the "First Egyptian Plague" Ex. 7:19-21, and read the account of the turning of the waters of the River Nile into **BLOOD.** "And all the waters that were in the river were turned to **BLOOD.** And the fish that was in the river **DIED;** and the river **STANK,** and the Egyptians could not drink of the water of the river: and there was **BLOOD** throughout **ALL THE LAND OF EGYPT."** The only difference between the "First Egyptian Plague," and the effect on the Mediterranean Sea by the falling of a "Meteor" into it at the sounding of the Second Trumpet, will be, that only $\frac{1}{3}$ **of the sea** shall become **BLOOD,** that where the "Meteor" strikes, and thus only $\frac{1}{3}$ **of the living creatures** in the sea shall **DIE.** One-third also of the ships shall be **DESTROYED,** possibly by a tidal wave, or the "Meteor" may fall on a fleet of **naval vessels,** like the storm that destroyed the Spanish Armada.

THIRD TRUMPET.
(The Star Wormwood.)
Rev. 8:10-11.

"And the **THIRD ANGEL** sounded, and there fell a 'GREAT STAR' from heaven, burning as it were a lamp, and it fell upon the **third part of the rivers,** and upon the **fountains of waters;** and the name of the 'Star' is 'WORMWOOD': and the third part of the waters (rivers) became **WORMWOOD;** and many men died of the waters, because they were made **bitter.**"

When the "Third Trumpet" sounded a "GREAT STAR" fell from heaven burning like a lamp (R. V. Torch). This will doubtless be another "Meteor," that will assume the form of a "Torch" in its blazing path through the heavens, and when its gaseous vapors are scattered as it explodes, they will be absorbed by the **third part of the rivers and fountains of waters,** and they will be **poisoned by the noxious gases,** and made **bitter,** and many men shall die from drinking of those waters. "Wormwood" is a perennial herb, very bitter, and is used in the manufacture of "Absinthe." It is much used in France as a beverage, and is more intoxicating and destructive than ordinary liquors. This time is foretold by the Prophet Jeremiah. "Therefore thus saith the Lord of Hosts, because they have forsaken my law, Behold, I will feed them, even this people (Israel), with **WORMWOOD,** and give them **WATER OF GALL** to drink." Jer. 9:13-15.

FOURTH TRUMPET.
(SUN, Moon and Stars Smitten.)
Rev. 8:12.

"And the 'FOURTH ANGEL' sounded, and the **third part of the SUN** was smitten, and the **third part of the MOON,** and the **third part of the STARS;** so as the **third part** of them was **DARKENED,** and the day shone not for a third part of it, and the night likewise."

What happens under the sounding of this "Trumpet" is so similar to what happened under the "Sixth Seal" that it is not necessary to further dwell on it here. These are some of the "Signs" spoken of by Christ, in Luke's Gospel, that shall precede His Second Coming. There shall be signs in the **SUN,** and in the **MOON,** and in the **STARS,** and upon the earth distress of nations, with **PERPLEXITY.**" Luke 21:25-28.

THE ANGEL WARNING.
("Three Woes" Announced.)
Rev. 8:13.

"And I beheld, and heard an **ANGEL (R. V. Eagle)** flying through the midst of heaven, saying with a loud voice, **WOE, WOE, WOE,** to the **inhabiters of the earth** by reason of the other voices of the Trumpet of the **THREE ANGELS,** which are yet to sound."

The Revised Version, and many Manuscripts substitute "Eagle" for **ANGEL,** but that does not affect the meaning, for if God could make Balaam's "ass" to speak, He can use an "Eagle" to announce a message.

FIFTH TRUMPET.

FIRST WOE.
(The Plague Of Locusts.)
Rev. 9: 1-12.

"And the FIFTH ANGEL sounded, and I saw a 'STAR' fall from Heaven unto the earth: and to HIM was given the 'Key' of the 'BOTTOMLESS PIT.' And he opened the 'BOTTOMLESS PIT,' and there arose a smoke out of the 'Pit,' as the smoke of a furnace; and the Sun and the air were darkened by reason of the smoke of the 'Pit.' And there came out of the smoke LOCUSTS upon the earth: and unto them was given power, as the Scorpions of the earth have power. And it was commanded them that they should not hurt the grass of the earth, neither any green thing, neither any tree; but only those men which have not the 'SEAL OF GOD' in their foreheads. And to them it was given that they should not kill them, but that they should be TORMENTED FIVE MONTHS: and their torment was as the TORMENT OF A SCORPION, when he striketh a man. And in those days shall men seek death, and shall not find it: and shall desire to die, and death shall flee from them. And the shape of the LOCUSTS were like unto HORSES PREPARED UNTO BATTLE: and on their heads were as it were crowns of gold, and their faces were as the faces of men. And they had hair as the hair of women, and their teeth were as the teeth of lions. And they had 'Breastplates,' as it were Breastplates of iron; and the sound of their wings was as the sound of chariots of many horses running to battle. And they had tails like unto SCORPIONS, and there were stings in their tails: and their power was to hurt men FIVE MONTHS. And they had a King over them, which is the ANGEL of the 'Bottomless Pit,' whose name in the Hebrew tongue is ABADDON, but in the Greek tongue hath his name APOLLYON. One 'WOE' is past; and, behold, there come 'TWO WOES' more hereafter."

At the sounding of the Fifth Trumpet John saw a "STAR" fall, or as the Revised Version has it, "fallen from Heaven." That it was not a literal star is clear, for in the next verse the "STAR" is spoken of as a PERSON (He), and in the Old Testament angels were called "Stars." Job 38:7. Because the "STAR" was "fallen from

Heaven" does not imply that the "ANGEL," for that is what it was, was a "FALLEN ANGEL," or SATAN himself, as some have supposed. John simply meant that he saw the descent of the "STAR," or Angel, and so rapidly did it descend that it appeared to be falling. This is the same "STAR ANGEL" that in Rev. 20:1-3 comes down from Heaven, having the "Key" of the "BOTTOMLESS PIT," and a great chain in his hand, and binds SATAN, and casts him into the "PIT." This makes it clear that the "STAR ANGEL" is not SATAN. The work of both Angels is the same, to unlock and lock the "Bottomless Pit." It does not look reasonable that God would entrust the "Key" of the "Prison House" of the "Demons" to a "Fallen Angel," or even Satan himself.

THE BOTTOMLESS PIT.

The "BOTTOMLESS PIT" is not Hell, or Hades, the place of abode of the "Spirits" of wicked men and women until the resurrection of the "Wicked Dead." See the Chart of "The Underworld." Neither is it "Tartarus" the "Prison House" of the "Fallen Angels" (Jude 6-7), nor the "Lake of Fire," the "Final Hell" (Gehenna), Matt. 25:41, but it is the place of confinement of the DEMONS, who are not Satan's Angels but a class of "disembodied Spirits," supposed by many to be the "disembodied spirits" of the inhabitants of the Pre-Adamite Earth, who, as they have liberty and opportunity, as in the days of Christ, try to re-embody themselves again in human bodies. They are wicked, unclean, vicious, and have power to derange both mind and body. Matt. 12:22; 15:22. Luke 4:35; 8:26-36; 9:42. They are the "Familiar Spirits" of the Old Testament and the "Seducing Spirits" of which Paul warned Timothy. 1. Tim. 4:1. They wander about in desolate places. Christ used them to illustrate the condition of the Jewish people in the "last days" when "Demoniacal Power" shall be increased over them SEVENFOLD. He said, "When the 'UNCLEAN SPIRIT' (or Demon) is gone out of a man, he (the Demon) walketh through dry places, seeking rest, and findeth none. Then he saith, I will return into my house from whence I came out: and when he is come, he findeth it empty, swept, and garnished. Then goeth he, and taketh with himself SEVEN OTHER SPIRITS more wicked than himself, and they enter in and dwell there: and the last state of that man is worse than the first. Even so shall it be also unto this WICKED GENERATION." Matt. 12:43-45. The word "Generation," means not simply the lifetime of an individual, but it means a "race," and by this "WICKED GENERATION," Christ meant those He was addressing, and they were the Jews. So we see that the Jews, as a "race," when Jesus comes back, will be SEVENFOLD DEMONICALLY POS-SESSED. This will account for their making a "Covenant" with Antichrist which the Prophet Isaiah calls a "Covenant with DEATH and HELL." Isa. 28:18. When Christ cast the "Legion" of devils (Demons) out of the Gadarene Demoniac, they besought Him to not cast them into the "deep," that is, not into the "ABYSS," the "BOTTOMLESS PIT." Luke 8:26-36.

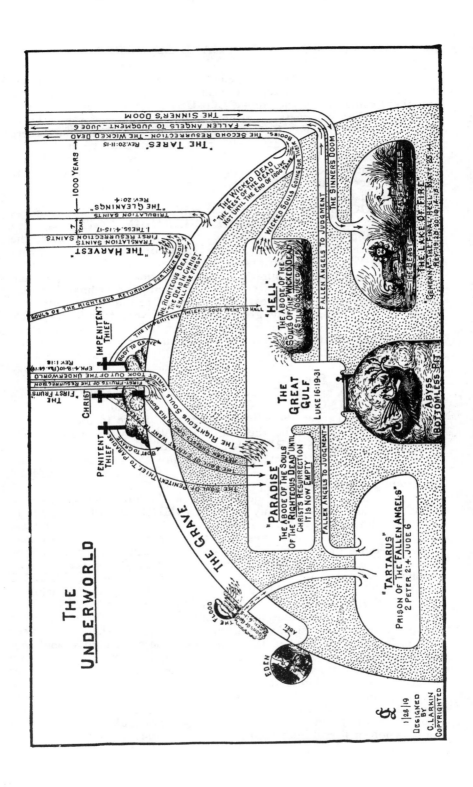

THE
UNDERWORLD

THE GRAVE

"PARADISE"
THE ABODE OF THE SOULS
OF THE "RIGHTEOUS DEAD" UNTIL
CHRIST'S RESURRECTION
IT IS NOW EMPTY

THE
GREAT
GULF
LUKE 16:19-31

"HELL"
THE ABODE OF THE
SOULS OF THE "WICKED DEAD"
STILL OCCUPIED

THE LAKE OF FIRE
GEHENNA — THE FINAL HELL MATT. 25:41
REV. 19:20; 20:14, 15

ABYSS
BOTTOMLESS PIT

"TARTARUS"
PRISON OF THE "FALLEN ANGELS"
2 PETER 2:4. JUDE 6

THE SINNER'S DOOM →
← FALLEN ANGELS TO JUDGMENT — JUDE 6
← Bodies. THE SECOND RESURRECTION — THE WICKED DEAD
"THE TARES." Rev. 20:11-15

1000 YEARS

"THE GLEANINGS"
Rev. 20:4

TRIBULATION SAINTS
1. THESS. 4:15-17

"THE HARVEST"
TRANSLATION SAINTS
FIRST RESURRECTION SAINTS

CHRIST — THE "FIRST-FRUITS OF THE RESURRECTION"

THE "FIRST FRUITS"

PENITENT THIEF

IMPENITENT THIEF

EPH. 4:8-10 (PSA. 68:18)
REV. 1:18

EDEN

THE FLOOD

ABEL

1/28/19
DESIGNED
BY
C. LARKIN
COPYRIGHTED

When the "Star Angel" opened the "Bottomless Pit," smoke, like the smoke of a great furnace, issued forth and darkened the sun, and there came out of the smoke **LOCUSTS** upon the earth. These were not ordinary locusts. Neither were the locusts of the "Eighth Egyptian Plague." Ex. 10: 3-20. For we read of them that **"there were no such locusts as they, neither after them shall be such,"** that is, just like them. Nevertheless they were **locusts,** not some **"composite creature"** such as John saw, for they acted like locusts and ate up every green thing. The difference must have been in their size and voraciousness.

The **LOCUSTS** that John saw come out of the "Bottomless Pit" were a kind of **"INFERNAL CHERUBIM."** That is, they were a combination of the **HORSE,** the **MAN,** the **WOMAN,** the **LION,** and the **SCORPION,** and the sound of their wings in flying was as the "sound of chariots of many horses running to battle." Their size is not given, but they were doubtless much larger than ordinary locusts, but they were not like them, for ordinary locusts feed on vegetation, but these locusts were forbidden to hurt the grass, or the **trees,** or any green thing, but were to afflict **ONLY MEN,** and they had **human intelligence,** for they afflicted only those men who had not the **"SEAL OF GOD"** in their foreheads. These men they were not permitted to kill, but only **torment,** and that for only a limited period—**FIVE MONTHS,** the time limit of ordinary locusts, which is from May to September. The length of time is mentioned twice, and the **character** of the torment was like that which follows the **STING OF A SCORPION,** which causes **excruciating pain** that often causes the afflicted person to desire to die. So fearfully excruciating will be the anguish of those who shall be tormented by these **"SCORPION LOCUSTS"** that they will "seek death, and shall not find it; and shall desire to die, but death shall flee from them," the inference being that the **LOCUST** or **DEMON** controlling them shall have power to prevent their death.

There is a remarkable description in the prophecy of Joel, of what is spoken of as an army of **HORSEMEN,** but which seems to refer to John's **"SCORPION LOCUSTS."** "The appearance of them is as the appearance of **horses,** and as **horsemen,** so shall they run. Like the noise of **CHARIOTS** on the tops of mountains shall they leap, like the noise of a flame of fire that devoureth the stubble, as a strong people set in battle array. Before their face the **PEOPLE SHALL BE MUCH PAINED:** all faces shall gather **blackness.** They shall run like mighty men; they shall **climb the wall** like men of war; and they shall march every one **his** ways, and they shall not break ranks; neither shall one thrust another; they shall walk every one in his path; and when they **fall upon the sword, they shall not be wounded.** They shall run to and fro in the city; they shall run upon the wall, they shall **climb up upon the houses;** they shall **enter in at the windows like a thief.** The earth shall quake before them; the heavens shall tremble; the **sun and the moon shall be dark, and the stars shall withdraw their shining."** Joel 2: 4-10. There are a number of things in this prophecy of Joel that makes us doubt that an invasion of **literal horsemen** is meant. Horses do not **climb walls,** or climb up upon roofs, or enter windows like a thief. They do not fly in the heavens and in such numbers as to darken the sun, moon, and stars, nor do they fall upon the sword and escape wounding. This could only be said of "spirit beings" as DEMONS. This prophecy looks more like a scourge of locusts; not literal locusts, but such "SCORPION LOCUSTS" as John describes, for they attack men, and cause them such great pain that their faces turn BLACK. This view is confirmed when we note the time of this "horsemen" invasion. Joel tells us that it will be in the "Day of the Lord" (Joel 2: 1, 11), that it will be accompanied with the "sound of a trumpet," that it will precede the pouring out of the Holy Spirit on all flesh, and that it will be at a time when the Lord will "shew wonders in the heavens and in the earth, BLOOD, and FIRE, and PILLARS OF SMOKE."

Now we know that the "Gift of the Holy Spirit" on the Day of Pentecost was only the "first fruits" and partial fulfilment of this prophecy of Joel, for none of these terrible things occurred at that time, and there was no invasion of enemy "horsemen," or a "scourge of locusts," on, or before, or after, the Day of Pentecost such as here described. As we have no historical record of such an invasion of "locust horsemen" as the Prophet Joel describes, the event must still be future, and the description in many respects corresponds with what John tells us will happen when the Fifth Trumpet sounds.

These "SCORPION LOCUSTS" have a King, which ordinary locusts have not. Prov. 30: 27. This King's name in the Hebrew is "ABADDON," but in the Greek is "APOLLYON." Now Satan is no where in the Scriptures called by either of these names, so Satan cannot be the King of the Demons, for their King is the King of the "Bottomless Pit," to which he is confined, while Satan and his angels are at liberty and roam the Heavenlies. The meaning then of this scourge of "SCORPION LOCUSTS" seems to be, that an Angel, the custodian of the "Pit," will open the "Bottomless Pit," and liberate a vast multitude of Demons who shall enter into and take possession of the bodies of men, and so torment them that they shall desire to die and shall not be able.

Those will be awful days in which to live, and especially so for those who have the "MARK OF THE BEAST," who will be the special mark of those "SCORPION LOCUSTS." They will be invisible to the natural eye, being "SPIRIT BEINGS," but their presence will be known by the suffering they inflict, which will be unavoidable because of their invisibility, and the inability to provide any material means as screens, to protect one's person from their attack. This invasion of "Scorpion Locusts" will last for 5 months and may well be called a "WOE," but it will be comparatively trifling in comparison with the two "WOES" that are to follow, that of the "Plague of Infernal Cavalry," and the "Vial Judgments," which are included under the "Third Woe."

THE SIXTH TRUMPET.

SECOND WOE
(The Plague Of Horsemen.)
Rev. 9: 13-21.

"And the 'SIXTH ANGEL' sounded, and I heard a voice from the 'Four Horns' of the 'Golden Altar' which is before God, saying to the 'SIXTH ANGEL' which had the Trumpet, Loose the "Four Angels' which are bound in the great river Euphrates, and the 'Four Angels' were loosed, which were prepared for an hour, and a day, and a month, and a year, for to slay the third part of men. And the number of the army of the horsemen were two hundred thousand thousand: and I heard the number of them. And thus I saw the horses in the Vision, and them that sat on them, having breastplates of fire, and of jacinth, and brimstone: and the heads of the horses were as the heads of lions: and out of their mouth issued fire and smoke and brimstone. By these three was the third part of men killed, by the fire, and by the smoke, and by the brimstone, which issued out of their mouths. For their power is in their mouth, and in their tails: for their tails were like unto serpents, and had heads, and with them do hurt. And the rest of the men which were not killed by these Plagues yet repented not of the works of their hands, that they should not worship devils (demons), and idols of gold, and silver, and brass, and stone, and of wood; which neither can see, or hear, nor walk: neither repented they of their murders, nor of their sorceries, nor of their fornication, nor of their thefts."

That these "Four Angels," who were bound at the river Euphrates, were bad angels is seen from the fact that they were bound, and that they are the leaders or commanders of an army of 200,-000,000 "INFERNAL CAVALRY." This army of 200,000,000 horsemen is a supernatural army. It is not composed of ordinary men and horses. The fact that these "Four Angels" were bound at the Euphrates, where Satan's seat was in ancient times, and where it is to be again in the City of Babylon restored, and from whence he sallied forth to do his diabolical work, makes it clear that this army is a part of Satan's forces. Supernatural armies are not unknown to the Scriptures. Horses and a chariot of fire separated Elijah from

Elisha in the day when Elijah was taken up by a **whirlwind into Heaven**, 2. Kings 2:11.   When Dothan was besieged by the army of Syria, God opened the eyes of Elisha's servant, and he saw the mountains around the city full of horses and **chariots of fire**. 2. Kings 6:13-17.   When the Lord Jesus Christ shall come to take "The Kingdom," He will be attended by the "Armies of Heaven" riding on "White Horses," and it stands to reason, if there is to be "War in Heaven" between Michael and his angels, and Satan and his angels (Rev. 12:7), that Satan has his armies, and among them **horsemen,** and that the 200,000,000 Horsemen mentioned here are Satan's Horsemen, for no such army of **ordinary horsemen** ever was, or ever could be, assembled on this earth.

Again the horses were not ordinary horses, for while their **bodies** were like the body of a **HORSE,** their **heads** were as the head of a **LION,** and their **tails** were like unto a **SERPENT,** the end of which had the **HEAD OF A SERPENT,** and it was the **SULPHUROUS SMOKE AND FIRE** that issued from their mouths, and the **SERPENT STING** of their **tails,** that killed all that crossed their path, that reveals the Satanic character of the horses and their riders.   The "Riders" upon these horses had "Breastplates of **FIRE, JACINTH,** and **BRIMSTONE,**" to match the **breath** of the horses upon which they rode.

The wonderful thing about this invasion of "INFERNAL CAVALRY" was the awful destruction they wrought.   They slew the **THIRD PART OF MEN.**   If that means of the whole world, and the present population of the earth is 1,700,000,000, then this army will destroy 566,666,666 persons.   It probably however refers to one-third of the men of the old Roman world.   Another remarkable thing is, that the "Four Angels" were prepared for THE (R. V.) **HOUR, MONTH,** and **YEAR,** that is, they were waiting for the **EXACT** year, month, day, and even hour, known only to God, on which to make the invasion, and not, as some think, to slay for a **year, month and day,** or 391 days.   "Known unto God are all His works from the beginning of the world."   Acts 15:18.   This Plague of "INFERNAL CAVALRY" was for a twofold purpose, retribution and reformation.   To punish the **idolatry** and **demon worship of** men, and their **sins** of **murder, sorcery, fornication,** and **theft,** and to keep others from following in their footsteps.   But it appears from verses 20 and 21, that the residue of men who were not killed, did not repent and turn from their sins, and so were left for later judgments.

This army of "INFERNAL CAVALRY," being composed of "SPIRIT BEINGS" like the "SCORPION LOCUSTS," will like them be **invisible** to the natural eye, and therefore cannot be resisted, or warred against, by carnal weapons.   Those attacked will therefore be without any means of protection, and this will account for the awful destruction of human life, for the **"third part"** of man will be killed.   The awful destructive judgments of the "Trumpets" and "Vials" that are to come upon the earth are doubtless for the purpose of weeding out the worst of the human race, so that only the better class of men shall be saved for the millennium.

The Interval Between the Sixth and Seventh Trumpets.

1. THE LITTLE BOOK.
Rev. 10: 1-11.

"And I saw another 'MIGHTY ANGEL' come down from Heaven, clothed with a cloud: and a Rainbow was upon His head, and His face was as it were the Sun, and His feet as Pillars of Fire: and He had in His hand a 'LITTLE BOOK' open: and He set His right foot on the SEA, and His left foot on the EARTH, and cried with a loud voice, as when a lion roareth: and when He had cried 'SEVEN THUNDERS' uttered their voices. And when the 'SEVEN THUNDERS' had uttered their voices, I was about to write: and I heard a voice from Heaven saying unto me, Seal up those things which the SEVEN THUNDERS uttered, and write them not. And the 'ANGEL' which I saw stand upon the sea and upon the earth lifted up His hand to Heaven, and swear by Him that LIVETH FOREVER AND EVER, who created heaven, and the things that therein are, and the earth, and the things that therein are, and the sea, and the things which are therein, that there should be TIME NO LONGER: but in the days of the voice of the 'SEVENTH ANGEL,' when he shall begin to sound, the 'MYSTERY OF GOD' SHOULD BE FINISHED, as He hath declared to His servants the Prophets. And the voice which I heard from Heaven spake unto me again, and said, Go and take the 'LITTLE BOOK' which is open in the hand of the 'ANGEL' which standeth upon the sea and upon the earth. And I went unto the 'ANGEL,' and said unto him, Give me the 'LITTLE BOOK.' And he said unto me, Take it, and eat it up; and it shall make thy belly bitter, but it shall be in thy mouth sweet as honey. And I took the 'LITTLE BOOK' out of the 'ANGEL'S' hand, and ate it up; and it was in my mouth sweet as honey; and as soon as I had eaten it, my belly was bitter. And He said unto me, Thou must prophesy again before many peoples, and nations, and tongues, and kings."

Who this "MIGHTY ANGEL" is we do not know unless he be Christ Himself. In the Old Testament the Son of God was called the "ANGEL OF THE LORD" (Ex. 3:2-18), and as we are now in that part of the Book of Revelation that deals mainly with Israel it is nothing less than what we should expect to hear, Christ spoken of as a "MIGHTY ANGEL." Then the description of this "MIGHTY ANGEL" seems to point to the same Person that John saw standing amid the "Lampstands" in chapter 1:12-16, or Christ Himself. The "ANGEL" was clothed in a CLOUD, there was a RAINBOW upon His head, His face was as it were the SUN, and His feet as PILLARS OF FIRE. No mere angel was ever before or since described in the Scriptures as appearing like that. Then He is described as crying with a loud voice, as a lion roareth, and Christ is spoken of in this Book (Rev. 5:5) as "THE LION OF THE TRIBE OF JUDAH"; and in the chapter that follows this the same "MIGHTY ANGEL" speaks of the "Two Witnesses," as "MY WITNESSES," which is further indisputable evidence that this "MIGHTY ANGEL" is no other than Christ Himself. This interpretation makes clear what follows. For when this "MIGHTY ANGEL" places His right foot upon the sea, and His left foot on the earth, and swears that there shall be "TIME NO LONGER," or "NO LONGER DELAY" (margin), it is Christ taking formal possession of the Earth and Sea, and declaring that there shall be no longer delay in dispossessing the false claimant Satan.

When the "MIGHTY ANGEL" cried with a loud voice, John heard "SEVEN THUNDERS" utter their voices. These "THUNDERS" spoke, for John heard what they said, and as he had been commanded to write what he should see and hear, he proceeded to write what the "voices" of the "SEVEN THUNDERS" uttered, but he was told to "seal up those things which the 'SEVEN THUNDERS' uttered, and write them not." What they said has never as yet been revealed, but doubtless will be when the time comes to make the revelation.

John was then told to—"Go, take the 'LITTLE BOOK' which is open in the hand of the 'ANGEL' which standeth upon the sea and upon the earth." John was at this time back again on the earth. And when John took the "LITTLE BOOK," the "ANGEL" said to him—"Take, and eat it up; and it shall make thy belly bitter, and it shall be in thy mouth sweet as honey." And when John had eaten the "BOOK" it was as the "ANGEL" had said, sweet to his mouth and bitter to his stomach.

What was this "LITTLE BOOK"? Some claim that it was the "SEVEN SEALED BOOK," now open, and therefore the "TITLE DEED" to the Earth, and that the "MIGHTY ANGEL" held it in His hand, as He stood with one foot on the sea and one foot on the earth, as His authority for claiming possession. But the "ANGEL" does not make that use of it, and if it were His "TITLE DEED" to the Earth it seems a strange procedure for Him to give it to John to eat. Then it is described as a "LITTLE BOOK," as if its contents were small. In that respect it stands in marked contrast with the "SEVEN SEALED BOOK" whose numerous "Seals" and the time taken to break them, imply that it was of considerable size. Then the effect upon John of the eating of the "LITTLE BOOK" seems to indicate that it was more than a "Title Deed." For it contained matter that when John first ate it (glanced over it) was sweet as honey to his mouth, but when he had thoroughly digested its contents was bitter to his belly. In other words the "LITTLE BOOK" contained matter connected with John's work as a Prophet, for the "ANGEL" immediately said to him— "Thou must prophecy again before many peoples, and nations, and tongues, and kings," which for ought we know John did.

This "LITTLE BOOK," here open, is probably the "BOOK" that Daniel was told to "SEAL UP." Dan. 12:4, 9. That "Book" contained things that were not to be revealed until the "TIME OF THE END." Not the "End Of Time," but the "End" of the "TIMES OF THE GENTILES," which synchronizes with the last half of Daniel's "SEVENTIETH WEEK," and therefore with "THE GREAT TRIBULATION PERIOD." If this supposition be true, then the "LITTLE BOOK" was a foreview of the things that are to befall Daniel's People in the last half of Daniel's "SEVENTIETH WEEK." The effect on John of reading the "LITTLE BOOK" seems to confirm this view, for as he read of the deliverances that were to come to his people, and of the final victory of the Lamb, and the setting up of "The Kingdom," the "Book" was as "sweet as honey" to his taste, but when he meditated upon the awful sufferings that would come upon the world, and upon the Jews, under the reign of the "BEAST" (Antichrist), and during the pouring out of the "VIALS," it was bitterness to his soul.

THE FINISHED MYSTERY.

When the "SEVENTH TRUMPET ANGEL" shall begin to sound the "MYSTERY OF GOD" shall be finished. This is not the "Mystery of the Church" for that was finished by the taking out of the Church in chapter four. That "Mystery" was unknown to the Prophets. The "MYSTERY OF GOD" is the "Mystery" of why God permitted Satan to cause the "Fall of Man" and thus bring sin, and misery, and death into the world. To the Old Testament Prophets God revealed the fact that in His own good time He would make clear this "MYSTERY," and when the "SEVENTH TRUMPET" (that includes all that happens from chapter 11:15) sounds, the "MYSTERY OF GOD" will be finished, for then the "MYSTERY of INIQUITY" (Antichrist, 2. Thess. 2:6-10) will be revealed, in whom Satan will incarnate himself after he is cast out of Heaven, and in his destruction, and the "Binding of Satan," and the setting up of the "Millennial Kingdom" of Christ, shall be fulfilled the promises to the Prophets, that peace and righteousness shall reign on the earth. And when, as the result of the "Renovation of the Earth by Fire," the redeemed human race shall take up its abode upon a redeemed and restored earth, and sin and rebellion shall forever be destroyed, the "MYSTERY OF GOD," or why sin was permitted to wreck this world, will be finished.

2. THE TWO WITNESSES.

Rev. 11:1-14.

"And there was given me a reed like unto a rod: and the 'ANGEL' stood, saying, Rise and measure the **TEMPLE OF GOD,'** and the **'ALTAR,'** and them that worship therein. But the **'COURT'** which is without the **TEMPLE** leave out; and measure it not; for it is given unto the **GENTILES:** and the Holy City shall they tread under foot **FORTY AND TWO MONTHS.** And I will give power unto **MY 'TWO WITNESSES,'** and they shall prophesy a **THOUSAND TWO HUNDRED AND THREE-SCORE DAYS,** clothed in sackcloth. These are the **'TWO OLIVE TREES'** and the **'TWO CANDLESTICKS'** standing before the God of the earth. And if any man will hurt them, fire proceedeth out of their mouth, and devoureth their enemies: and if any man will hurt them, he must in this manner be killed. These have power to **SHUT HEAVEN,** that it rain not in the days of their prophecy: and have power over waters to **TURN THEM TO BLOOD,** and to smite the earth with **ALL PLAGUES,** as often as they will. And when they shall have finished their testimony, the **BEAST THAT ASCENDETH OUT OF THE 'BOTTOMLESSS PIT'** shall make war against them, and shall overcome them, and kill them. And their dead bodies shall lie in the street of the **'GREAT CITY,'** which spiritually is called **SODOM** and **EGYPT,** where also our Lord **WAS CRUCIFIED.** And they of the people and kindreds and tongues and nations shall see their dead bodies **THREE DAYS AND A HALF,** and shall not suffer their dead bodies to be put in graves. And they that dwell upon the earth shall rejoice over them, and make merry, and shall send gifts one to another; because these **TWO PROPHETS** tormented them that dwelt on the earth. And after three days and a half the **SPIRIT OF LIFE** from God entered into them, and they stood upon their feet; and great fear fell upon them which saw them. And they heard a great voice from Heaven saying unto them **'COME UP HITHER,'** and they ascended up to Heaven **in a cloud;** and their enemies beheld them. And the **same hour** was there a **GREAT EARTHQUAKE,** and the **tenth part of the City fell,** and in the earthquake were slain of men **seven thousand:** and the remnant were affrighted, and gave glory to the God of Heaven."

The "ANGEL" that told John to rise and measure the **TEMPLE** was the same "MIGHTY ANGEL" that handed him the "LITTLE BOOK" to eat. And as they were both still on the earth, the "TEMPLE" that John was told to measure was the Temple at Jerusalem. Not the Temple of Herod, for that had been destroyed over 25 years before by Titus, in A. D. 70. This then must be a future temple that is to be built at Jerusalem. It is clear that there will be a Temple at Jerusalem during the reign of Antichrist, for he shall sit in it, and proclaim himself **GOD.** 2. Thess. 2:3-4. And he shall cause the "ABOMINATION OF DESOLATION" spoken of by Daniel the Prophet (Dan. 9:27), probably the "IMAGE OF THE BEAST," to be set up in the "HOLY PLACE." Matt. 24:15. This will not be the Millennial Temple described by Ezekiel (Ez. 4:1; 42:20), for that will be built at Shiloh, in the midst of the Holy Oblation (Ez. 48:8, 21), and not until after the physical changes that will take place at the return of Christ (Zech. 14:4) shall have changed the surface of the Land of Palestine. The Temple that the Jews will build on their return to Jerusalem will probably be destroyed by the Earthquake that destroys the **tenth part** of the City, for that Earthquake will synchronize with the "Great Earthquake" that shall occur at the breaking of the "Seventh Seal," the sounding of the "Seventh Trumpet," and the pouring out of the "Seventh Vial." Rev. 8:5, 11:19, 16:18.

John was told to measure only the Temple proper, and to leave out the "Court" that surrounded it. The Temple of Herod had four Courts: the Court of the Priests, the Court of Israel, the Court of the Women, and the Court of the Gentiles. The Tabernacle had but **one** Court; while Solomon's Temple had **two,** the Court of the Priests, and the Court of the Gentiles. As the "Court" of this new Temple, as well as the Holy City (Jerusalem), is to be trodden under foot of the Gentiles for 42 months, or 3½ years, this period must refer to the **last half** of the "Seventieth Week," after Antichrist breaks his "Covenant" with the Jews, and desecrates the Temple, for Jerusalem must be trodden down of the Gentiles until the "Times of the Gentiles" is fulfilled (Luke 21:24), and that will not end until the Battle of Armageddon.

After the **"MIGHTY ANGEL"** had given John instructions as to measuring the Temple, He said—"And I will give power unto **MY 'TWO WITNESSES,'** and they shall prophesy a 'thousand two hundred and threescore days'." As a "thousand two hundred and threescore days" are equal to 42 months of 30 days each, or to 3½ years, then the **time** when these **"TWO WITNESSES"** are to prophesy must correspond with the **last half** of the "Week," or the time of **THE GREAT TRIBULATION.**

Who are these **"TWO WITNESSES"?** They are **men:** not systems, or churches, or a body of witnesses, for they **prophesy** and **are clothed in sackcloth,** neither of which can be said of other than **persons,** and there are **TWO** of them. It is very easy to identify them. They have power to **shut heaven that it rain not in the DAYS OF THEIR PROPHECY.** This can refer to no other than Elijah, who had power in the days of King Ahab to shut up the heavens for the space of three years and six months (1. Kings 17:1. Luke 4:25. James 5:17), and this is the same length of time, 42 months, or 1260 days, or 3½ years, that these **"TWO WITNESSES"** are to prophesy. Then we know that Elijah was translated, and did not see death, that he might come back before **"THE GREAT AND DREADFUL DAY OF THE LORD"** for the purpose of "turning the heart of the children to their fathers," and this is the purpose of the prophesying of these **"TWO WITNESSES."** Mal. 4:5-6. It is clear from the **time** that the Prophet Malachi said that Elijah would come again, **JUST BEFORE "The Great And Dreadful Day Of The Lord,"** that this prophecy was not fulfilled in John the Baptist. He announced the "First Coming" of Christ, but no **"Great And Dreadful Day Of The Lord"** followed. That event is yet **future,** and follows the testimony of these **"TWO WITNESSES."**

When the Jews sent Priests and Levites from Jerusalem to John to ask him "Who Art Thou?" he confessed—"I AM NOT THE CHRIST." And they asked him, "What then? Art thou ELIJAH?"

And he said—"I AM NOT." It is clear from John's answers to these questions that he was NOT ELIJAH. When Gabriel announced to Zacharias the birth of John the Baptist, he said, he shall go before Him (Christ) in the "SPIRIT AND POWER" of Elijah. That is, he will not be Elijah, but shall be like him in spirit and power. When John from his prison cell sent messengers to Jesus to ask Him if He were the Christ, after Christ had dismissed those messengers He said to the multitude of John, "IF YE WILL RECEIVE 'IT,' THIS IS ELIJAH WHICH WAS FOR TO COME." Matt. 11:1-14. Jesus here simply affirms that John was ELIJAH if men would RECEIVE "IT." Not receive "HIM" (John), but receive "IT." What did Jesus mean by "IT"? The context shows that Jesus was talking about the "KINGDOM" (Verses 11 and 12), and if they had received "THE KINGDOM" that John announced was at hand, then John, instead of being John, would have been ELIJAH come back, but because God foresaw that the Jews would not receive the KINGDOM, He could not send ELIJAH at that time, so He had to send a substitute with the "spirit" and "power" of Elijah in his place, so He sent John the Baptist.

But you say, did not Jesus say to the Disciples when they were coming down from the Mt. of Transfiguration, where they had seen Elijah—"Elias truly shall first come, and restore all things. But I say unto you that ELIAS IS COME ALREADY, and they knew him not, but have done unto him whatsoever they listed. Then the Disciples understood that He spake unto them of JOHN THE BAPTIST"? Matt. 17:11-13. Now whatever this may mean, it cannot contradict John's own declaration that he WAS NOT ELIJAH, or Christ's statement that if God had foreseen that the Jews would have received the Kingdom, He would have sent ELIJAH instead of John. And Christ's statement in the above reference, that Elijah's purpose in coming is to "RESTORE ALL THINGS," which John did not do, and Malachi's declaration that Elijah would not come until just before the 'GREAT AND DREADFUL DAY OF THE LORD,' makes it clear that John the Baptist was not Elijah, and that Elijah is yet to come.

It is clear then that one of the "TWO WITNESSES" will be Elijah, but who will be the other? Many claim that Moses will be the second Witness, while some say he will be Enoch, because they say Moses being a resurrected person cannot die again, and the "Two Witnesses" are both to die. They claim that both Enoch and Elijah were caught up in their bodies, without dying, that they might come back again in their bodies and die. There is no scriptural ground for declaring that Moses cannot die again. Lazarus was raised from the dead and he died again, and the "Wicked Dead" shall be raised from the dead, and after Judgment at the "Great White Throne," they shall be sentenced to die again, which is the "SECOND DEATH." Rev. 20:12-15.

It is said of these "TWO WITNESSES" that they have power—

1. "To SHUT HEAVEN, that it RAIN NOT in the days of their prophecy."

2. "And have power over **WATERS** to **TURN THEM TO BLOOD,** and to smite the earth with **ALL PLAGUES,** as often as they will."

Now we know that Moses had power to turn water into **BLOOD,** and to smite the earth with **PLAGUES,** but we are not told that Enoch had such power.

If we study carefully what shall happen during the period the **"TWO WITNESSES"** shall testify, which as we have seen will be the last half of the "Week," or 3½ years, we shall see that the **"TWO WITNESSES"** can be no other than **MOSES** and **ELIJAH.** It is probable that Elijah will shut up the heavens that there shall be no rain, during the 3½ years of their witnessing, for we read that there is to be a "FIRE TEST" such as Elijah appointed on Mt. Carmel in the days of King Ahab (1. Kings 18: 17-40), and the contest will be between Elijah and the "FALSE PROPHET," and that the "FALSE PROPHET" shall have power to do what the Priests of Baal could not do, bring **FIRE FROM HEAVEN.** Rev. 13: 13. The crucial question on Mt. Carmel was, who is **GOD, JEHOVAH** or **BAAL?** In the days of Antichrist it will be, who is **GOD, JEHOVAH** or **ANTICHRIST?** The test will be the power to bring down **FIRE FROM HEAVEN.** As the "False Prophet" will imitate the power of Elijah and bring down **FIRE FROM HEAVEN,** the test will not be decisive. The true Israel of God however will acknowledge the claim of Jehovah, while the followers of "The Beast" will continue to believe in him. But Elijah shall not be as fortunate as he was in the days of Ahab, for then he escaped the vengeance of Jezebel, but he will not be able to escape the vengeance of Antichrist who will see to it that both he and Moses are slain.

As the Plagues that are to accompany the pouring out of the "Vials," are **four** of them similar to the "Plagues of Egypt," who more likely to bring them to pass than Moses? The evidence seems conclusive that the **"TWO WITNESSES"** will be **MOSES** and **ELIJAH.**

In passing it is worth noting the "TITLE" of these two men. The **"MIGHTY ANGEL"** (Christ) calls them My **"TWO WITNESSES."** This implies that "WITNESSING" was their business. And when we recall their witnessing on the Mt. of Transfiguration (Matt. 17: 3), and that it was **TWO MEN** that witnessed to the women at the Tomb that Jesus had risen (Luke 24: 4-7), and that it was **TWO MEN** who stood by and witnessed to the Disciples as Jesus ascended into Heaven (Acts 1: 10-11), and that in all three incidents the **MEN** were clothed in "shining garments," it seems clear that Moses was resurrected and Elijah translated for the express office of "WITNESSES."

These **"TWO WITNESSES"** are called the **"TWO OLIVE TREES"** and the **"TWO CANDLESTICKS"** which stand before the God of the earth. For an explanation of this symbol we must turn back to the Old Testament. The Prophet Zechariah saw in a vision a **"GOLDEN CANDLESTICK,"** with a bowl upon the top of it, and the seven lamps thereon, and seven pipes to the seven lamps; and **TWO OLIVE TREES** by it, one upon the right side of the bowl, and the other upon the left side thereof. And he turned to the angel that talked with him and said "What are these 'TWO OLIVE TREES' upon the right side of the CANDLESTICK and upon the left side thereof?" And he said, "These are the 'TWO ANOINTED ONES,' that stand by the Lord of the whole earth." Zech. 4:1-14. These "TWO ANOINTED ONES" were Zerubbabel the Governor, and Joshua the High Priest. Haggai 1:1, 14. Zech. 3:1; 4:6. They had been anointed by the Holy Spirit to rebuild and restore Jerusalem and the Temple after the Babylonian Captivity, against which Satan was raising up much opposition. Zech. 3:1-7. What more appropriate type could have been used than this? Zerubbabel and Joshua are types of the "TWO WITNESSES" whose work it will be to proclaim that the time has come to rebuild Jerusalem and re-establish the Temple worship, for the "KINGDOM OF HEAVEN" is at hand. And they will have to do it in the face of the opposition of Satan, who at that time will have incarnated himself in the Antichrist. How beautifully this illustrates the fact that every Type in the Scriptures has its Anti-Type, and that the Old Testament infolds and unfolds the New Testament, and that until the Anti-Type appears the plan and purpose of God remains unfulfilled and incomplete.

These "TWO WITNESSES" are to prophecy for 1260 days, or 3½ years, and for that length of time they are immune from death. For if any man attempt to hurt them, "fire will proceed out of their mouths and devour their enemies." But when they have "finished their testimony," they shall be overcome by "THE BEAST" (Antichrist), who will make war against them, and shall kill them, and their dead bodies shall lie in the streets of Jerusalem, which is spiritually called Sodom and Egypt at that time, because the character of its inhabitants will resemble the character of the inhabitants of Sodom in the days of Lot, and the conduct of Israel in Egypt (Ezek. 23:3-4, 8, 19), for the space of "three days and a half," and the people of all nationalities shall not suffer their dead bodies to be buried, and they shall rejoice over them, and make merry, and shall send gifts one to another, because these "TWO WITNESSES" who tormented them by their testimony and their plagues are dead. How foolish men are. They think that when they kill God's Prophets they have destroyed His law, and cannot be punished.

But the people's rejoicing will be short-lived, for at the end of the 3½ days the "SPIRIT OF LIFE" will re-enter the bodies of the "TWO WITNESSES," and they shall stand upon their feet, and great fear shall be upon their enemies, and a voice from Heaven will be heard saying—"COME UP HITHER," and they shall ascend up to Heaven in a cloud as Christ Himself ascended, and their enemies shall witness their ascent. They are first resurrected and then translated. The same hour of their ascension there will be a "Great Earthquake" that will destroy a tenth part of the city of Jerusalem and 7000 of its inhabitants, and the remainder of its inhabitants will turn to God from fright. But this repentance will be short-lived, like that of Pharoah's.

It must not be supposed that because this description of the "Two Witnesses" is given to John in the "INTERVAL" between the "Sixth" and "Seventh" Trumpets, that the "Two Witnesses" testify only during that "INTERVAL." The time is too short, for they testify for 1260 days, or 42 months. Their witnessing was still future when John was told about them, for the "MIGHTY ANGEL" said to John—"I WILL give," showing that the "Two Witnesses" had not as yet appeared, for John did not see them, he simply recorded what the "MIGHTY ANGEL" told him about them. As we have seen, the period of their witnessing is during the "last half" of the Week, and therefore they do not appear until the "Middle" of the Week.

"The 'SECOND WOE' is past: and, behold, the 'THIRD WOE' cometh quickly."

SEVENTH TRUMPET.

THIRD WOE.
(Covers The Rest Of The Week.)
Rev. 11 : 15-19.

"And the 'SEVENTH ANGEL' sounded: and there were great voices in Heaven, saying, THE KINGDOMS OF THIS WORLD ARE BECOME THE KINGDOMS OF OUR LORD, AND OF HIS CHRIST; AND HE SHALL REIGN FOR EVER AND EVER. And the four and Twenty Elders, which sat before God on their seats, fell upon their faces, and worshiped God, saying, We give Thee thanks, O Lord God Almighty, which art, and wast, and art to come; because Thou hast taken to Thee Thy great power, and hast reigned. And the nations were angry, and Thy wrath is come, and the time of the dead, that they should be judged, and that Thou shouldest give reward unto Thy Servants the Prophets, and to the Saints, and them that fear Thy Name, small and great; and shouldest destroy them which destroy the earth. And the TEMPLE OF GOD was opened IN HEAVEN, and there was seen in His Temple the 'Ark of His Testament': and there were LIGHTNINGS, and VOICES, and THUNDERINGS and an EARTHQUAKE, and GREAT HAIL."

The sounding of the "SEVENTH TRUMPET" includes all that happens down to chapter 20:3. When it sounded John heard "Great Voices" in Heaven saying—"THE KINGDOMS OF THIS WORLD ARE BECOME THE KINGDOMS OF OUR LORD, AND OF HIS CHRIST; AND HE SHALL REIGN FOR EVER AND EVER." This is the announcement that the time had come for Christ to take "THE KINGDOM," though "The Kingdom" does not fully come into His possession for $3\frac{1}{2}$ years. The whole of this passage is anticipative, for the "sayings" of the Four and Twenty Elders look forward to the Resurrections and Judgments of chapter 20. The scene is located in Heaven. For it is there that John hears the Trumpet sound, and sees the "Temple of God" opened, and hears the "voices" and "thunderings" that accompany the devastation of the earth by "earthquake" and "hail." This announcement is preliminary to the great events that are to follow, which will be the most remarkable and momentous that have ever happened on this earth.

The "THIRD WOE" includes the "VIALS," and all other judgments down to chapter 20:3. The "Time Limit" of the "SEVENTH TRUMPET" is given in chapter 10:7, and is spoken of as "THE 'DAYS'" of the "Voice" of the "SEVENTH ANGEL" when he shall BEGIN TO SOUND. Implying that the blast or blasts, of the "SEVENTH TRUMPET" shall be long continued, that is, extend over the whole of the last half of the "Week."

The Middle of the Week

The Seven Personages

1. THE SUN-CLOTHED WOMAN.
Rev. 12:1-2.

"And there appeared a **'GREAT WONDER'** in Heaven; a Woman **CLOTHED WITH THE SUN**, and the **MOON UNDER HER FEET**, and upon her head a **CROWN OF TWELVE STARS:** and she being with child cried, travailing in birth, and pained to be delivered."

In the "Middle of the Week" two **"Wonders"** will appear in Heaven, for John is back again in Heaven. The Revised Version calls them **"SIGNS,"** that is, they are **"SYMBOLS"** of something, and must be thus interpreted. The first will be a **"SUN CLOTHED WOMAN."** Who does this "Sun Clothed Woman" represent? Some would have us believe that this "Woman" is the Virgin Mary, others that she represents the Church. Those who say she represents the

Church claim that she represents the **visible** or outward Church, **and** her "Child" represents the "True Church" or those who are to be "caught out" at the Rapture. If this be true, and the "Child" is not caught out until the "Middle of the Week," then the Church will have to go half way through the "Tribulation." The fact is, the "Woman" is neither the Virgin Mary or the Church. She is **ISRAEL.** We have only to be reminded of "Joseph's Dream," where he says— "Behold, I have dreamed a dream more; and, behold, the 'SUN' and the 'MOON' and the 'ELEVEN STARS' made Obeisance to me" (Gen. 37:9), to see the Jewish character of this "Woman." Joseph was the "Twelfth" star.

Israel is again and again compared to a woman, and a married woman, in the Old Testament. Isa. 54:1. And in the period of her rejection she is spoken of as a **WIDOW** (Isa. 47:7-9. Luke 18:1-8), and a **DIVORCED** Woman (Isa. 50:1), and an **ADULTEROUS WIFE** (Jer. 3:1-25, Hosea 2:1-23) but the Church is a **VIRGIN,** and an **ESPOUSED** Virgin at that. 2. Cor. 11:2. Eph. 5:25-27. The "Sun Clothed Woman," is described as being "**WITH CHILD,**" and "**TRAVAILING TO BRING FORTH.**" When was the Church in such a condition? To be found in such a condition would unfit her to be the Bride of Christ. Nowhere in the scriptures is it intimated that the Church is ever to be a **Mother.** But it is so prophesied of Israel. Speaking of the sevenfold privilege of Israel, Paul says— "Who are Israelites; to whom pertaineth the **adoption,** and the **glory,** and the **covenants,** and the **giving of the law,** and the **service of God,** and the **promises,** whose are **the fathers,** and of whom **AS CONCERNING THE FLESH CHRIST CAME.**" Rom. 9:4-5. Here we see that Christ was to come from **ISRAEL.** Then we know that the "**PROMISED SEED**" was to come through **ISRAEL,** and the Prophet Isaiah looked forward to the time when Israel could say— "**UNTO US A CHILD IS BORN UNTO US A SON IS GIVEN.**" Isa. 9:6-7. Before the promised heir could be born Israel had to pass through many sore afflictions and judgments. These were her "**TRAVAIL TIME.**" There can be no question but what the "Sun Clothed Woman" represents **ISRAEL.**

2. THE DRAGON.
Rev. 12:3-4.

"And there appeared another 'WONDER' in Heaven; and behold a 'GREAT RED DRAGON,' having SEVEN HEADS and TEN HORNS, and SEVEN CROWNS upon his heads. And his tail drew the THIRD PART OF THE STARS OF HEAVEN, and did cast them to the earth: and the DRAGON stood before the WOMAN which was ready to be delivered, for to devour her CHILD as soon as it was born."

The second "WONDER" that will appear in Heaven will be a "**GREAT RED DRAGON.**" We are not left in doubt as to who is meant, for in verse 9 he is called that "**OLD SERPENT, THE DEVIL,**" and "**SATAN.**" His color is RED, the color of blood, for he was a murderer from the beginning. John 8:44.

He has "SEVEN HEADS" and "TEN HORNS," and upon his heads are "SEVEN CROWNS." These are the emblems of the universality of his earthly dominion, and typify the sevenfold perfection of his power: for he is the

PRINCE OF THE "POWERS OF THE AIR."
And the
"PRINCE OF THIS WORLD."
(Eph. 6:12.   John 12:31, 14:30, 16:11.)

As such Jesus did not dispute his claim when in the Wilderness Temptation he offered Him the "Kingdoms of this World" and the glory of them. Luke 4:5-7. His "Seven Heads," "Ten Horns," and "Crowns," associate him with the **BEAST OUT OF THE SEA"** of the first verse of the next chapter, the only difference being that the Dragon's "Crowns" are on his "Heads," while those of the Beast are on his "Horns," and therefore differ in number. These features, common to both, reveal the fact that there is some relation between the "Dragon" and the "Beast," and that the "Beast" is an earthly embodiment or incarnation of the **"DRAGON,"** for the "Beast" does not appear on the earth until after the "Dragon" is cast out of Heaven. Though the "Antichrist" exists from the beginning of the Week, he does not become **"THE BEAST"** until in the "Middle of the Week." Satan is cast out of Heaven and incarnates himself in him. Then the "Antichrist" breaks his "Covenant" with Israel, desecrates the Temple, and becomes the "Satanic Person" that rules during the last half of the Week.

The **"STARS OF HEAVEN"** attached to his "tail" reveal the fact that Satan will take with him in his expulsion from Heaven, a third of the Angels, for the Angels are spoken of as "Stars" in the Old Testament. Job 38:7. These "Angels" will be cast with him into the earth. They will not be visible but they will secretly sow the seeds of rebellion, and ultimately they will be cast with Satan into the "Lake of Fire" which will be prepared for them. Matt. 25:41. While we are not told that Satan's "Angels" are cast bound with him into the "Bottomless Pit," yet the inference is that they are, for during the Millennium they do not appear to be present on the earth.

John tells us that the "Dragon" stood before the "Sun Clothed Woman" ready to "devour her child" as soon as it was born. It is intensely interesting reading to trace in the Scriptures the story of Satan's efforts to prevent the birth of the "Man-Child" **CHRIST,** and then after His birth to destroy Him before He could reach the Cross and purchase man's redemption. As soon as Satan had accomplished the Fall of Adam and Eve, he found himself under the curse of God, and was told that the **"SEED"** of the Woman should bruise his head. Gen. 3:14-15. This aroused the enmity of Satan and he determined to prevent the birth of the promised "Seed," or, if that were not possible, to destroy the "Seed" after birth. So as soon as Abel was born, from whom the promised "Seed" was to come, Satan schemed for his destruction, and finally got his brother Cain to kill him. Then the "Sons of God" (Angels) doubtless at Satan's instigation, married the "Daughters of Men" (Cainites), and their "sin," and the character of their offspring moved God to destroy mankind from off the earth. This was what Satan planned for, and would have been a victory for Satan and a defeat for God, so God decided to spare the race, and begin over again with a representative man, Noah. But it was not long before Noah planted a vineyard and drank himself drunk with the wine therefrom, the result the curse of Canaan the Son of Ham. Gen. 9: 18-27. Then the people began to multiply and Satan filled their heart with pride and presumption and they rose and built the "Tower of Babel," the result the "Confusion of Tongues" and the unity of the race broken up. Gen. 11: 1-9. Then the Lord called Abraham and the fight narrowed down to his seed. Abraham was 75 years old, and had no children, and Sarah his wife was 65 years of age and barren. Gen. 16: 1. Doubtless Satan laughed at the situation because of Sarah's barrenness, in which probably he had a hand, but to show Satan that He could work a miracle if necessary, to produce the promised "seed," God waited until Sarah was "past age," until she was 90 years old (Gen. 17: 17), and then He caused her to conceive and bear the promised "seed." Gen. 18: 9-15; 21: 1-3. When Isaac was about 12 years of age Satan moved God to test Abraham by commanding him to offer up Isaac as a sacrifice upon Mount Moriah. It was similar to the test of Job. Job 1: 6-12; 2: 3-6. The plan for Isaac's destruction failed, for when God saw that Abraham was willing and ready to slay his son, He intervened and spared his life. When Isaac grew up and married Rebekah, Satan, to prevent her having offspring, caused her to be barren, but Isaac prayed and God heard his prayer (Gen. 25: 20-21), and twins were born. Then Satan, when they had grown up, stirred up enmity between them hoping that the tragedy of Cain and Abel would be repeated, and Jacob, through whom Christ was to come, would be slain. When the time came for Moses to be born, Satan put it into the heart of Pharaoh to order that all male Hebrew children should be destroyed at birth, his purpose being to destroy the male line of descent altogether. But his plan was frustrated by a baby's tear. Ex. 2: 5-10. And so it went on, until at the death of King Jehoshaphat his son Jehoram slew all his brethren with the sword (2. Chron. 21: 13), thus reducing the "seed royal" down to one life. But Jehoram had children. Then the Arabians slew all his children but one, Ahaziah the youngest. 2. Chron. 21: 17 (margin). 2. Chron. 22: 1. But Ahaziah had children. These in turn were slain by Athaliah his mother, doubtless at the instigation of Satan. She thought she had slain them all, but God interposed and rescued the infant son at the hands of his aunt, who hid him in the Temple (2. Cor. 22: 10-12), and for 6 years all the hopes of God's people as to the promised "seed" rested on that infant's life. During the Captivity Satan tried to destroy the whole Hebrew nation at the hands of Haman, but a very little thing, a king's sleepless night, frustrated that plan. Esther 3: 8-15, 6: 1-11. But the story is too long.

At last the promised "SEED" was born. Then Satan, failing to prevent His birth, determined to destroy Him before He could reach the Cross. To that end he prompted Herod, through jealousy and fear, to slay all the male children at Bethlehem under 2 years of age, but Joseph warned of God in a dream, had fled with the infant Christ to Egypt. When Christ entered on His ministry Satan met Him in the Wilderness and suggested that He throw Himself from the Pinnacle of the Temple. Foiled in that Satan sought Christ's life by getting His own townspeople to attempt to cast Him over a precipice. Luke 4:29. The two storms on the Sea of Galilee were but attempts of Satan to destroy Christ. You cannot rebuke a thing, you can only rebuke a **person**, and when Christ rebuked the winds and the sea, He rebuked the **person** (Satan) who had caused their disturbance. Matt. 8:24-27.

Then Satan renewed the fight through Priests and Pharisees until he succeeded at last in getting one of Christ's own disciples, Judas, to sell his Master. Then amid the shades of Gethsemane, through physical exhaustion, he sought to kill Christ. And when he at last succeeded in having Christ crucified, through the agency of Pilate, he thought he had conquered, but to be doubly sure he took good care to have the place of burial sealed and guarded. But when Christ rose from the dead Satan's rage knew no bounds. In all probability Satan and his angels contested the Ascension of Christ, for only thus can we account for the necessity of His going up 10 days before Pentecost, that He might have ample time, convoyed by "Twelve Legions of Angels," for any "Battle of the Clouds" that Satan might attempt. The history of the Christian Church is but one long story of the "Irrepressible Conflict" between Satan and God's people. Paul writing to the Thessalonians said—"We would have come unto you, even I Paul, once and again, but **SATAN hindered us.**" 1. Thess. 2:18. And now as the time draws nigh for Christ to receive "The Kingdom," which means that He will come back to the earth, and that Satan's power and dominion over the earth shall cease, and Satan be bound for 1000 years, Satan filled with wrath will oppose His return with his armies and there will be "**WAR IN HEAVEN.**"

3. THE MAN-CHILD.
Rev. 12:5-6.

"And she brought forth a 'MAN-CHILD,' who was to rule all nations with a 'ROD OF IRON': and her child was caught up unto God, and to His Throne."

As the result of her "**travail**" the "**Sun Clothed Woman**" brought forth a "**MAN-CHILD**" who was to rule the nations with a "**ROD OF IRON.**" There can be no question as to who is meant by the "Man-Child." He is **CHRIST.** The Second Psalm settles that— "Ask of me, and I shall give Thee the heathen for Thine inheritance, and the uttermost parts of the earth for Thy possession. Thou shalt break them with a 'ROD OF IRON': Thou shalt dash them in pieces like a potter's vessel." The "Man-Child" cannot be the Church, as some claim, because the "Man-Child" is caught up to the **FATHER'S THRONE**, where He is now seated, while the Church, which is **not as yet caught up**, is to be caught up to **CHRIST IN THE AIR.** 1. Thess. 4:17.

Those who claim that Christ and the Church **together** constitute the "Man-Child," because in the Message to the Church at Thyatira, the promise to the "Overcomers" is, that they shall rule the Nations with a "ROD OF IRON," forget that this promise is not to the Church as a whole, but only to the "Overcomers" of the "Thyatiran Church Period," A. D. 606-1520. In other words the "Overcomers" of the "Thyatiran Church Period" shall hold some prominent "Ruling Power" with Christ in the Millennial Kingdom.

"And the 'WOMAN' fled into the 'Wilderness,' where she hath a place prepared of God, that they should feed her there a thousand two hundred and threescore days."

Here is where many interpreters of this chapter have been led astray. They have supposed that the "Woman" flees into the Wilderness **immediately after the birth of her child**, and because the **time** of her flight is in the "Middle of the Week" (for the 1260 days of her preservation in the Wilderness corresponds with the "last half" of the "Week"), they cannot see how her "Child" can be Christ, for Christ was born and "caught up" to His Father's Throne centuries ago, while this event is still future. But they overlook the fact that between the 5th and 6th verses of this chapter the present CHURCH PERIOD comes in. Between these verses the "GAP" between the "Sixty-ninth" and the "Seventieth" Week of Daniel's "Seventy Weeks" is found. The 5th verse describes the "BIRTH" of Christ, and His "ASCENSION," and then John jumps over the "GAP," and describes in the 6th verse the "Flight" of the Woman ISRAEL into the Wilderness to escape from the Antichrist. The reason for this is that John is not dealing here with the Church, and having introduced the "Woman" and her "Child" to account for the "Dragon's" wrath against her because he did not succeed in destroying her "Child" (Christ) when He was born, John jumps over the "GAP," that he may again take up God's dealing with ISRAEL. The "Flight" of the "Woman" is mentioned here by anticipation, for she does not flee until after the "War in Heaven."

Here is evidence that the "Sun Clothed Woman" is not the "Virgin Mary," for she does not flee into Egypt, as Joseph and the Virgin did (Matt. 2: 12-15), but into the WILDERNESS. Neither does she flee "with her child," for it was taken away from her and caught up to the "Throne of God." Neither does she flee for her child's protection, but for her **own** safety.

From this passage we learn that Christ's Millennial rule will be AUTOCRATIC, for He shall rule over the Nations with a "ROD OF IRON." This does not signify that His rule will be tyrannical. It simply means that His WILL shall be supreme. We cannot imagine Christ's rule to be other than a rule of love. Politics will have no place in the government, the masses will not be oppressed by those in power, equal rights will be accorded to everyone, and every man shall sit under his own vine and figtree.

4. THE ARCHANGEL.
(War In Heaven.)

Rev. 12:7-12.

"And there was 'WAR IN HEAVEN': MICHAEL and his angels fought against the DRAGON: and the DRAGON fought and his angels, and prevailed not: neither was their place found any more in Heaven. And the GREAT DRAGON was cast out, that old SERPENT, called the DEVIL, and SATAN, which deceiveth the whole world: he was cast out into the earth, and his angels were cast out with him. And I heard a loud voice saying in Heaven, Now is come salvation, and strength, and the Kingdom of God, and the power of His Christ: for the ACCUSER OF OUR BRETHREN IS CAST DOWN, which accused them before our God day and night. And they overcame him (the Dragon) by the BLOOD OF THE LAMB, and by the WORD OF THEIR TESTIMONY; and they loved not their lives unto the death (Martyr's Death). Therefore rejoice, ye heavens, and ye that dwell in them. Woe to the INHABITERS OF THE EARTH AND OF THE SEA! for the DEVIL is come down unto you, having great wrath, because he knoweth that he hath but a SHORT TIME." (3½ years.)

The "WAR IN HEAVEN" is started by the attempt to expel the DRAGON and his angels From the Heavenlies. That the DRAGON (Satan) and his angels were not cast out of Heaven at the time of his "Rebellion" (which antedates the present earth), and confined in some "prison house," is clear, for he was at liberty to visit the Garden of Eden and tempt Adam and Eve, and he had access to God in Heaven in the days of Job, 2000 years before Christ (Job 1:1; 2:8), and he was free to visit the earth in Christ's day and tempt Him in the Wilderness, and later to sift Peter. His origin is more or less shrouded in mystery, but one thing is certain, he is a "created being," and that of the most exalted type. He was before his rebellion "The Anointed Cherub That Covereth." That is, he was the guardian or protector of the "Throne of God." He was perfect in all his ways from the day that he was created until iniquity was found in him. In him was the "fulness of wisdom," and the "perfection of beauty," but it was his "beauty" that caused the pride (1. Tim. 3:6) that was his downfall. He was clothed in a garment that was covered with the most rare and precious gems, the sardius, topaz, diamond, beryl, onyx, jasper, sapphire, emerald, carbuncle, all woven in with gold. He dwelt in Eden, the Garden of God. This probably refers not to the earthly Eden, but to the "Paradise of God" on high, for Satan dwelt on the "Holy Mount of God." All this we learn from Ezek. 28:11-19, where the Prophet has a "foreview" of the Antichrist under the title of the "King of Tyrus," and as Antichrist when he becomes the "Beast" is to be an incarnation of Satan, the Prophet here describes Satan's original glory from which he fell, for there has never as yet been such a King of Tyrus as here described. The cause of Satan's rebellion, or fall, is given in Isa. 14:12-20. He is there called "LUCIFER, SON OF THE MORNING." This was his glorious title when he was created, and this world of ours was made, at which time—"The 'Morning Stars' (probably other glorious created ruling beings like himself), sang together, and all the 'Sons of God' (angels) shouted for joy." Job 38:7.

It is well to note that the one here called "LUCIFER," is in verse four (Isa. 14:4), also called the "King of Babylon." As there never has been a King of Babylon like the one here described, the description must be that of a future King of Babylon. And as "Antichrist" is to have for his Capital City Babylon rebuilt, this is probably a "foreview" by the Prophet of Antichrist as indwelt by "LUCIFER" (Satan) in that day when he shall be King of Babylon, and also King of Tyrus.

The common notion is that Satan and his angels are imprisoned in Hell. This is not true. The angels described in 2. Pet. 2:4, and Jude 6, as having left their "first estate," and being "reserved in everlasting chains under darkness," are not Satan's angels. They are a special class of angels, spoken of as "Sons of God," whose sin of marrying the "Daughters of Men" caused the Flood. Gen. 6:1-8. They are the "Spirits in Prison" of whom Peter speaks in 1. Pet. 3:18-20. They are now confined in "Tartarus" awaiting the "Great White Throne" Judgment. Jude 6. As this Book of Revelation that we are now studying is a prophecy of "Things To Come" that were

future in the Apostle John's day, and it declares that Satan was still in the Heavenlies at that time, A. D. 96, as he has not been cast out since he must still be there.

He is a great "Celestial Potentate." He is the "**PRINCE OF THE POWERS OF THE AIR**" (Eph. 2:2), and the "**GOD OF THIS WORLD.**" 2. Cor. 4:4. He is the "God" not of the earth, for that belongs to its Maker—**GOD**. "The earth is the Lord's and the fulness thereof." He is the "God" of the "**WORLD SYSTEMS**" of the habitable earth. These "**World Systems**" embrace business, society, politics, and religion. He is the Ruler of the "Powers of Darkness" of the "Spirit World" (Eph. 6:11-12), and his position is so exalted that even Michael the Archangel dare not insult him. Jude 9. So mighty is he that man cannot successfully resist him without Divine help.

Satan is a **King**, and has a **KINGDOM**. Of it Christ said—"If Satan cast out Satan he is divided against himself; how then shall his 'KINGDOM' stand"? (Matt. 12:24-30.) Speaking of the "Evil Powers" Paul wrote—"We wrestle not against flesh and blood, but against 'Principalities,' against 'Powers,' against the 'Rulers of Darkness Of This World' (Age), against 'Spiritual Wickedness' in HIGH PLACES" (the Heavenlies). Eph. 6:12. From this we see that Satan's Kingdom consists of "Principalities," "Powers," "Age Rulers of Darkness," and "Wicked Spirits" in the Heavenlies. These "Principalities" are ruled by "Princes" who control the nations of the earth as in the days of Daniel the Prophet, when a Heavenly Messenger was sent to Daniel, but was hindered "three weeks" from reaching him by the "**Prince of the Kingdom of Persia**," Satan's ruling "Prince of Persia," until Michael the Archangel came to his rescue. Dan. 10:10-14.

The opposing "Commanders in Chief" of the "War in Heaven" will be **MICHAEL** and the **DRAGON** (Satan). We are first introduced to Michael in the Book of Daniel, and his appearance here is a confirmation that this part of the Book of Revelation is Jewish, and a continuation or supplement to the Book of Daniel. Michael is called in the Book of Daniel "**one of the CHIEF PRINCES**" (Dan. 10:13), "**YOUR PRINCE**" (Dan. 10:21), and the "**GREAT PRINCE WHICH STANDETH FOR THY PEOPLE.**" Dan. 12:1. That is, Michael has been chosen from among the "Chief Princes" that stand before God, to be the protector of Daniel's People, the Jews. In Jude 9 he is called the "**ARCHANGEL**," and as there is but one "Archangel" spoken of in the Bible, Michael must be he. He also has something to do with the resurrection of the dead, for he is associated with the "Resurrection" mentioned in Dan. 12:1-2, and he contested with the Devil the resurrection of Moses (Jude 9), and the "Voice" of the Archangel that will be heard when the "Dead in Christ" shall rise (1. Thess. 4:16), will be the "voice" of **MICHAEL**.

When the "Dragon" is cast out of the "Heavenlies" there will be great rejoicing in Heaven because the "Accuser" of Christ's "Brethren" (the Jews) is cast down, but there will be "woe" for the "inhabitants of the earth," for the "Dragon" will be filled with "great wrath" because he knows that he will have but a "**short time**" (3½ years) to vent his wrath on the inhabitants of the earth before he is chained and cast into the Bottomless Pit.

While Satan has been the "Accuser of the Brethren" in all Ages, the context shows that reference is here made to the "Jewish Remnant" (the brethren of Christ), who during the first 3½ years of the "Tribulation Period" pass through great persecution, and die as "martyrs." They are referred to in Rev. 6:9-11 as the "souls of them that were slain for the Word of God," and we are here told (Rev. 12:11) that they overcame by the "Blood of the Lamb," and the "Word of their Testimony," and died as "martyrs," for they "loved not their lives unto the death." As they overcame by the "Blood Of The Lamb," then the "TIME" of their overcoming must be subsequent to the shedding of Christ's blood on Calvary, that is, Satan according to this account, could not have been cast out of the "Heavenlies" prior to the Crucifixion of Christ. When Jesus said—"I beheld Satan as lightning fall from heaven" (Luke 10:18), He was not referring to some past fall of Satan, but it was a prophetic utterance, by way of anticipation, of his future fall, when he shall be hurled headfirst out of Heaven by Michael the Archangel. As further evidence as to the time of Satan's casting out, Daniel the Prophet tells us that it will be at the "Time of Trouble" that is to come upon Daniel's People, the Jews, and that "Time of Trouble" is the "GREAT TRIBULATION." At that time Michael shall "stand up" to deliver Daniel's People, and the result will be "WAR IN HEAVEN" and Daniel's People shall be delivered, not from the "Great Tribulation," but out of it.

When the Dragon and all the Principalities and Powers of evil that now occupy the "Middle Heaven" of the Heavenlies, that is, the Heaven between the atmosphere of our earth, and the "Third Heaven" where God dwells, are cast out and down, then the Heavens will be **CLEAN**, for they are not now clean in God's sight. Job 15:15. And as all these "Evil Powers" will doubtless be imprisoned during the Millennium, with Satan, the Heavens will be **CLEAN** during that period, and this will account for the universal rule of righteousness and peace of those days.

"THE PERSECUTION OF THE "SUN CLOTHED WOMAN."
Rev. 12:13-16.

"And when the 'Dragon' saw that he was cast unto the earth, he persecuted the 'Woman' which brought forth the 'MAN-CHILD.' And to the 'Woman' were given two wings of a Great Eagle, that she might fly into the Wilderness, into her place, where she is nourished for a 'time,' and 'times,' and 'half a time' (3½ years), from the face of the 'Serpent' (The Dragon). And the 'Serpent' cast out of his mouth water as a flood after the 'Woman,' that he might cause her to be carried away of the flood. And the earth helped the 'Woman'; and the earth opened her mouth, and swallowed up the flood which the Dragon cast out of his mouth."

When the Dragon is cast out of Heaven into the Earth, knowing that his defeat has been brought about by the elevation of the "MAN-CHILD" to the place of power, he will concentrate his hatred and malice on the "Sun-Clothed Woman" (Israel), who gave the "Man-Child" birth. To the "Woman" will be given the "WINGS OF A GREAT EAGLE" that she may fly into the "Wilderness," into "HER PLACE" where she shall be nourished for a "TIME, TIMES and HALF A TIME," or 3½ years. This takes us back to the flight of Israel from Egypt, of which God said—"Ye have seen what I did unto the Egyptians, and how I bare you on 'EAGLE'S WINGS,' and brought you unto myself." Ex. 19:4. As the "Woman" and the "Dragon" are symbols, so are the "Eagle's Wings." They speak of the rapid and safe flight of the "Woman" (ISRAEL) into the "Wilderness" where she shall be safely kept and nourished for 3½ years until the Dragon is bound.

The Prophet Isaiah speaks of this time when he says—"Come, my people (ISRAEL) enter thou into thy CHAMBERS, and SHUT THY DOORS ABOUT THEE: HIDE THYSELF AS IT WERE FOR A LITTLE WHILE (3½ years) UNTIL THE INDIGNATION (The Great Tribulation) IS OVERPAST. . . . In THAT DAY (the Day of the casting out of the Dragon) the Lord with His sore and great and strong sword shall punish 'LEVIATHAN' (the "Dragon" or "Serpent") the piercing SERPENT, even 'LEVIATHAN' the crooked SERPENT, and He shall slay 'THE DRAGON' that is in the sea." Isa. 26:20; 27:1. This may mean the "BEAST" that comes up out of the sea, the "ANTICHRIST." Rev. 13:1-2.

This is the time that Christ refers to in Matt. 24:15-22. "When ye therefore shall see the 'ABOMINATION OF DESOLATION,' spoken of by Daniel the Prophet (Dan. 9:27), stand in the Holy Place (whoso readeth, let him understand), then let them which be in Judea flee into the mountains: let him which is on the housetop not come down to take anything out of his house: neither let him which is in the field return back to take his clothes. And woe unto them that are with child, and to them that give suck in those days! But pray ye that your flight be not in the winter, neither on the Sabbath day: for then shall be GREAT TRIBULATION, such as was not since the beginning of the world to this time, no, nor ever shall be. And except those days should be shortened, there should no flesh be saved; but for the ELECT'S SAKE (the elect of Israel) those days shall be shortened." The flight that Matthew here speaks about is not the same flight that Luke speaks about. "And when ye shall see Jerusalem COMPASSED WITH ARMIES, then know that the desolation thereof is nigh. Then let them which are in Judea flee to the mountains: and let them which are in the midst of it depart out: and let not them that are in the countries enter thereinto. For these be the days of vengeance, that all things which are written may be fulfilled. But woe unto them that are with child, and to them that give suck, in those days! for there shall be great distress in the land, and wrath upon this people. And they shall fall by the edge of the sword, and shall be led away captive into all nations: and JERUSALEM SHALL BE TRODDEN DOWN OF THE GENTILES, UNTIL THE TIMES OF THE GENTILES BE FULFILLED." Luke 21:20-24.

A careful comparison of these two passages will reveal their difference. Luke refers to the "Destruction of Jerusalem" by Titus, A. D. 70, at which time Jerusalem was compassed by the Roman Army, and the sufferings of the inhabitants of the city were so great that mothers cooked and ate their own children. This is **past**. And verse 24 has been fulfilled for the Jews have been "**led away captive into ALL NATIONS**," where they still remain, and Jerusalem has since then been "**TRODDEN DOWN OF THE GENTILES**," and will continue to be until the "**TIMES OF THE GENTILES**" shall **be fulfilled**. But the "flight" that Matthew speaks about is still future. He locates it at the time of the "Great Tribulation," which he says is to be preceded by the **setting up** of the "**ABOMINATION OF DESOLATION**," spoken of by Daniel the Prophet. The gods, or idols of the heathen, are spoken of as "**ABOMINATIONS**." Milcom, or Molech, was the "**abomination**" of the Ammonites; Chemosh, the "**abomination**" of Moab. 1. Kings 11 : 5-7. This interprets the "**ABOMINATION**" spoken of by Daniel, as nothing other than an "**IDOL**" or "**FALSE GOD**." In the "Middle of the Week," a "**DESOLATOR**" (Antichrist) will appear and cause the sacrifices and oblations to cease, and set up in the "Holy Place" of the Temple an "**IDOL**," and that "Idol" will be an "**IMAGE OF THE BEAST**." Rev. 13 : 14-15.

Let us now return to the "Flight of the Woman" and see if we can locate "**her place**," the "**chamber**" to which she is to flee, and "**shut to the door**," and "**hide herself for a little while**," and be **nourished by God** for a "Time, and Times, and Half a Time," or 3½ years.

THE CITIES OF REFUGE.

The "Cities of Refuge" of Old Testament times are a type of this "Wilderness Refuge" of the Children of Israel.

The "Cities of Refuge" were designated cities, 3 on each side the river Jordan, where the "Man-Slayer" could flee for safety from the "Avenger of Blood." If it was proved after trial that he had slain a man "wilfully," he was turned over to the "Avenger of Blood," but if he did it unwittingly, his life was spared, but he had to remain in the city until the death of the High Priest. If there were no "Man-Slayer" there would be no "Avenger of Blood," and therefore no need for a "City of Refuge."

Now if I find in the New Testament that a certain class of people are called upon to flee to a "Place of Refuge" for the protection of their lives, then I must believe that they flee because an "Avenger of Blood" is after them, and that they flee because they are guilty of "Manslaughter."

Such a class of people I find in the Jewish Race. They were the cause of the death of Christ, and though He was crucified by the Roman authorities they assumed the guilt for they cried—"His **blood** be on **Us**, and on **Our Children**." Matt. 27 : 25. At first sight it looks like "wilful" murder, yet from the prayer of Jesus on the Cross— "Father, forgive them for they **know not what they do**," it is clear that Jesus' death was not so much a premeditated murder as it **was a** murder committed in a blind religious frenzy. Paul says—"had they known they would not have crucified the Lord of Glory." 1. Cor. 2: 8.

It is clear then that the Jewish race is only guilty of "Man-slaughter." As the "Man-Slayer" of Jesus they have been for over 1800 years running for a "City of Refuge" and have not as yet reached it. The "Avenger of Blood" has been on their track and has hounded them from nation to nation, and the epithet of

"The Wandering Jew"

has followed them down the centuries, and the prophecy of Moses is being fulfilled that they should find no rest for the sole of their foot. Deut. 28: 64-67.

If the Jews are the "Man-Slayer" who is the "Avenger of Blood"? Antichrist.

And now as to the "City of Refuge" that God will provide for Israel when the "Avenger of Blood" (Antichrist), who shall then be indwelt by the Dragon, is on her track.

When the Lord God brought the Children of Israel out of Egypt they journeyed from the Red Sea, tarrying for a while at Mt. Sinai to receive the Law and build the Tabernacle, until they came, one year, after leaving Egypt, to Kadesh Barnea. There they sent up spies to spy out the land of Canaan, but refused to go up and take possession of the land, and were compelled to wander in the Wilderness south of the Dead Sea. There God took care of them and fed them for 40 years. Now it is in the same Wilderness that God is going to provide for them a place of "Refuge" in the day when the "Avenger of Blood" shall seek to destroy them.

Speaking of the Antichrist, the Prophet Daniel says—

"He shall enter also into the Glorious Land (Palestine) and many countries shall be overthrown; but these shall escape out of his hand, even **Edom** and **Moab** and the chief of the **Children of Ammon.**" Dan. 11: 41.

Now Edom takes in the Wilderness where Israel wandered for 40 years. And it is here in Edom that the "City of Refuge" that God has provided for Israel is located, and is known today as Petra. It was a great commercial centre in the days of King Solomon. In A. D. 105 the Romans conquered the country and called the province Arabia Petra. When the power of Rome waned Petra gradually fell into the hands of the Arabs and became completely lost to the civilized world in the seventh century, and remained so until it was rediscovered by Burckhardt in 1812.

It is located in the mountains like as in the crater of a volcano. It has but one entrance, and that is through a narrow, winding defile or canyon from 12 to 40 feet wide, the sides of which are precipitous and at times so close together as to almost shut out the blue sky above and make you think you are passing through a subterranean passage-way. The height of the sides varies from 200 to 1000 feet, and the length of the canyon is about two miles. No other city in the world has such a wonderful gateway. The sides of the canyon are lined with wonderful monuments and temples carved out of the rocky sandstone of the sides. Once inside the rocky inclosure of the city we find the ruins of magnificent buildings, tombs and monuments. The cliffs that surround the city are carved and honeycombed with excavations to a height of 300 feet above the floor of the valley, and the excavations cut as they are out of different colored strata of the rock, such as red, purple, blue, black, white and yellow, lend a beauty to their appearance that is indescribable and overpowering to the beholder.

When the time comes for the "Man-Slayer" (Israel), to escape from the hands of the "Avenger of Blood" (Antichrist), the rocky fastness of the ancient city of Petra will be her "City of Refuge." We read that when the "Woman" (Israel) shall flee into the Wilderness that the "Serpent" (Antichrist, indwelt by Satan) shall cast a flood of water out of his mouth after her to destroy her, but that the earth shall open her mouth and swallow the flood. That is, Antichrist will send his army after the fleeing Israelites, and it will probably be swallowed up in a "Sand storm" of the desert, and Israel shall safely reach her place of refuge, where she shall be safe, not until the death of the High Priest, but until the return of "The High Priest" (Jesus) from Heaven, who as "King-Priest" of the Armies of Heaven will deliver her and allow her to leave her place of refuge. During the period of Israel's "hiding" in the Wilderness God will "nourish" her as He did during her 40 years' wandering in the same Wilderness in the days of Moses.

5. THE JEWISH REMNANT.
Rev. 12:17.

"And the Dragon was wroth with the 'WOMAN,' and went to make war with the 'REMNANT OF HER SEED,' which keep the commandments of God, and have the testimony of Jesus Christ."

Baffled in his attempt to destroy the "Woman," the Dragon, in his rage will make war against the "REMNANT OF HER SEED," that is, against those Israelites left in Palestine or among the nations that keep the "commandments of God," and have the "testimony of Jesus Christ." To this end he will give to the "BEAST" (Antichrist) his "Power," and his "Seat," and "Great Authority." Rev. 13:2.

Here again we have indirect evidence that the "Woman" is not the Church but ISRAEL. When the Church is caught out no REMNANT is left behind, all that are "IN CHRIST" are taken away; but when the "Woman" (ISRAEL) flees into the wilderness a "REMNANT" is left behind. This "Remnant" is composed of two classes. First, those who "keep the Commandments of God," that is, Orthodox Jews who observe the Old Testament Law, and second, those who "accept the testimony of Jesus Christ," that is, accept Jesus as their promised Messiah. The latter class will be converted by the preaching of the "Gospel of the Kingdom" by the "Two Witnesses." Those will be trying times for those Israelites who will not commit idolatry by bowing the knee to the "Image of the Beast," for it will be a remorseless war of persecution that Antichrist will wage against them, and thousands will die a martyr's death.

6. THE BEAST OUT OF THE SEA.
The Incarnation Of "The Dragon," "The Anti-God."
In "The Beast" Or "Anti-Christ."
Rev. 13:1-10.

"And I (**He,** the Dragon, R. V.) stood upon the sand of the sea **and** (I) saw a 'BEAST' rise up **out** of the SEA having 'SEVEN HEADS' and 'TEN HORNS,' and upon his horns 'TEN CROWNS,' and upon his heads the name of BLASPHEMY. And the 'BEAST' which I saw was like a **LEOPARD,** and his **feet** were as the **feet of a BEAR,** and his **mouth** as the **mouth** of a LION: and the 'DRAGON' gave him his **POWER,** and his SEAT (Throne), and GREAT AUTHORITY. And I saw one of his HEADS as it were **wounded to death:** and his deadly **wound was healed:** and **all the world wondered after the 'BEAST.'** And they wor- shipped the 'DRAGON' which gave power unto the 'BEAST,' and they **worshipped the 'BEAST,'** saying, **Who is like unto the** 'BEAST'? **Who is able to make war with him?** And there was given unto him a mouth **speaking great things and blasphemies;** and power was given unto him to continue **forty and two months.** And he opened his mouth in **blasphemy against God,** to blaspheme His **name,** and **His Tabernacle, and them that dwell in Heaven.** And it was given unto him to **make war with the saints, and to overcome them:** and power was given him over **all kindreds, and tongues, and nations.** And **all that dwell upon the earth shall** WORSHIP HIM, whose names are **not written in the** 'BOOK OF LIFE' of the Lamb slain from the foundation of the world. If any man have an ear, let him hear. He that leadeth into cap- tivity shall go into captivity: he that killeth with the sword must be killed with the sword. Here is the patience and the faith of the saints."

John next saw the "Dragon" standing on the seashore, and **as he** stood, a "Beast" rose up out of the sea having **"SEVEN HEADS"** and **"TEN HORNS,"** and upon his **"Horns" "TEN CROWNS,"** and upon his **"Heads"** the name of BLASPHEMY, and the body of the **"Beast"** was like a **LEOPARD,** and his **feet** were as the **feet of a BEAR,** and his **mouth** as the **mouth of a LION,** and the **"DRAGON"** gave him his **POWER**, and his **SEAT** (Throne), and **GREAT AUTHORITY.** This does not necessarily mean that the "Dragon" gave him his **own** throne, but he gave him **power**, and **a throne**, and **great authority.** As John was back on the Isle of Patmos, the "sea" from which he saw the "Beast" arise was probably the Mediterranean, though the "sea" in prophecy signifies the nations.

What does this "**COMPOSITE BEAST**" signify? This is not the first time we have read in the Scriptures of a "Beast" coming up out of the sea, so we must go back to the Book of Daniel for an explanation. While Daniel was a Statesman and did not hold the "Prophetic Office," he had the "Prophetic Gift," and was not only an interpreter of dreams, but a Prophet, and to him was revealed the whole course of the "Times of the Gentiles," and the character of its last "Great Leader" the "**ANTICHRIST.**" His prophecy is mainly concerned with the things that shall befall his people, **the Jews,** in the "**LATTER DAYS**" (Dan. 10:14), and as we are now dealing with the things that shall come to pass in the "Last" or "Seventieth Week," of Daniel's "Seventy Weeks," we necessarily must turn back to the Book of Daniel for an explanation of this symbol of the "**BEAST.**" But before we take that up it is important **to** note that both the Old and New Testaments speak of a

"**MYSTERIOUS AND TERRIBLE PERSONAGE**"

who shall be revealed in the "Last Times." He is called by various names.

In The Old Testament

"**The Assyrian.**"—Isaiah 10:5-6; 30:27-33.
"**King of Babylon.**"—Isaiah 14:4.
"**Lucifer.**"—Isaiah 14:12.
"**The Little Horn.**"—Daniel 7:8; 8:9-12.
"**A King Of Fierce Countenance.**"—Dan. 8:23.
"**The Prince That Shall Come.**"—Dan. 9:26.
"**The Wilful King.**"—Dan. 11:36.

In The New Testament

"**The Man Of Sin.**"—2. Thess. 2:3-8.
"**Son Of Perdition.**"—2. Thess. 2:3-8.
"**That Wicked.**"—2. Thess. 2:3-8.
"**Antichrist.**"—1. John 2:18.
"**The Beast.**"—Rev. 13:1-2.

Jesus also made **a** prophetic reference to him. "I am come in my Father's Name, and ye receive me not; if another shall come in his own name, him ye will receive." John 5:43.

I. ISAIAH'S FOREVIEW.

The Prophet Isaiah sees the Antichrist as the "**ASSYRIAN.**" Isa. 10:5, 12, 24; 30:27-33. In Isa. 11:4, a chapter which is evidently Messianic, we read that among other things which the Messiah will do—"He shall smite the earth with the 'rod of His mouth,' and with the 'breath of His lips' shall He slay 'THE WICKED'." **The** word translated "THE WICKED," is in the singular number, and cannot refer to wicked persons in general, but to some **one person who is conspicuously wicked.** The expression is strikingly like that of Paul's in 2. Thess. 2: 8. "Then shall that 'WICKED' be revealed, whom the Lord shall consume with the 'Spirit of His Mouth,' and shall destroy with the 'Brightness of His Coming'." It is evident that Isaiah and Paul refer to the same individual, who can be no other than the Antichrist.

In Isa. 14: 4-17 there is a description of a **"King of Babylon"** who shall smite the people in his wrath, and rule the nations in anger. He is called **"LUCIFER, Son of the Morning,"** and his fall is described. He is cast down to Hell (Sheol, the Underworld), where his coming creates a great stir among the kings of the earth that have preceded him, and who exclaim when they see him—"Art thou also become weak as we? Art thou become like unto us? . . . Is this the man that made the earth to tremble, that did shake kingdoms; that made the world as a wilderness and destroyed the cities thereof; that opened not the house of his prisoners?" There has never as yet been such a King of Babylon as is here described. It must therefore refer to some **future** King of Babylon, when Babylon shall be rebuilt, as we shall see it is to be. Verses 12 to 14 evidently refer to Satan, and are descriptive of him before his fall, but as he is to incarnate himself in the Antichrist, who is to be a future King of Babylon, it explains the source of the pride and presumption of Antichrist, which will lead to his downfall, as it did to Satan's.

II. DANIEL'S FOREVIEW.

1. The Colossus.

We now turn to Daniel. The Book of Daniel may be divided into two parts. The first six chapters are Historical, the last six are Prophetical. The Book contains one "Dream" by Nebuchadnezzar, and four "Visions" by Daniel, all relating to the "Times of the Gentiles." Nebuchadnezzar in his "Dream" saw a **"Great Image"** or **"COLOSSUS."** The Head of the "Image" was of fine gold, its Breast and Arms of silver, its Belly (Abdomen) and Thighs (Hips) of brass, its Legs of iron, and its Feet of iron and clay. This Image was destroyed by a "Stone" cut out of a mountain supernaturally. The "Stone" in turn became a great mountain and filled the WHOLE EARTH. Dan. 2: 31-35. The four metals of which the "COLOSSUS" was composed represented **Four Worldwide Empires** which were to arise in succession. Dan. 2: 37-40. Four great Empires, and only four, were to succeed each other in the government of the world, from Nebuchadnezzar (B. C. 606) to the "Second Coming" of Christ—the Babylonian, Medo-Persian, Grecian, and Roman. These Empires are not only made known as to **number**, but their names, in the **order of their succession**, are given. The First— **"BABYLONIAN"** is indicated by Daniel while interpreting the vision to Nebuchadnezzar. **"THOU** art this **Head of Gold."** Dan. 2: 38. The Second—the **"MEDO-PERSIAN,"** Daniel points out in

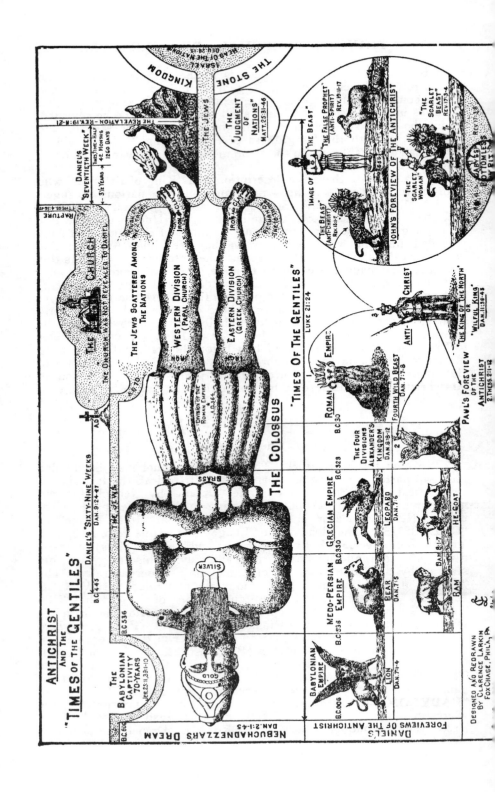

ANTICHRIST
AND THE
"TIMES OF THE GENTILES"

THE
BABYLONIAN
CAPTIVITY
70 YEARS
JER.25:11,39:1-10

DANIEL'S "SIXTY-NINE" WEEKS
DAN.9:24-27

THE JEWS

DANIEL'S "SEVENTIETH WEEK"
3½ YEARS — TIME, TIMES, HALF
42 MONTHS
1260 DAYS
THE REVELATION — REV.19:11-21

RAPTURE
1 THESS.4:16,17

THE CHURCH
THE CHURCH WAS NOT REVEALED TO DANIEL

THE JEWS SCATTERED AMONG
THE NATIONS

WESTERN DIVISION
(PAPAL CHURCH)
NOW

EASTERN DIVISION
(GREEK CHURCH)
NOW

DIVISION OF THE
ROMAN EMPIRE
A.D.364

BRASS

SILVER

GOLD

NEBUCHADNEZZAR'S DREAM
DAN.2:1-45

THE COLOSSUS

B.C.606

B.C.536

B.C.445

A.D.

A.D.70

THE STONE

THE JEWS

KINGDOM

ISRAEL
HEAD OF THE NATIONS
DEU.28:13

THE
"JUDGMENT"
OF
NATIONS"
MATT.25:31-46

JOHN'S FOREVIEW OF THE ANTICHRIST

"The Beast"

"The False Prophet"
(ANTI-SPIRIT)
REV.19:11-17

"THE
SCARLET
BEAST"
REV.17:3-4

"The Beast"
(ANTI-CHRIST)
REV.18:1-7

"THE
SCARLET
WOMAN"

IMAGE OF

APPEARS
BOTTOMLESS PIT
REV.17:3,8

"TIMES OF THE GENTILES"
LUKE 21:24

ANTI-CHRIST

ROMAN
EMPIRE
B.C.30

GRECIAN EMPIRE
B.C.330

MEDO-PERSIAN
EMPIRE
B.C.538

BABYLONIAN
EMPIRE
B.C.606

THE FOUR
DIVISIONS
ALEXANDER'S
KINGDOM
DAN.8:8-12

FOURTH WILD BEAST
DAN.7:7-8

LEOPARD
DAN.7:6

BEAR
DAN.7:5

LION
DAN.7:1-4

HE-GOAT
DAN.8:1-7

RAM

PAUL'S FOREVIEW
OF THE
ANTICHRIST
2.THESS.2:1-12

ANTI-CHRIST
OR
"THE KING OF THE NORTH"
"WILFUL KING"
DAN.11:36-45

DANIEL'S
FOREVIEWS OF THE ANTICHRIST

DESIGNED AND REDRAWN
BY CLARENCE LARKIN
FOX CHASE, PHILA., PA

his account of "Belshazzar's Feast," by the emphatic words—"In that night was Belshazzar the King of the Chaldeans slain, and Darius the **MEDIAN** took the Kingdom." Dan. 5:30-31. The Third —the "GRECIAN," is mentioned in Dan. 8:20-21, "the **Ram** which thou sawest having 'two horns' are the kings of Media and Persia, and the 'Rough Goat' is the **King of Grecia** (Greece)." The Fourth— the "ROMAN," is referred to in Dan. 9:26 as—"the **PEOPLE** of the 'Prince' that should destroy the city (Jerusalem) and the Sanctuary," and we know that it was the **ROMANS** under Titus, that destroyed Jerusalem in A. D. 70. While these Four Great Empires were to follow each other in the order named, they were not to follow without a break. The Babylonian lasted from B. C. 606 to B. C. 538. The Medo-Persian from B. C. 538 to B. C. 330. The Grecian from B. C. 330 to B. C. 323. Then the Grecian was broken up into four parts, Thrace, Macedonia, Syria, and Egypt, and the last of these was conquered by the Romans in B. C. 30, and the Roman Empire lasted from B. C. 30 to A. D. 364, when it was divided into its Eastern and Western Divisions. Since then there has been no leading world Empire, and cannot be according to this prophecy until Christ sets up His "STONE" or "Millennial Kingdom," as represented by the "Stone" that smites the "COLOSSUS" on its **feet**, for this "STONE KINGDOM" is to fill the whole earth, and thus be universal. This "STONE" cannot be Christianity, for it does not fill the earth **by degrees,** and thus **crowd out** the "COLOSSUS," but it at **One Blow DEMOLISHES IT.** The action of the "STONE" is that of **JUDGMENT** not **Grace,** and is **SUDDEN** and **CALAMITOUS.** Again the **TIME** of the destruction is not until **after the formation of the Toes,** and we know that the "TWO LIMBS" did not appear until A. D. 364, and the "TEN TOES" have not yet developed. The **TIME** when the "STONE" falls on the "FEET" we are told is "in the days of THOSE KINGS" (Dan. 2:44), that is the Kings represented by the "Ten Toes," which as we shall see corresponds with the "Ten Horns" of Daniel's "Fourth Wild Beast," Dan. 7:7-8, and with the "Ten Kings" of John's "Beast." Rev. 17:12. The first Four Kingdoms were **literal Kingdoms,** and so must the "Stone Kingdom" be, for it is to take the place of those Kingdoms and **fill the whole** earth. It represents therefore the "Millennial Kingdom" of Christ, for He is the "STONE" of the Scriptures. Matt. 21:44.

From what has been said we see that the "COLOSSUS" of "Nebuchadnezzar's Dream" symbolized the "World Kingdoms" in their **Unity** and **Historical Succession.** Gentile dominion is represented by a huge "METALLIC MAN." The **degeneration** of the "World Kingdoms" is seen in the diminishing **value** of the metals used. Silver is worth less than gold, brass than silver, iron than brass, and clay than iron. The **weight** of the "COLOSSUS" also declines; the specific gravity of gold is 19.5, of silver 10.47, of brass 8, of cast-iron 5, and of clay 1.93. The "Colossus" is **TOP HEAVY.** The character of the governing power also **deteriorates** from an "Absolute Monarchy" under Nebuchadnezzar, to an "Autocratic Democracy" symbolized by the mixture of the **iron** and clay of the

Feet. In other words the governing power passes from the **Head,** the organ that ought to direct the members of the body, to the **Feet,** which are only made to carry the body whither the Head directs. We have dwelt thus at length on the "Colossus," for it is only as we understand it, that we can understand the meaning of the "Wild Beasts" that Daniel saw come up out of the sea.

2. The Vision of the "FOUR BEASTS."

Forty-eight years after Nebuchadnezzar had his "Dream," B. C. 555, Daniel in vision stood upon the shore of the "Great Sea" (the Mediterranean), and saw four **"Great Beasts"** come up out of the sea in succession.

FIRST BEAST. The "First Beast" was like a **LION** and had Eagle's Wings, and as the Prophet watched it, he saw it lifted up from the earth, and made to stand upon its feet as a **Man,** and a **Man's Heart** was given to it. Dan. 7:4. We have only to visit the British Museum, London, and examine the Colossal Stone Lions with the **"wings of an eagle"** and the **"head of a man,"** disinterred from the ruins of Babylon and Assyria by Sir Henry Layard between the years 1840 and 1850 A. D., to see that this "FIRST BEAST" stands for Babylon and its King—Nebuchadnezzar. The peculiarity of this "FIRST BEAST" was that it had "Eagle's Wings." This combination of the **LION,** the "King of Beasts," and the EAGLE, the "King of Birds," corresponded to the Royalty of the "Head of Gold" of the "COLOSSUS," and typified the "Eagle-like" swiftness of the armies of Nebuchadnezzar. The **"Plucking of the Wings"** doubtless referred to the **"Beastly Insanity"** of Nebuchadnezzar (Dan. 4:20-27), and the **"lifting up,"** and causing to stand upon its feet **"as a MAN,"** to his restoration to sanity.

SECOND BEAST. The "Second Beast" was "like to a **BEAR**, and it raised up itself on one side, and it had "**Three Ribs**" in the mouth of it, between the teeth of it: and they said thus unto it **Arise, devour much flesh.**" Dan. 7:5. The bear is the strongest beast after the lion and is distinguished for its voracity, but it has none of the agility and majesty of the lion, is awkward in its movements, and effects its purpose with comparative slowness, and by brute force and sheer strength. These were the characteristics of the Medo-Persian Empire. It was ponderous in its movements. It did not gain its victories by bravery or skill, but overwhelmed its enemies by hurling vast masses of troops upon them. Xerxes' expedition against Greece was undertaken with 2,500,000 fighting men, who with the camp followers made up an army of 5,000,000. Other Persian generals had armies running up into the 100,000's of men. It is easy to be seen that the movements of such enormous bodies of men would "devour much flesh," not only in the destruction of their enemies, but thousands would die of disease and exposure and the countries through which they passed would become famine-stricken by the loss of food seized to feed such armies. The side of the "BEAR" which raised up to attack signifies Persia, in which lay the greatest military strength, and corresponded to the "right shoulder and arm" of the "Colossus." The "Three Ribs" stood for the three Kingdoms of **Lydia, Babylon** and **Egypt**, which formed a "**Triple Alliance**" to check the Medo-Persian power, but were all destroyed by it.

THIRD BEAST. The "Third Beast" was "like a **LEOPARD,** which had upon the back of it **four wings of a fowl;** the 'BEAST' had also **four heads;** and dominion was given to it." Dan. 7:6. The Leopard is the most agile and graceful of creatures; but its speed is here still further assisted by "wings." Slight in its frame, but strong, swift and fierce, its characteristics render it a fitting symbol of the rapid conquests of the Greeks under Alexander the Great, who, followed by small but well-equipped and splendidly brave armies, moved with great celerity and in about 10 years overthrew the unwieldy forces of Persia, and subdued the whole civilized world. The "four wings of a Fowl" indicate, that, as a "fowl" does not fly high, the armies of Alexander were fitted mainly for lowland fighting. There is an incongruity between the number of "wings" and the number of "heads" of the Leopard. "Four heads" call for "four pair of wings." Why only "four" wings we do not know, unless they denote the four quarters of the earth into which Alexander sought to extend his Kingdom.

The **"Four Heads"** of the **LEOPARD** represent the **"Four Kingdoms"** into which the Empire of Alexander was divided by his generals, namely **Thrace, Macedonia, Syria** and **Egypt.** The "Third Beast" corresponds to the "Abdomen" and "Hips" of the "COLOSSUS."

FOURTH BEAST. The "Fourth Beast" was unlike any Beast that Daniel had ever seen or heard about. It was "dreadful and terrible, and strong exceedingly, and it had great IRON TEETH. It devoured and brake in pieces, and stamped the residue (the other Beasts) with the feet of it; and it was diverse from all the 'BEASTS' that were before it, and it had 'TEN HORNS'." Dan. 7:7. The fact that the "Fourth Beast" had "Iron Teeth," and that there were "Ten Horns" on its Head, the "iron" corresponding to the "Iron Limbs," and the "Ten Horns" to the "Ten Toes" of the "CO-LOSSUS," would cause Daniel to see that the "Fourth Beast" stood for the Fourth World Empire, the ROMAN.

But as Daniel "considered" the "Ten Horns," he was amazed to see another "Horn," a LITTLE one, come up among them, and before whom there were "three" of the "First Horns" plucked up by the roots, that is destroyed. And as he examined the "LITTLE HORN" more closely he noticed that it had Eyes like the eyes of a Man, and the Mouth of a Man speaking great things. Dan. 7:8. This mystified and troubled Daniel. He had seen nothing corresponding to it on the "Ten Toes" of the "COLOSSUS." It must mean some new and additional revelation that God had not seen fit to impart to the Gentile King Nebuchadnezzar, and that was reserved for Daniel and his people (the Jews), for we must not forget that Daniel's own visions, in the last six chapters of the Book, have to do with God's dealings with the Jewish People in the "LATTER DAYS." Dan. 10:14. So Daniel approached one of the "Heavenly Messengers" that stood by and asked him the meaning of what he had seen. He was told that the "Four Beasts" stood for "FOUR KINGS" or "KINGDOMS" (vs. 23), that should arise out of the earth. Then Daniel wanted to know the "truth" about the "FOURTH Beast," which was so diverse from the other three, and particularly about the "LITTLE HORN" that came up among the "Ten Horns" on its head. In explanation Daniel was told that the "Ten Horns" on the "Fourth Beast" represented "TEN KINGS" that shall arise, and that the "Little Horn" was a "King" that should rise among them and sub-due three of them, and that he would be a "PERSON" of remark-able intelligence and great oratorical powers, having a mouth speak-ing great things. That he would be audacious, arrogant, imperious, and persecuting, and change "times and laws," and that the "Saints of the Most High" (Daniel's People) would be given into his hands for a "Time, and Times, and the Dividing of Time," or 3½ years.

In this Vision of the "Four Beasts" we see "Degeneration" just as we saw it in the metals of the "COLOSSUS." The descent is from the LION, the "King of Beasts," to a nondescript "MONSTER" that defies description. The reason why these "Four Kingdoms" are rep-resented first as a "Golden Headed Metallic Image," and then as a succession of "Wild Beasts," is to show the difference between Man's view and GOD'S view of the World Kingdoms. Man sees in them the concentration of wealth, majesty and power; GOD sees them as a succession of rapacious Wild Beasts devouring one another.

3. The Vision Of The "RAM" And The "HE-GOAT."

The explanation as to the meaning of the **"LITTLE HORN"** perplexed Daniel, and he voiced it by saying "My **'cogitations'** much troubled me, and my **countenance changed in me** (he had a sad look) ; but I kept the matter in **my heart."** Dan. 7:28. To comfort His Servant, God, two years later, transported Daniel in vision to Shushan, the Capital of Persia, and as he stood on the bank of the river Ulai, he saw a **RAM** which had **"Two Horns,"** one higher than the other, and the higher came up last. He saw the **RAM** push **"Westward,"** and **"Northward,"** and **"Southward,"** and nothing could stand before it, and it did according to its will. Dan. 8:4. While Daniel was "considering" what the Vision of the **RAM** meant, he saw a **HE-GOAT** come from the West unmolested, and he noticed it had a **"NOTABLE HORN"** between its eyes, and when it reached the **RAM** it was moved with "choler" or anger against it, and smote it with "fury," and broke its **"Two Horns,"** and **knocked it down** and **stamped upon it.** Then the **HE-GOAT** waxed great, but when it became strong its **"GREAT HORN"** was broken off, and "Four Notable Horns" came up in its place, and out of one of them sprang a **"LITTLE HORN"** which waxed exceedingly great toward the "South," and toward the "East," and toward the **"Pleasant Land"** (Palestine). Dan. 8:5-9.

When Daniel sought for the meaning of this Vision he heard a voice say—"Gabriel, make this man to understand the Vision." Then Gabriel said to Daniel the Vision belongs to the **"Time of the End"** (the End of the Times of the Gentiles), and is to make thee know what shall come to pass in the **"Last End of the Indignation"** (the Great Tribulation). Dan. 8:15-19. Gabriel then informed Daniel that the **"RAM"** stood for the "Medo-Persian Empire," with its two Kings, Darius and his nephew Cyrus, that the **"HE-GOAT"** stood for the "Grecian Empire," the **"GREAT HORN"** between its eyes for its first King (Alexander the Great), and that the **"FOUR HORNS"** that took the place of the **"GREAT HORN,"** stood for **"Four Kingdoms"** into which the "Grecian Empire" should be divided.

This explanation cleared up things considerably for Daniel. It revealed to him that the **"TWO HORNS"** of the RAM, one higher than the other, and the **"TWO SHOULDERS"** of the BEAR, one higher than the other, and the **"TWO ARMS"** of the COLOSSUS, stood for the same thing, the double Empire of Medo-Persia. He also saw that the **"FOUR HORNS"** that came up in the place of the **"GREAT HORN"** corresponded to the **"FOUR HEADS"** of the LEOPARD, and therefore must correspond with the **"ABDOMEN"** and **"HIPS"** of the COLOSSUS, and stand for the Grecian Empire, and its **"Fourfold Division"** among the Generals of Alexander the Great.

But Daniel was still troubled as to the meaning of the **"LITTLE HORN"** that he saw come out of one of the **"Four Horns"** of the HE-GOAT, and Gabriel told him that it stood for a King of **"Fierce Countenance"** who should stand up in the **"LATTER TIME"** of the Kingdom, and who should stand up against the **"PRINCE OF PRINCES"** (Christ). Dan. 8:23-25. The description of this **"LITTLE HORN"** so clearly corresponded to the description of the **"LITTLE HORN"** that Daniel saw arise amid the **"Ten Horns"** of the "Fourth Wild Beast," that he saw they described and stood for the **same Person.** The revelation so overcame Daniel that he "fainted," and was sick certain days. Dan. 8:27

4. The Vision Of The **"KINGS OF THE NORTH AND SOUTH."**

While Daniel had revealed to him that the **"LITTLE HORN"** should come out of one of the **"Four Kingdoms"** into which the Empire of Alexander the Great was divided, he was not at that time told which one, but 20 years later, in B. C. 533, the information was imparted to him in a Fourth Vision. He saw in vision two Kings warring against each other. One was called the **"King of the North,"** the other the **"King of the South."** This chapter (Dan. 11:1-45) is one of the most wonderfully minute as to prophetic details of any chapter in the Bible. It corresponds exactly with the profane history of the kings of Egypt and Syria for over 350 years. From verse 5 to verse 31 we have an account of what is called the "wars" of the "Kings of the North" (Syria) and of the "Kings of the South" **(Egypt).** These end with the close of the reign of Antiochus Epiphanes, B. C. 164. Verses 32-35 cover the whole period from B. C. 164 down to the **"Time of the End,"** that is, until the "Seventieth Week" of Daniel's "Seventy Weeks." At verse 36 the **"WILFUL KING"** appears, and from that verse down until the end of the Book of Daniel we have an account of what is to befall Daniel's People in the "Latter Days." As the description of the **"WILFUL KING"** corresponded with the description of the **"LITTLE HORN"** of the **"Fourth Wild Beast"** and the **"LITTLE HORN"** of the **"He-Goat,"** and they were all to appear at the **same time**—the "Time of the End." Daniel understood that they referred to one and the **same Person,** and as the **"WILFUL KING"** would be the **"King of the NORTH,"** that is, of **Syria,** Daniel saw that the **"LITTLE HORN"** was to rise on the **"SYRIAN HORN"** of the **"He-Goat,"** in other words that the **"LITTLE HORN,"** or **"Antichrist,"** shall come out of **SYRIA,** and as **Syria** included **Assyria** that the **"LITTLE HORN"** of Daniel is the same as the **"Assyrian"** of Isaiah. "When the Lord hath performed His **whole work** upon Mount Zion and on Jerusalem (which will not be until Christ comes back), I will punish the fruit of the stout heart of the **KING OF ASSYRIA** (Antichrist) and the glory of his **high looks.**" Isa. 10:12. I will break the **ASSYRIAN** (Antichrist) in **My Land** (Palestine), and upon My mountains **tread him under foot;** then shall his yoke depart from off them (Israel), and his burden from off their shoulders." Isa. 14:25. The context shows that this prophecy is connected with the restoration of Israel to their own land, not after the Babylonian Captivity, but a restoration that is still future, for the Assyrian Empire had been swallowed up by the Babylonian when the Prophet wrote and the **ASSYRIAN** King here mentioned must be some **future** Assyrian King, for he is to be brought to **Palestine** and **destroyed there.**

We must not allow ourselves to be confused by the different names given the Antichrist, as the "King of Tyrus," the "King of Babylon," and the "King of Assyria," for that section of the world will comprise one territory in the days of the Antichrist and he will be known by all of these titles.

From what we have thus far learned of the Antichrist, the probability is that he will be a **SYRIAN JEW,** for it is not likely that the Jews will accept as their Messiah one who is not a Jew, unless the claimant by false pretense makes them believe he is one. This, however, does not prevent the Antichrist being a **Roman citizen,** and the political head of the revived Roman Empire, for Saul of Tarsus was both a Jew and a Roman citizen.

Those who claim that the **"LITTLE HORN"** of Dan. 7, and the **"LITTLE HORN"** of Dan. 8, are not the same, because the **"LITTLE HORN"** of Dan. 7 arises amid the "Ten Horns" of the "Fourth Wild Beast," which represents the Roman Empire, and the **"LITTLE HORN"** of Dan. 8, arises on one of the Horns of the "He-Goat" which represents the Grecian Empire, and corresponds to the "Third Wild Beast," forget that the Vision that the Apostle John had of the revived Roman Empire (Rev. 13:1-2), the Roman Empire in its last stage, reveals the fact that the "last stage" of the Roman Empire will include **all the characteristics** of the whole Four Empires, Baby-

Ionian, Medo-Persian, Grecian and old Roman. This is seen in the character of the "**BEAST**" John saw come up out of the sea. It was like unto a **LEOPARD** (Greece), with the feet of a **BEAR** (Medo-Persia), and the mouth of a **LION** (Babylon). The fact that the **BODY** of the "**BEAST**" was like a **LEOPARD** (Greece), reveals the fact that the preponderating feature of the revived Roman Empire will be **GRECIAN**, and that therefore the "Ten Federated Kingdoms," represented by the "**Ten Horns**" of the "**Beast**," will include the **FOUR KINGDOMS** into which the **GRECIAN** Empire was divided, viz., Egypt, Macedon, Thrace and **SYRIA**. It follows therefore that the "**LITTLE HORN**" of the "**He-Goat**" (Greece), will be the **LITTLE HORN** that rises among the "**Ten Horns**" of the "**Fourth Wild Beast**" (Rome), for **Syria**, one of the four divisions of the Grecian Empire, will be one of the component parts of the Revived Roman Empire.

Again those who claim that Antiochus Epiphanes (B. C. 175-165), a king of Syria, was the "**LITTLE HORN**" of the "**He-Goat**," overlook the fact, that, while Antiochus Epiphanes devastated Palestine and caused an "**idol altar**" to be erected on the Brazen Altar of the Temple, on which he offered swine-flesh, which was an abomination to the Jews, he does not fulfil the description of the "**LITTLE HORN**" of the "**He-Goat**" (Dan. 8:9-12, 23-25), for Antiochus Epiphanes, nor any other ruler of the past, ever stood up against **JESUS**, the "**Prince of Princes**." Neither was Antiochus Epiphanes "**broken without hand**." He died a natural death at Tabae in B. C. 165. But the "**LITTLE HORN**" of the "**He-Goat**" is to be "**broken without hand**." His Kingdom is to be destroyed by a "**stone cut out of the mountain WITHOUT HANDS**," and he himself shall be "**paralyzed**" by the "**brightness of the Lord's Coming**" (1. Thess. 2:8), and he shall be cast **ALIVE** into the "Lake of Fire." Rev. 19:20. There is no intimation in Scripture that Antiochus Epiphanes is even to be regarded as a "type" of Antichrist. They are distinct historical personages, and though they resemble each other in some respects, yet they must not be confounded with each other. After this prolonged exposition of Daniel's "Foreview" of the Antichrist, which has seemed necessary to a proper understanding of the meaning of the "Beast" which John saw come up out of the sea, we now turn to—

III. PAUL'S FOREVIEW.

"Let no man deceive you by any means: for 'that Day' (the Day of the Lord) shall not come except there come a 'falling away first,' and that 'MAN OF SIN' be revealed. The
'SON OF PERDITION,'
who opposeth and exalteth himself above all that is called God, or that is worshipped; so that he As God sitteth in the Temple of God (the rebuilt Temple at Jerusalem), showing himself that he is God . . . For the
'MYSTERY OF INIQUITY'
doth already work (in Paul's day); only He (the Holy Spirit) who now letteth (restraineth R. V.) will let (restrain), until He be taken out of the way. And then shall
'THAT WICKED'
be revealed, whom the Lord shall consume with the spirit (breath) of His mouth, and shall destroy with the brightness (manifestation R. V.) of His Coming. Even him, whose coming is after the working of Satan with all power and signs and lying wonders, and with all deceivableness of unrighteousness in them that perish; because they received not the love of the truth (Christ) that they might be saved." 2. Thess. 2: 3-10.

In the American Standard Edition of the Bible the Antichrist is called the "MYSTERY OF LAWLESSNESS" or the "LAWLESS ONE." As such he is not the cause of Lawlessness, he is the result or fruit of it, for he will arise out of the seething cauldron of Lawlessness that is now becoming more pronounced and manifest in the world.

The name that the Apostle Paul gives the Antichrist—the "SON OF PERDITION," is not without significance. The name is used but twice in the Scriptures. It is first used by Christ of Judas (John 17: 12), and then here of Antichrist. The Apostle also calls the Antichrist in this passage the "MYSTERY OF INIQUITY." What does that mean? In 1. Tim. 3: 16 Christ is spoken of as the "MYSTERY OF GODLINESS," that is, that He was God MANIFEST IN THE FLESH. How did He become "manifest in the flesh"? By being born of the Virgin Mary by the Holy Spirit. Thus it was that Jesus became the SON OF GOD. Luke 1: 35. Now as iniquity is the opposite of godliness, then the "MYSTERY OF INIQUITY" must be the opposite of the "MYSTERY OF GODLINESS." That is, if Christ is the "MYSTERY OF GODLINESS," Antichrist must be the "MYSTERY OF INIQUITY," and as Christ was the "Son of God," then Antichrist must be the "SON OF PERDITION," that is, of SATAN. And as Christ was born of a virgin by the Holy Spirit, so Antichrist will be born of a woman (not necessarily a virgin) by Satan. This is no new view for it has been held by many of God's spiritually minded children since the days of the Apostle John, and there is some warrant for it in the Scriptures. In Gen. 3:15, God said to the Serpent (Satan), "I will put enmity between thee and the woman, and between 'THY SEED' and 'HER SEED'." Now the Woman's **SEED** was **CHRIST**, then the Serpent's **SEED** must be **ANTICHRIST**. In John 8:44 Jesus said to the Jews—"Ye are of your father **THE DEVIL** . . . When he speaketh a **lie**, he speaketh of his own; for he is a liar, and the father of **IT**." In the Greek there is the definite article before "lie," and it should read "THE LIE," so when the Devil speaks of "THE LIE," he is speaking of **his own** (child), for he is a liar, and the **FATHER OF "IT"**— "THE LIE." And it is worthy of note that in the verse (vs. 11) that follows the passage we are considering that the Apostle says— "And for this cause God shall send them strong delusion that they should believe **a lie**." Here again the definite article is found in the Greek, and it should read "The LIE," the "SON OF PERDITION," the **ANTICHRIST**.

But why was Judas called the "SON OF PERDITION"? Was he a child of Satan by some woman, or was he simply indwelt by Satan? Here we must let the Scriptures speak for themselves. In John 6:70-71 we read that Jesus said "Have not I chosen you Twelve, and one of you is a **DEVIL**? He spake of **Judas Iscariot** the son of Simon; for he it was that should betray Him, being one of the Twelve." In no other passage than this is the word "Devil" applied to anyone but to Satan himself. Here the word is "diabolus," the definite article is employed, and it should read—"and one of you is **THE DEVIL**." This would make Judas the Devil **incarnate**, or the "MYSTERY OF INIQUITY," and explains why Jesus in John 17:12, calls him the "SON OF PERDITION."

This is the only place in the Scriptures where the word "diabolus" is applied to a human being, and it implies an incarnation.

While "Perdition" is a **PLACE** (Rev. 17:8, 11), it is also a "condition" into which men may fall (1. Tim. 6:9; Heb. 10:39), and while men who have committed the "Unpardonable Sin" are "sons of perdition," because they are destined to the place of the irrevocably lost, yet Judas and Antichrist are the "SONS OF PERDITION" in a special sense, for they are the **SONS** or the author of "Perdition"— **THE DEVIL**. That is they are not merely "obsessed" or controlled by the Devil, the Devil has **incarnated** himself in them, and for the time being, to all practical purposes, they are the very Devil himself.

The next question that arises is, "If Judas and the Antichrist are both called the 'SON OF PERDITION,' are they one and the same, or are there **two** 'Sons of Perdition'?" Here we must anticipate. Turning to Rev. 11:7, we read that the "Beast" that slays the "Two Witnesses" ascends out of the "Bottomless Pit" (ABYSS), and that "Beast" is the **ANTICHRIST**. Now how did he get into the "ABYSS"? Well, if there is only **one** "SON OF PERDITION," and Judas and Antichrist are one and the same, then he got in the ABYSS when Judas went to his "Own Place" (the ABYSS). Acts 1:25. Of no other person is it said anywhere in the Scriptures that he went "to his own place." Again in Rev. 17:8 it is said—"The 'Beast' that thou sawest was, and is not: and shall ascend out of the

'Bottomless Pit' (Abyss), and go into PERDITION." As this "Beast" is the same that slays the "Two Witnesses" he is the ANTI-CHRIST. Now there are four things said of him. First, he "WAS." Second, he "IS NOT." Third, he shall "ASCEND OUT OF THE BOTTOMLESS PIT." Fourth, he shall "GO INTO PERDITION." From this we learn that in John's day the "Beast" "Was Not," but that he had been before on the earth, and was to come again, that he was to ASCEND FROM THE BOTTOMLESS PIT. This is positive proof that the ANTICHRIST has been on the earth before, and that when he comes in the future he will come from the "ABYSS."

The question then arises, when was "Antichrist" on the earth before? If Judas and Antichrist are one and the same the enigma is solved. When Judas was on the earth, he WAS; when Judas went to his "Own Place" he "WAS NOT"; when Judas comes back from the "Abyss" he will be—THE ANTICHRIST. The Author does not insist on this view of Judas and Antichrist being correct, but with open mind he accepts it, because it seems to be the only logical solution of both Judas and Antichrist being called the "SON OF PERDITION."

IV.   JOHN'S FOREVIEW.

John saw "A 'BEAST' rise up out of the sea, having 'SEVEN HEADS' and 'TEN HORNS,' and upon his horns 'TEN CROWNS,' and upon his heads the name of BLASPHEMY. And the 'BEAST' which I saw was like a LEOPARD, and his feet were as the feet of a BEAR, and his mouth as the mouth of a LION: and the 'DRAGON' gave him his POWER, and his SEAT (Throne), and GREAT AUTHORITY. And I saw one of his HEADS as it were wounded to death: and his deadly wound was healed: and all the world wondered after the 'BEAST.' And they worshipped the 'DRAGON' which gave power unto the 'BEAST,' and they worshipped the 'BEAST,' saying, who is like unto the 'BEAST'? Who is able to make war with him? And there was given unto him a mouth speaking great things and blasphemies; and power was given unto him to continue forty and two months."

When we compare these "Foreviews," and note the similarity of conduct of Daniel's "LITTLE HORN," Paul's "MAN OF SIN," and John's "BEAST," and that Daniel's "LITTLE HORN" and John's "BEAST" are to continue for the same length of time—"Forty and Two Months," or 3½ years, and that Daniel's "LITTLE HORN," Paul's "MAN OF SIN," and John's "BEAST," are all to be destroyed in the same manner at Christ's "Second Coming," we see that they all prefigure the same "Evil Power," which is after the "Working of Satan," and which John in 1. John 2:18, calls THE ANTICHRIST. In other words when we find in prophecy "Three Symbolic Personages" that come upon the stage of action at the same time, occupy the same territory, exhibit the same character, do the same work, exist the same length of time, and meet the same fate, they must symbolize the SAME THING.

Before we examine in detail John's "BEAST," it would be well for us to compare it with Daniel's "FOURTH WILD BEAST."

In comparing these two "BEASTS" we find that they both come up out of the sea (the nations), and that they are utterly unlike

Daniel's Fourth Wild Beast Dan. 7:7, 8, 19, 20, 23-25.	John's Beast Out Of The Sea Rev. 13:1-7

"After this I saw in the night visions, and behold a FOURTH BEAST, dreadful and terrible, and strong exceedingly; and it had great iron teeth; it devoured and brake in pieces, and stamped the residue (the 3 preceding Beasts) with the feet of it; and it was diverse from all the Beasts that were before it; and it had TEN HORNS. I considered the HORNS, and, behold, there came up among them another LITTLE HORN, before whom there were THREE of the FIRST HORNS plucked up by the roots; and, behold, in THIS HORN were eyes like the eyes of a MAN, and a mouth speaking great things."

"Then I would know the truth of the FOURTH BEAST, which was diverse from all the others, exceeding dreadful, whose teeth were of iron, and his nails of brass; which devoured, brake in pieces, and stamped the residue with his feet; and of the TEN HORNS that were in his head, and of the OTHER which came up, and before whom three fell; even of THAT HORN that had eyes, and a mouth that spake very great things, whose look was more stout than his fellows."

"Thus he said, the FOURTH BEAST shall be the FOURTH KINGDOM upon earth, which shall be diverse from all kingdoms, and shall devour the whole earth, and shall tread it down and break it in pieces. And the TEN HORNS out of this Kingdom are TEN KINGS that shall arise; and another (King) shall rise after them; and he shall be diverse from the first, and he shall subdue THREE KINGS. And he shall speak great words against the Most High, and shall wear out the saints of the Most High, and think to change times and laws; and they shall be given into his hand until a TIME and TIMES and the DIVIDING OF TIME."

"I saw a BEAST rise up out of the SEA, having SEVEN HEADS and TEN HORNS, and upon his horns TEN CROWNS, and upon his heads the NAMES OF BLASPHEMY. And the BEAST which I saw was like unto a LEOPARD, and his feet were as the feet of a BEAR, and his mouth as the mouth of a LION; and the Dragon gave him his power, and his seat, and great authority. And I saw one of his HEADS as it were wounded to death; and his deadly wound was healed; and all the world wondered after the BEAST. . . . And there was given unto him a mouth speaking great things and blasphemies; and power was given unto him to continue FORTY AND TWO MONTHS. And he opened his mouth in blasphemy against God, to blaspheme His Name, and His Tabernacle, and them that dwell in Heaven. And it was given unto him to make war with the saints, and to overcome them; and power was given him over all kindreds, and tongues, and nations."

any beast we have ever heard of. Daniel's "Beast" was dreadful and terrible, and strong exceedingly; and it had great iron teeth, and nails of brass; while John's "Beast" was like a LEOPARD, with the

feet of a **BEAR**, and the mouth of a **LION**. As Daniel's "Beast"
represented the "**FOURTH KINGDOM**" upon the earth, the Roman
Empire, it is evident that its characteristics describe the old Roman
Empire, while the characteristics of John's Beast represent the **revived**
Roman Empire. We know that the Old Roman Empire was "**strong
exceedingly**" and its grip and power were like a beast with "**great
iron teeth**" and "**nails of brass,**" and from the description of John's
"Beast" we learn that the revived Roman Empire shall embody all
the characteristics of the Four World Empires, as seen in its
LEOPARD like body, its feet of a **BEAR**, and its mouth of a **LION**.
That both "Beasts" have **TEN HORNS** reveals the fact that they will
be in existence at the time indicated by the **TEN TOES** of the Colossus, with which they correspond, which will be just before the
setting up of the "Stone" or Millennial Kingdom of Christ. We are
told that the "**TEN HORNS**" of Daniel's "Beast" stand for "**TEN
KINGS,**" and the "**TEN HORNS**" of John's "Beast" stand for the
same. Rev. 17:12. From this we see that both Daniel and John
foresaw that the Roman Empire was to be eventually divided into
"Ten Separate but Federated Kingdoms."

While both "Beasts" have **TEN HORNS,** they differ in that
John's had "**SEVEN HEADS**" while Daniel's had but **ONE**, and
among the "**TEN HORNS**" on Daniel's "Beast" there came up a
"**LITTLE HORN,**" which is not seen amid the "**TEN HORNS**" of
John's Beast. These, as we shall see, are features that refer to the
last stage of the "Beast" and show that we cannot understand the
last stage of the "Beast" without carefully comparing Daniel's and
John's "Beasts," for the "**LITTLE HORN**" of Daniel's "Beast"
plucks up **THREE** of the "**TEN HORNS**" and destroys them, or
takes their kingdom away, a thing that John omits to tell us. Again
the Antichristian character of Daniel's "Beast" is seen in its "**LIT-
TLE HORN**" whose conduct corresponds with not a part, but the
whole of John's "Beast," and that for the same length of time, "**TIME**"
and "**TIMES**" and the "**DIVIDING OF TIME**" which equals
"**FORTY AND TWO MONTHS.**"

It now remains to analyze the "**Beast**" that John saw come up
out of the sea, and try to discover the meaning of its various members.

We have two descriptions of this "**Beast.**"

Daniel's "Fourth Wild Beast" as we have seen, represents the
Roman Empire as it existed from B. C. 30, until as a nation it shall
cease to exist. While it was divided in A. D. 364, as the result of an
ecclesiastical schism, into its Eastern and Western Divisions, and lost
its national life as a world power, yet it has never lost its religious
existence or influence as seen in the continuance of the Greek and
Roman Churches, and Roman Law is still a controlling power in our
laws. In this sense the Roman Empire in its influence has never
ceased to exist. We are now to consider it in its last stage as out-
lined in John's "Beast."

In the two descriptions of John's Beast as given above it is very
important to see that the "Beast" has a "Dual" meaning. It represents both the revived Roman Empire, and its Imperial Head the

JOHN'S TWO VISIONS OF THE BEAST

BEAST OUT OF THE SEA

Rev. 13:1-7

"I saw a BEAST rise up out of the SEA, having SEVEN HEADS and TEN HORNS, and upon his horns TEN CROWNS, and upon his heads the NAMES OF BLASPHEMY. And the BEAST which I saw was like unto a LEOPARD, and his feet were as the feet of a BEAR, and his mouth as the mouth of a LION; and the Dragon gave him his power, and his seat, and great authority. And I saw one of his HEADS as it were wounded to death; and his deadly wound was healed; and all the world wondered after the BEAST. . . . And there was given unto him a mouth speaking great things and blasphemies; and power was given unto him to continue FORTY AND TWO MONTHS. And he opened his mouth in blasphemy against God, to blaspheme His Name, and His Tabernacle, and them that dwell in Heaven. And it was given unto him to make war with the saints, and to overcome them; and power was given him over all kindreds, and tongues, and nations."

SCARLET COLORED BEAST

Rev. 17:3, 7-17

"I saw a Woman sit upon a scarlet colored BEAST, full of names of blasphemy, having SEVEN HEADS and TEN HORNS. . . . I will tell thee the mystery of the Woman, and of the BEAST that carried her, which hath the SEVEN HEADS and TEN HORNS. The BEAST that thou sawest WAS, and IS NOT; and shall ascend out of the BOTTOMLESS PIT, and go into perdition. . . The SEVEN HEADS are SEVEN MOUNTAINS, on which the Woman sitteth. And they (the Seven Heads, R. V.) are SEVEN KINGS; FIVE are fallen, and ONE is, and the OTHER is not yet come; and when he cometh, he must continue a short space. And the BEAST that WAS, and IS NOT, even he is the EIGHTH, and is of the SEVEN, and goeth into perdition. And the TEN HORNS which thou sawest are TEN KINGS, which have received no kingdom as yet; but receive power as kings one hour with the BEAST. These have one mind, and shall give their power and strength unto the BEAST. . . . And the TEN HORNS which thou sawest upon the BEAST, these shall hate the WHORE, and shall make her desolate and naked, and shall eat her flesh, and burn her with fire. For God hath put in their hearts to fulfil His will, and to agree, and give their kingdom unto the BEAST, until the words of God shall be fulfilled."

Antichrist. As the revived Roman Empire it is seen coming up out of the sea of the nations, as the Antichrist it comes up out of the ABYSS. For instance it cannot be said of the Roman Empire of John's day, that it WAS, and IS NOT, for it was at the height of its power in John's day. Neither can it be said of it that it shall ascend out of the pit and go into PERDITION, that could only be said of a person. Again we must distinguish between the body of the "Beast" and its heads and horns. The body being that of a LEOPARD, with the feet of a BEAR, and the mouth of a LION is to show that the revived Roman Empire in its last stage will include the characteristics of the first "Three Wild Beasts" of Daniel, that is, of the **LION** (Babylon), the **BEAR** (Medo-Persia), and the **LEOP-ARD** (Greece), and as the largest part of the "Beast," the body, is represented by the **LEOPARD,** the prevailing characteristic of the revived Roman Empire will be **GRECIAN.**

The "Beast" that comes up out of the sea (Chap. 13), has **SEVEN HEADS** and **TEN HORNS,** and the "Horns" are **CROWNED.** This represents the "Beast," or Empire, at the height of its power, when it will have all its "Heads," and when the **TEN KINGS,** the heads of the **TEN KINGDOMS** into which the Empire shall be divided, will have been crowned. The "Beast" that comes up out of the **ABYSS** also has **SEVEN HEADS** and **TEN HORNS,** but they are not crowned, for the **TEN KINGS** represented by the **TEN HORNS,** have not as yet received their kingdom. (Rev. 17: 12.) This implies that the "Beast" of Rev. 17, represents the Antichrist at the beginning of the "Week." As confirmation of this view the "WOMAN" is seen at this stage riding the "Beast." For while the "Scarlet Clothed Woman" is not seen until chapter 17, it is clear that she rides the "Beast" from the beginning of the "Week," for she represents the "PAPAL CHURCH" that comes into power after the true Church has been caught out. During the wars preceding the rise of Antichrist the nations that will then be found in the geographical limits of the Old Roman Empire will form an "Alliance" for mutual protection. Those nations will be ten in number, represented by the "TEN HORNS" of the Beast. No doubt the "Papal Church" will play a prominent part in those proceedings. She will be rewarded by restoration to political power, and this union of Church and State, in which the Church will have control, is shown by the **WOMAN** riding the Beast, thus dominating it. But when the "Ten Kings" shall receive their Kingdoms and be **CROWNED,** they "shall hate the **WHORE,** and shall make her desolate and naked, and shall eat her flesh, and burn her with fire." (Vs. 16.)

While we are told in Rev. 17 : 9 that the "SEVEN HEADS" of the "Beast" represent "SEVEN MOUNTAINS" (this is to identify it with the Roman Empire), we are told in the next verse (R. V.) that they (the "Seven Heads") also represent "SEVEN KINGS" of whom "Five are fallen, and one is, and the other is not yet come; and when he cometh he must continue a short space." That is, in John's day "Five" of these Kings had fallen, one was the then ruling Emperor, and the "Seventh" was yet to come. Who are meant by the first "Five Kings" that had fallen we do not know. The King that was on the throne in John's day was Domitian, who had banished John to the Isle of Patmos. The last or "SEVENTH KING" who is yet to come is undoubtedly the **ANTICHRIST.** We are told in Rev. 13: 3, that one of the "SEVEN HEADS," or "KINGS," received a deadly wound. Which one is not stated. The inference is that it is the last, for the Beast has all of his "HEADS" before one of them is wounded. In Rev. 17: 11 he is called the Beast that **WAS,** and **IS NOT,** even he is the "EIGHTH," and is of the "SEVENTH," and goeth into PERDITION. The only clear explanation of this passage is that the "SEVENTH HEAD"—THE ANTICHRIST, is the one who receives the "deadly wound," probably at the hand of an

THE ANTICHRIST

Daniel's Foreview

Fourth Wild Beast
Dan. 7: 7, 8, 19, 20, 23-25.

"After this I saw in the night visions, and behold a FOURTH BEAST, dreadful and terrible, and strong exceedingly; and it had great iron teeth; it devoured and brake in pieces, and stamped the residue (the 3 preceding Beasts) with the feet of it; and it was diverse from all the Beasts that were before it; and it had TEN HORNS. I considered the HORNS, and, behold, there came up among them another LITTLE HORN, before whom there were THREE of the FIRST HORNS plucked up by the roots; and, behold, in THIS HORN were eyes like the eyes of a MAN, and a mouth speaking great things."

"Then I would know the truth of the FOURTH BEAST, which was diverse from all the others, exceeding dreadful, whose teeth were of iron, and his nails of brass; which devoured, brake in pieces, and stamped the residue with his feet; and of the TEN HORNS that were in his head, and of the OTHER which came up, and before whom three fell; even of THAT HORN that had eyes, and a mouth that spake very great things, whose look was more stout than his fellows."

"Thus he said, the FOURTH BEAST shall be the FOURTH KINGDOM upon earth, which shall be diverse from all kingdoms, and shall devour the whole earth, and shall tread it down and break it in pieces. And the TEN HORNS out of this Kingdom are TEN KINGS that shall arise; and another (King) shall rise after them; and he shall be diverse from the first, and he shall subdue THREE KINGS. And he shall speak great words against the Most High, and shall wear out the saints of the Most High, and think to change times and laws; and they shall be given into his hand until a TIME and TIMES and the DIVIDING OF TIME."

Daniel's Foreview

The Little Horn Of The He-Goat
Dan. 8: 8-12, 23-25.

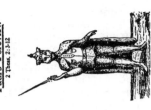

"Therefore the He-Goat waxed very great; and when he was strong, the GREAT HORN was broken; and for it came up FOUR NOTABLE ONES toward the four winds of heaven. And out of one of them came forth a LITTLE HORN, which waxed exceeding great, toward the South and toward the East, and toward the Pleasant Land (Palestine). And it waxed great, even to the Host of Heaven, and it cast down some of the Host and of the Stars to the ground, and stamped upon them. Yea, he magnified himself even to the Prince of the Host and by him the daily sacrifice was taken away, and the place of his Sanctuary was cast down. And an host was given him against the daily sacrifice by reason of transgression, and it (the, the LITTLE HORN) cast down the truth to the ground; and it (the LITTLE HORN) practised and prospered."

"And in the LATTER TIME of their kingdom, when the TRANSGRESSORS ARE COME TO THE FULL, a King of FIERCE COUNTENANCE, and understanding dark sentences, shall stand up. And his power shall be mighty, but not by his own power; and he shall destroy wonderfully, and shall prosper, and practice, and shall destroy the mighty and the Holy People. And through his policy also he shall cause craft (all kinds of business) to prosper in his hand; and he shall magnify himself in his heart, and by peace shall destroy many. He shall also stand up against the PRINCE OF PRINCES (Christ); but he shall be broken without hand."

The Wilful King
Dan. 11: 36-39.

"And the KING shall do according to his WILL; and he shall exalt himself and magnify himself above every god, and shall speak marvellous things against the God of gods, and shall prosper till the indignation be accomplished: for that, that is determined, shall be done. Neither shall he regard the God of his fathers, nor the desire of women, nor regard any god: for he shall magnify himself above all. But in his estate shall he honor the God of forces: and a god whom his fathers knew not shall he honor with gold, and silver, and with precious stones, and pleasant things. Thus shall he do in the most strong holds with a strange god, whom he shall acknowledge and increase with glory; and he shall cause them to rule over many, and shall divide the land for gain."

Paul's Foreview

2 Thess. 2: 3-12

"Let no man deceive you by any means; for THAT DAY (the "Day of the Lord") shall not come except there come a falling away first, and that

be revealed. The **'MAN OF SIN'**

'SON OF PERDITION,'

who opposeth and exalteth himself above all that is called God, or that is worshipped; so that he AS GOD sitteth in the Temple of God (the rebuilt Temple of Jerusalem), showing himself that he IS GOD."

"For the **'MYSTERY OF INIQUITY'**

doth already work (in Paul's day); only He (the Holy Spirit) who now letteth (restraineth, R. V.) will let (restrain), until He be taken out of the way. And then shall **'THAT WICKED'**

be revealed, whom the Lord shall consume with the spirit (breath) of His Mouth, and shall destroy with the brightness (manifestation, R. V.) of His Coming. Even him, whose coming is after the working of Satan with all power and signs and lying wonders, and with all deceivableness of unrighteousness in them that perish; because they received not the love of the Truth (Christ) that they might be saved. And for this cause God shall send them strong delusion that they should believe a lie. (THE LIE, American RSV, that shall arise; may, that they all might be damned who believed not the truth, but had pleasure in unrighteousness."

John's Foreview

Beast Out Of The Sea
Rev. 13: 1-7

"I saw a BEAST rise up out of the SE, having SEVEN HEADS and TEN HORNS, and upon his horns TEN CROWNS, and upon his heads the NAMES OF BLASPHEMY. And the BEAST which I saw was like unto a LEOPARD, and his feet were as the feet of a BEAR, and his mouth as the mouth of a LION: and the Dragon gave him his power, and his seat, and great authority. And I saw one of his HEADS as it were wounded to death; and his deadly wound was healed; and all the world wondered after the BEAST. . . . And there was given unto him a mouth speaking great things and blasphemies; and power was given unto him to continue FORTY AND TWO MONTHS. And he opened his mouth in blasphemy against God, to blaspheme His Name, and His Tabernacle, and them that dwell in Heaven. And it was given unto him to make war with the saints, and to overcome them; and power was given him over all kindreds, and tongues, and nations."

assassin, and as his body is lying in state prepared for burial, he rises from the dead (Vs. 14), and thus becomes the "EIGHTH," though he is of the "SEVENTH." By this resurrection of the Antichrist, Satan imitates the Resurrection of Christ and makes the world "wonder after the Beast" (Rev. 13:3), and this adds to his prestige and power. If this happens at the "Middle of the Week," at the time the Dragon is cast out of Heaven, it will account for the great change that takes place in the Antichrist, for before receiving his "deadly wound" he will be sweet and lovable, but after his resurrection or recovery he will become Devilish, the result of the Dragon incarnating himself in him. It is at this time that he breaks the Covenant with the Jews and desecrates the Temple by setting up the "Abomination of Desolation" which is an "Idol Image" of himself—the "DESOLATOR." As the "LITTLE HORN" of Daniel's "Fourth Wild Beast" he will destroy three of the "Ten Kings" and firmly establish himself in the place of power, and as he, as the "LITTLE HORN," does not appear until after the "TEN HORNS," or "Ten Federated Kingdoms," come into existence, it is clear that the Antichrist does not form the Federation. but is the outgrowth of it.

He will be a "composite" man. One who embraces in his character the abilities and powers of Nebuchadnezzar, Xerxes, Alexander the Great and Caesar Augustus. He will have the marvelous gift of attracting unregenerate men, and the irresistible fascination of his personality, his versatile attainments, superhuman wisdom, great administrative and executive ability, along with his powers as a consummate flatterer, a brilliant diplomatist, a superb strategist, will make him the most conspicuous and prominent of men. All these gifts will be conferred on him by Satan, whose tool he will be, and who will thus make him the—

SUPERMAN.

He will pose as a great humanitarian, the friend of men, and the especial friend of the Jewish race, whom he will persuade that he has come to usher in the "Golden Age" as pictured by the prophets, and who will receive him as their Messiah.

He will intoxicate men with a strong delusion and his never varying success. And when he shall be slain and rise again he will have lost none of these powers, but will be in addition the embodiment of all kinds of wickedness and blasphemy.

"He shall speak great words against the Most High, and shall wear out the saints of the Most High, and think to change times and laws." Dan. 7:25.

"He shall also stand up against the 'Prince of Princes'" (Jesus). Dan. 8:25.

"He shall do according to his will; and he shall exalt himself and magnify himself above every god, and shall speak marvellous things against the God of Gods." Dan. 11:36.

"Who opposeth and exalteth himself above all that is called God, or that is worshipped; so that he AS GOD sitteth in the Temple of God (at Jerusalem) showing himself that he IS GOD . . . whose coming is after the Working of Satan with all Power and Signs and Lying Wonders." 2. Thess. 2:3-9.

There has never as yet appeared on this earth a person who answers the description given in the above Scriptures. Such a character is almost inconceivable. No writer would have invented such a character.

7. THE BEAST OUT OF THE EARTH.
The "False Prophet" Or "Anti-Spirit."
Rev. 13 : 11-18.

"And I beheld **another** '**BEAST**' coming up **out of the EARTH**; and he had **two horns like a lamb,** and he **spake as a DRAGON.** And he exerciseth all the power of the 'First Beast' before him, and causeth the earth and them which dwell therein to worship the 'First Beast,' whose **deadly wound was healed.** And he doeth great wonders, so that he maketh **fire come down from heaven on the earth in the sight of men,** and deceiveth them that dwell on the earth by the means of those miracles which he had power to do in the sight of the 'Beast'; saying to them that dwell on the earth, that they should make an '**IMAGE TO THE BEAST**,' which had the wound by a sword, and did live. And he had power to give **LIFE UNTO THE** '**IMAGE OF THE** '**BEAST**,' that the '**IMAGE OF THE BEAST**' **SHOULD BOTH SPEAK, AND CAUSE THAT AS MANY AS WOULD NOT WORSHIP THE** '**IMAGE OF THE BEAST**' **SHOULD BE KILLED.** And he causeth all, both small and great, rich and poor, free and bond, to receive a '**MARK**' in their **right hand,** or in their **foreheads;** and that no man might **BUY** or **SELL,** save he that had the '**MARK**,' or the '**NAME OF THE BEAST**,' or the '**NUMBER OF HIS NAME.**' Here is wisdom. Let him that hath understanding count the '**NUMBER OF THE BEAST**': for it is the '**NUMBER OF MAN**': and his number is **SIX HUNDRED THREESCORE AND SIX.**"

After the Apostle John had seen and described the "Beast" that came up **out of the SEA,** he saw another "Beast" come up out of the EARTH. This "Second Beast," while John does not say it was a lamb, had "Two Horns" "like a lamb," that is, it was **LAMB-LIKE.** Because of this resemblance many claim that the "Second Beast" is the Antichrist, for Antichrist is supposed to imitate Christ. While the **LAMB** (Christ) is mentioned in the Book of Revelation **22 times,** the description given of Him in chapter 5:6, is that of a lamb having "SEVEN HORNS" and not "TWO." This differentiates Him from the "lamb-like Beast" that comes up out of the earth, who, though he is "lamb-like in appearance SPEAKS AS A DRAGON."

The "Second Beast" has a name. He is called the "FALSE PROPHET" three times. First in chapter 16:13, then in chapter 19:20, and again in chapter 20:10. Twice he is associated with the "First Beast" (Antichrist) and once with the "Dragon" (Satan) and the "First Beast," and as they are PERSONS so must he be. The fact that he is called the "False Prophet" is proof that he is not the "Antichrist." Jesus had a foreview of him when He said—"There shall arise 'FALSE CHRISTS' and 'FALSE PROPHETS,' and shall show GREAT SIGNS AND WONDERS: insomuch that, if it were possible they shall deceive the very elect." Matt. 24:24. Here Jesus differentiates between "FALSE CHRISTS" and "FALSE PROPHETS," therefore the "ANTICHRIST" and the "FALSE PROPHET" cannot be the same.

That the "Second Beast" comes up out of the EARTH may signify that he will be a resurrected person. If, as was hinted at, "Antichrist" was Judas resurrected, why should not the "False Prophet" also be a resurrected person? There will be two persons, as we have seen, who shall come back from Heaven as the "Two Witnesses," Moses and Elijah, why not two persons come up from "The Underworld," brought up by Satan to counteract the work of the "Two Witnesses"? The fact that the "First Beast" (Antichrist), and the "Second Beast" (False Prophet) are cast ALIVE into the "Lake of Fire" (Rev. 19:20) is further proof that they are more than ordinary mortals, and that the "First Beast" is more than the last ruling Emperor of the revived Roman Empire. He is the Antichrist, Satan's SUPERMAN.

In the "Dragon," the "Beast," and the "False Prophet," we have the "SATANIC TRINITY," Satan's imitation of the "Divine Trinity." In the unseen and invisible "Dragon" we have the FATHER (the ANTI-GOD). In the "Beast" we have the "SON OF PERDITION" (the ANTI-CHRIST), begotten of the Dragon, who appears on the earth, dies, and is resurrected, and to whom is given a throne by his Father the Dragon. In the "False Prophet" we have the "ANTI-SPIRIT," who proceeds from the "Dragon Father" and "Dragon Son," and whose speech is like the Dragon's. The "Dragon" then will be the "ANTI-GOD," the "Beast" the "ANTI-CHRIST," and the "False Prophet" the "ANTI-SPIRIT," and the fact that all three are cast ALIVE into the "Lake of Fire" (Rev. 20:10) is proof that they together form a "Triumvirate" which we may well call—"THE SATANIC TRINITY."

Again the "Antichrist" is to be a KING and rule over a KINGDOM. He will accept the "Kingdoms of this world" that Satan offered Christ, and that Christ refused. Matt. 4:8-10. He will also EXALT himself, and claim to be God. 2. Thess. 2:4. But the "False Prophet" is not a King, He does not exalt himself, he exalts the "First Beast" (Antichrist). His relation to the "First Beast" is the same as the Holy Spirit's relation to Christ. He causeth the earth

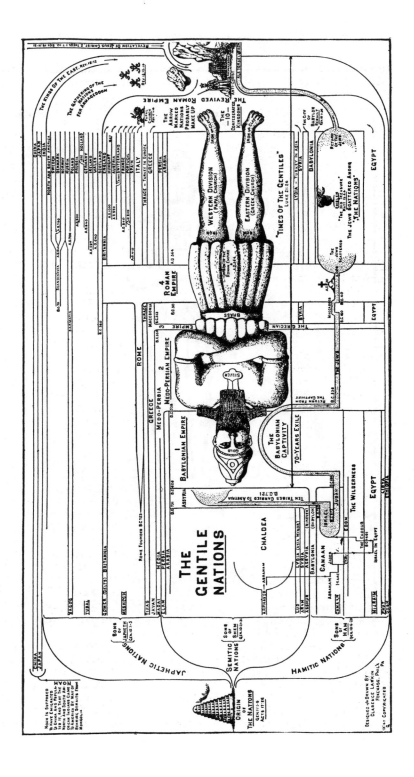

IMAGE OF THE BEAST

and them which dwell therein to worship the "First Beast." He also has power to give life, and in this he imitates the Holy Spirit. And as the followers of Christ are sealed by the Holy Spirit until the "Day of Redemption" (Eph. 4:30); so, the followers of Antichrist shall be sealed by the False Prophet until the "Day of Perdition." Rev. 13:16-17.

The False Prophet will be a "Miracle Worker." While Jesus was a "miracle worker," He did all His mighty works in the "power" of the Holy Spirit. Acts 10:38. Among the miracles that the False Prophet will perform he will bring down FIRE FROM HEAVEN. As we have seen under the work of the "Two Witnesses," chapter 11:1-14, there will probably be a "FIRE-TEST" between Elijah and the False Prophet, and the test as to who is God of Mt. Carmel will be repeated. That Satan, who will then energize the False Prophet, can do this is clear from Job 1:16, where Satan, having secured permission from God to touch all that Job had, brought down "fire from heaven" and burned up Job's sheep and servants.

The False Prophet then commands the people to make an

"IMAGE OF THE BEAST."

This is further proof that the "First Beast" is the Antichrist. It is a strange weakness of mankind that they must have some VISIBLE God to worship, and when the Children of Israel, who had been delivered from Egypt under Moses' leadership, thought he had forsaken them because he did not come down from the Mount, they called Aaron to make them gods which should go before them, and Aaron made for them the "GOLDEN CALF." Ex. 32:1-6. So the False Prophet will have the people make for the purpose of worship an "IMAGE OF THE BEAST." But the wonderful thing about the "IMAGE" is that the False Prophet will have power to give LIFE to it, and cause it to SPEAK, and to demand that all who will not worship it shall be put to death. In other words the "IMAGE" will be a living, speaking, AUTOMATON.

This "Image" reminds us of the "GOLDEN IMAGE" that Nebuchadnezzar commanded to be made and set up in the "Plain of Dura," in the Province of Babylon (Dan. 3:1-30), before which, at the sounding of musical instruments, the people were commanded to bow down and worship under penalty, for those who disobeyed, of being cast into a "BURNING FIERY FURNACE." Doubtless there will be many in the "Day of Antichrist" who will refuse to bow down and worship the "Image of the Beast," and who will not escape as did the "Three Hebrew Children," though God may interpose in a miraculous way to deliver some. And as if this was not enough the False Prophet shall cause—"ALL, both small and great, rich and poor, free and bond, to receive a 'MARK' in their RIGHT HAND, or in their FOREHEAD; and that no man might BUY or SELL, save he that has the 'MARK' or the 'NAME OF THE BEAST,' or the 'NUMBER OF HIS NAME'." This "MARK" will be known as the

"BRAND OF HELL."

This is what the world is fast coming to. The time is not far distant when the various "Trusts" and "Combinations of Capital" will be merged into a "FEDERATION OF TRUSTS," at the head of which shall be a "NAPOLEON OF CAPITAL." Ultimately this "Federation of Trusts" will extend to the whole world, at the head of which shall be THE ANTICHRIST, and the producer and consumer will be powerless in the tentacles of this OCTOPUS, and no man shall be able to BUY or SELL who has not the "MARK OF THE BEAST" either upon his "right hand" or on his "forehead." This "Mark" will be BRANDED or burnt on. It will probably be the "NUMBER OF THE BEAST" or "666." The number "666" is the "NUMBER OF MAN," and stops short of the perfect number SEVEN. Man was created on the SIXTH day. Goliath, the opposer of God's people, a type of Satan, was 6 cubits in height, he had 6 pieces of armor, and his spearhead weighed 600 shekels. 1. Sam. 17:4-7. Nebuchadnezzar's Image, a type of the "Image of the Beast," was 60 cubits in height, 6 cubits wide, and 6 instruments of music summoned the worshippers. Dan. 3:1-7.

In that day men will doubtless prefer to have the "MARK" on the back of their right hand so it can be readily seen in the act of signing checks, drafts, and receipts. There will doubtless be public officials in all public places of business to see that no one buys or sells who has not the "MARK." This will apply to women as well as men. No one can shop, or even buy from the huckster at the door, without the "MARK," under penalty of DEATH. Those will be awful times for those who will not WORSHIP THE BEAST. If they can neither buy or sell without the "MARK," they must beg, or starve or be killed. The instrument of death will be the guillotine (Rev. 20:4), and the daily papers will contain a list of the names of those who were beheaded the day before so as to frighten the people into obedience to the law. The doom of the "Satanic Trinity" will be, that at the close of that awful time of Tribulation the Lord Jesus Christ will return, and the "Dragon," the "Anti-God," will be cast into the "BOTTOMLESS PIT" for a 1000 years (Rev. 20:1-3), and the "Beast," the "Anti-Christ," and the "False Prophet," the "Anti-Spirit," will be cast ALIVE into the "LAKE OF FIRE." Rev. 19:20.

THE INTERVAL BETWEEN THE "SEVEN PERSONAGES" AND THE "SEVEN VIALS."

1. THE LAMB ON MOUNT ZION.
Rev. 14:1-5.

"And I looked, and, lo, a LAMB stood on MOUNT ZION, and with Him a Hundred Forty and Four Thousand, having His Father's name written in their foreheads. And I heard a voice from Heaven, as the voice of many waters, and as the voice of a great thunder: and I heard the voice of HARPERS harping with their harps: and they sung as it were a NEW SONG before the Throne, and before the Four Beasts, and the Elders: and no man could learn that song but The Hundred and Forty and Four Thousand, which were redeemed from the earth. These are they which were not defiled with women: for they are virgins. These are they which follow the Lamb whithersoever He goeth. These were redeemed from among men, being the first fruits unto God and to the Lamb. And in their mouth was found no guile: for they are without fault before the Throne of God."

The Lamb here is Christ, and the Mount Zion is not Mount Zion of the earthly Jerusalem but of the Heavenly of which Paul speaks in Heb. 12:22-23. "But ye are come unto Mount Zion, and unto the city of the living God, 'THE HEAVENLY JERUSALEM,' and to an innumerable company of angels, to the General Assembly and Church of the 'First Born' (New Born), which are written in Heaven, and to God the Judge of all, and to the spirits of just (justified) men made perfect."

The 144,000 standing with the Lamb on Mount Zion, are the 144,000 "SEALED ONES," 12,000 from each Tribe of Israel, of chapter 7:3-8. There we are told they were sealed, here we are told why. In chapter seven we are told they were sealed in their foreheads, here we are told that that sealing was the writing on their foreheads of the name of the Lamb (R. V.) and of the Lamb's Father. As John looked at the Lamb and the 144,000 "Sealed Ones" who stood with Him, he heard a voice from Heaven, as the "voice of many waters," and as the voice of a "great thunder," which identifies the Speaker with the one who spoke from the midst of the "Lamp-Stands" of chapter 1:10, 15, or the Lamb Himself.

What the "voice" said is not told us, but it was followed with the voice or singing of "Harpers" accompanied by their harps. These "Harpers" sung a "NEW SONG" before the Throne, and the "Four Living Creatures," and the "Elders." As the "Elders" represent the Church, these "Harpers" are not the Church, for they sing before the "Elders." Who these "Harpers" are we are told in chapter 15:2-4. They are those who stand on the "Sea of Glass" before the Throne. Rev. 4:6. The "New Song" they sing is a "double song," the "SONG OF MOSES" and the "SONG OF THE LAMB," and we are told that no man could learn the Song but the 144,000 who were redeemed from the earth. This is further evidence that the 144,000 "Sealed Ones" are in Heaven, either having been translated or died a Martyr's death, and from Rev. 14:4 we learn that they are the "FIRST-FRUITS" of the restored nation of Israel, not the "First-Fruits" of the Church, for that is represented by the "Elders," and was gathered out long before.

These 144,000 "Sealed Ones" are called "VIRGINS"; and the fact that they are spoken of as not having been "defiled with women," shows that they are either all men of the character of the Apostle Paul, who did not marry, or, as is most likely, and as the word translated "virgins" means persons of either sex, they are "virgins" in the sense that they kept themselves clean of the crowning sin of that day —FORNICATION, for the crowning sin of the Tribulation Period will be fornication (Rev. 9:21; 14:8), or looseness and laxity of the marriage tie, of which "free-love," and the doctrine of "affinities," and multiplied divorce in these days are but the opening wedge to the looseness of morals of those Anti-Christian times. The 144,000 "Sealed Ones" will be especially delivered from this sin, and so they, and they only, as a special class, can sing this "New Song" of redemption, not so much by the Blood, as from the sin of fornication.   The teaching of **"seducing spirits"** mentioned in 1. Tim. 4: 1-3, as belonging to those Anti-Christian times, of **"forbidding to marry and commanding to abstain from meats,"** has a deeper significance than that of the practice of the Church of Rome that requires the celibacy of the priesthood and clergy, and fasting of the laity.   Such teaching comes from the "Pit," and belongs to Antichrist's religion, and its purpose is to weaken the body by fasting and make it more susceptible to the influence of evil angels and demons, and to cause it to gratify the desires of the flesh in other ways than by lawful means. These **"Sealed Ones"** are a chosen class who follow the Lamb whithersoever He goeth, and they are without fault **before the Throne of God.**

2. THE THREE ANGEL MESSENGERS.

FIRST ANGEL.
THE EVERLASTING GOSPEL.
Rev. 14: 6-7.

"And I saw another angel fly, in the midst of heaven, having the 'EVERLASTING GOSPEL' to preach unto them that dwell on the earth, and to **every nation, and kindred, and tongue,** and **people;** saying with a loud voice 'FEAR GOD, AND GIVE GLORY TO HIM; FOR THE HOUR OF HIS JUDGMENT IS COME: AND WORSHIP HIM THAT MADE HEAVEN, AND EARTH, AND THE SEA, AND THE FOUNTAINS OF WATERS."

In his vision of Apocalyptic Judgments John sees many angels at work. Here he sees one flying in **"MID-HEAVEN."** That is, in the heaven or atmosphere that surrounds our earth. The mission of this Angel is to preach the

"EVERLASTING GOSPEL"

unto every nation, kindred, tongue, and people on the earth. Here is the first and only place in the Bible where an **angel** is commissioned to preach the Gospel. An angel could not tell Cornelius how to be saved, he could only tell him to send for Peter for that purpose. Acts **10: 3-6. In** this "Gospel Age" only redeemed men can preach the ьospel, but at the "End Time," just before the return of the Lord. an angel will go forth to preach the "EVERLASTING GOSPEL," or as the revised Version puts it, the "ETERNAL GOSPEL." The word "Gospel" means "**Good News.**" Four forms of the Gospel are mentioned in the New Testament, and we must distinguish carefully between them.

(1). THE GOSPEL OF "THE KINGDOM."
Matt. 24: 14.

This is the "Good News" that God purposes to set up a Kingdom on this earth over which David's Son, **JESUS,** shall reign, as prophesied in Luke 1: 32-33.   Two preachings of this Gospel are mentioned, one past, beginning with the ministry of John the Baptist, and preached by Jesus and His Disciples, but it ended with the rejection of Jesus as King.   This Gospel is to be preached again after the Church is taken out.   It will be the fulfilment of Matt. 24: 14, where it says: "This Gospel of '**THE KINGDOM**' shall be preached in all the world for a **WITNESS** unto all nations: and then shall the end come." This has no reference to the Gospel that is now being preached to the nations.   It is the Gospel of **SALVATION,** but the "Gospel of the Kingdom" is not for "Salvation" but for a **WITNESS,** that is. it is the **a**nnouncement that the time has come to SET UP THE KING-**DOM.** It will be preached first by Elijah the forerunner (Mal. 4: 5-6), and by others who shall be commissioned to bear the news to all nations as a proclamation of the Coming of Christ as King to occupy the Throne of David, and for the purpose of regathering Israel to the Promised Land.

(2). THE GOSPEL OF THE "GRACE OF GOD."
Acts 20: 24.

This is the "Good News" that Jesus Christ the rejected King died on the Cross for our **SALVATION.** This form of the Gospel is described in many ways.   It is called the "**GOSPEL OF GOD**" (Rom. 1: 1), because it has its **source** in the **LOVE OF GOD.** John 3: 16. Its **Character** is "**GRACE.**" Acts 20: 24. Its subject is **CHRIST** (Rom. 1: 16; 2. Cor. 10: 14), and it is the **POWER OF GOD UNTIL SALVATION.** It is also a "**GLORIOUS GOSPEL**" because it speaks of Him who is in the **GLORY,** and has been **GLORIFIED,** and who is bringing many sons to **GLORY.**   1. Tim. 1: 11, 2. Cor. 4: 4, Heb. 2: 10. And it is the "**GOSPEL OF PEACE,**" because it makes peace between the sinner and God, and brings peace to the soul.   Eph. 6: 15.

(3). MY GOSPEL.
Rom. 2: 16. (Acts 26: 16-18.)

This is the same as the "Gospel of the Grace of God," or of Salvation, with the additional revelations that were made known to Paul as to the Church (Eph. 3: 1-7), and as to Israel.   Rom. 11: 1-36.

(4) THE "EVERLASTING GOSPEL."
Rev. 14:6.

This is what the Angel preaches in this chapter. It is neither the "Gospel of the Kingdom," nor of "Grace." Its burden is **not Salvation** but **JUDGMENT.** "Fear God, and give glory to Him: for the **HOUR OF HIS JUDGMENT IS COME."** It is "Good News" to Israel, and all who are passing through the "fires of Judgment," because it declares that their troubles will soon end in the judgment and destruction of Antichrist. It calls on men to worship God as **"Creator,"** and not as "Saviour," and so it is called in the Revised Version—**"THE ETERNAL GOSPEL,"** the Gospel that has been proclaimed from Eden down by Patriarchs and Prophets, and not an "Everlasting Gospel" in the sense that it saves men for all eternity.

There is **"ANOTHER GOSPEL"** (Gal. 1: 6-12, 2. Cor. 11: 4), **which is not another,** and which Paul repudiated. It is a perversion of the true Gospel and has many seductive forms, and in the main teaches that **"faith" is not sufficient to Salvation,** nor able to keep and perfect, and so emphasizes "Good Works." Col. 2: 18-23, Heb. 6: 1, 9: 14. The Apostle pronounces a fearful "Anathema" upon its preachers and teachers. Gal. 1: 8-9. Our message is: **"Believe on the Lord Jesus Christ and thou shalt be saved."** Acts 16: 31. The Angel's message is: **"Fear God for the HOUR of His Judgment is come."** Men reject the human messenger and they will also reject the Angelic messenger, they will not believe even though **ONE** (Jesus) rose from the dead.

SECOND ANGEL.

FALL OF BABYLON PROCLAIMED.
Chap. 14: 8.

"And there followed another angel, saying **BABYLON IS FALLEN, IS FALLEN,** that great **City,** because she made all nations drink of the wine of the wrath of her fornication."

Here is proof that the City of Babylon is to be rebuilt. For further proof see chapter eighteen. As to the fall and destruction of the literal City of Babylon this proclamation is anticipative, but as a declaration that Babylon **had fallen** to fearful depths of wickedness and apostasy, and had become **"the habitation of demons, and the hold of every foul spirit, and a cage of every unclean and hateful bird,"** as described in chapter 18: 2, it was already true, for the City of Babylon will have been rebuilt at the time when this Angel utters his proclamation. The Angel's warning was that God's people might hear His voice saying: "Come out of her, **MY PEOPLE**, that ye be not **partakers** of her sins, and that ye receive not of her plagues." Rev. 18: 4.

THIRD ANGEL.
THE DOOM OF ANTICHRIST'S FOLLOWERS.
Rev. 14: 9-11.

"And the third Angel followed them, saying with a loud voice, If any man worship the Beast and his Image, and receive his mark in his forehead, or in his hand, the same shall drink of the wine of the 'wrath of God,' which is poured out without mixture into the 'cup of His Indignation'; and he shall be **tormented with fire and brimstone** in the presence of the Holy Angels, and in the presence of the **LAMB**: and the smoke of their torment ascendeth up for **ever and ever**: and they have no rest **day or night**, who **worship the Beast and his Image**, and whosoever receiveth the 'Mark' of his name."

This is a most awful warning. Any man who worships **the** Beast, and receives his 'Mark' in forehead or hand, his doom is fixed **FOREVER**, and he shall be tormented with fire and brimstone in **the** presence of the Holy Angels and of the Lamb, and the smoke of his torment shall ascend for **ever and ever**, and they shall have no rest day or night. That means during the 3½ years of Antichrist's reign, after they have received the "Mark," for there is no day or night in eternity. If "Eternal Punishment" is taught nowhere else in the Bible it is taught here, and if here, why is it not true as to other classes of sinners? Just think of the horror of remorse in the "Lake of Fire," as these worshippers of the Beast shall recall the "Mark of the Beast" as it was imprinted on their forehead or right hand with their own consent because of their desire to enrich themselves in the markets of their day.

3. THE BLESSED DEAD.
Rev. 14: 12-13.

"Here is the patience of the saints: here are they that keep the Commandments of God, and the Faith of Jesus. And I heard a voice from Heaven saying unto me, Write, blessed are the dead which die in the Lord FROM HENCEFORTH: Yea, saith the Spirit, that they may rest from their labors: and their works do follow them."

This is blessedly true of all saints but refers here to those who die **after** the False Prophet has issued the command that all who will not worship the "Image of the Beast" shall be killed." Rev. 13:15. This is settled by the word **HENCEFORTH.** This warning is given for the benefit of those who in that day shall be tempted to compromise with evil in order to preserve their lives. Better to live and reign with Christ a **1000 years,** than with Antichrist **3½ years.** This special class of dead who "DIE IN THE LORD" will be blessed because they will be delivered from the trials and sufferings of the Great Tribulation, and will receive the "MARTYR'S CROWN" (Rev. 2:10), and they shall rest from their labors of stemming the tide of iniquity of those days, and their works follow **with them** (R. V.). During the "Great Tribulation" they that are loyal to God have no prospect before them but martyrdom, hence the need at this time of a special message of blessing to those who are faithful **until death.** What a contrast between the "Blessed Dead," and those who have the "Mark of the Beast." The former will **rest** from their labors, while the latter shall **not rest** day or night.

4. THE HARVEST AND VINTAGE.
Rev. 14:14-20.

THE REAPER
REV. 14:14-20

"And I looked, and behold a white cloud, and upon the cloud one sat like unto the **SON OF MAN,** having on His head a Golden Crown, and in His hand a sharp Sickle. And another angel came out of the Temple, crying with a loud voice to Him that sat on the cloud, Thrust in Thy **SICKLE, and reap:** for the time is come for Thee to reap: for the 'Harvest of the Earth' **IS RIPE.** And He that sat on the cloud thrust in His Sickle on the earth: and the earth was reaped. And another angel came out of the Temple which is in Heaven, he also having a sharp Sickle. And another angel came out from the Altar, which had **power over** fire; and cried with a loud **cry** to him that had the sharp Sickle, saying Thrust in thy sharp Sickle,

and gather the clusters of the 'VINE OF THE EARTH';
for her grapes are **fully ripe.** And the angel thrust in his Sickle
into the earth, and gathered the 'VINE OF THE EARTH,'
and cast it into the great **WINEPRESS** of the 'Wrath of
God.' And the **WINEPRESS** was trodden without the city,
and **BLOOD** came out of the **WINEPRESS,** even unto the horse
bridles, by the space of a thousand and six hundred furlongs."

There can be no question as to who is the "Reaper" of the
"HARVEST OF THE EARTH." It is the "SON OF MAN,"
Christ Himself. He was the "Sower" and He shall be the "Reaper."
This is not the "Harvest of the Church." That was harvested in
chapters four and five, and the "Reapers" were the angels. Matt.
13: 39. This is the "Harvest" of the Gentile Nations. In Joel 3:
9-17 we have a description of this "Harvest and Vintage." The
"Harvest and Vintage" are **JUDICIAL.** That is, they are for the
purpose of Judgment. The account here is anticipative. It looks
forward to chapter 16: 13-16, which speaks of how the armies of the
world are to be gathered together by **"THREE UNCLEAN
SPIRITS"** to the Battle of the Great Day of God Almighty at Armageddon. This Battle takes place **after** the "Fall of Babylon," and is
more fully described in chapter 19: 17-19.

Here we are told that the Harvest is **RIPE,** and the "Son of
Man" is commanded to thrust in His Sickle, which He does, and
while the pouring out of the "Vials" is a part of the reaping, the
Harvest is not finished until the end of the "Battle of Armageddon."

The difference between the "Harvest and the Vintage" is, that
the "harvest" in the natural world precedes the "vintage," but often,
as in this case, continues until they become one.

The "Vintage" is of the "VINE OF THE EARTH." Israel
was a "VINE" brought out of Egypt (Psa. 80: 8) and planted in
Canaan, but when God looked for it to bring forth "good grapes"
it brought forth "WILD GRAPES" (Isa. 5: 1-7), and fruit unto
itself. Hosea 10: 1. When the Lord of the "Vineyard" sent His
servants for the "Fruit of the Vineyard," the husbandmen beat one,
killed another, and stoned another. At last He sent His Son, Him
they took and cast out of the Vineyard and slew. Matt. 21: 33-43.
Then Jesus Himself became the **"TRUE VINE,"** of which His
disciples are the branches. John 15: 5. The **"VINE OF THE
EARTH"** is Antichrist and all who belong to his pernicious system.

The **"WINEPRESS"** is the winepress of the **"FIERCENESS
AND WRATH OF ALMIGHTY GOD." Rev. 19: 15.** The Prophet
Isaiah (Isa. 63: 1-6) describes Christ's share in it. It will cover the
whole Land of Palestine, and extend as far south as Edom and
Bozrah. So great shall be the slaughter that the blood shall be up
to the horses' bridles in the valleys over the whole of Palestine for
1600 furlongs, or 200 miles. It will be the time of which the Prophet
Isaiah speaks, when the land shall be **DRUNK WITH BLOOD.**
Isa. 34: 7-8. We will consider it more in detail when we study the
Battle of Armageddon in chapter nineteen.

The Seven Last Plagues or Vial Judgments.

Rev. 15:1.

"And I saw another **SIGN** in Heaven, great and marvellous, **SEVEN ANGELS** having the 'SEVEN LAST PLAGUES'; for in them is filled up the **WRATH OF GOD.**"

This is another "SIGN" or "Wonder." It was great and marvellous, because it "FILLED UP THE WRATH OF GOD," that is, it completed the pouring out of the accumulated "WRATH OF GOD."

PRELUDE.

THE SEA OF GLASS.
Rev. 15:2-4.

"And I saw as it were a 'SEA OF GLASS' MINGLED WITH FIRE : and them that had gotten the victory over the Beast, and over his Image, and over his Mark, and over the NUMBER OF HIS NAME, stand on the SEA OF GLASS, having the Harps of God. And they sing the SONG OF MOSES the servant of God, and the SONG OF THE LAMB, saying, Great and Marvellous are Thy Works, Lord God Almighty; just and true are Thy Ways, Thou King of Saints. Who shall not fear Thee, O Lord, and glorify Thy name? for thou only art holy! for all nations shall come and worship before Thee; for Thy judgments are made manifest."

This "SEA OF GLASS" is the same "Sea of Glass" that we saw before the Throne in chapter 4:6. Then it was unoccupied, now it is occupied. Then its surface was crystal clear and plain, now its surface is of a "fiery" aspect, symbolizing the "fiery trials" of its occupants. The occupants of this "Sea of Glass" come out of the Great Tribulation, for they have gotten the victory over the "Beast," and over his "Image," and over his Mark, and over the "Number of His Name," and they have harps, and they sing the "SONG OF MOSES" and the "SONG OF THE LAMB." They are the "Harpers" of chapter 14:2, whose song only the 144,000 "Sealed Ones" could sing. John only heard them then, now he sees them. That they could sing both the "Song of Moses" and the "Song of the Lamb" implies that they were all or in part Israelites. Some think that the "Song of Moses" that they sung was the song the Children of Israel sang on the shore of the Red Sea after their escape from Egypt, as given in Ex. 15:1-22, while others think it is Moses' "SWAN SONG" as found in Deu. 31:19, 22; 31:30; 32:43. They sang the "Song of the Lamb" because as Israelites they had been redeemed by the blood of the Lamb.

THE TABERNACLE OF TESTIMONY.
Rev. 15:5-8.

"And after that I looked, and behold, the Temple of the 'TABERNACLE OF TESTIMONY' in Heaven was opened: and the 'Seven Angels' came out of the Temple, having the 'SEVEN PLAGUES,' clothed in pure and white linen, and having their breasts girded with Golden Girdles. And one of the 'Four Beasts' gave unto the 'Seven Angels' 'SEVEN GOLDEN VIALS' full of the 'WRATH OF GOD,' who liveth for ever and ever. And the Temple was filled with smoke from the Glory of God, and from His Power: and no man was able to enter into the Temple, till the 'SEVEN PLAGUES' of the 'Seven Angels' were fulfilled."

Here again we see the Heavenly Temple. The "Seven Angels" that come out of it are clothed in priestly garments, and the "Golden Vials" that they carry were given them by one of the "Beasts" or Living Creatures, which one is not mentioned, and when he gave them to them the Heavenly Temple was filled with smoke. When the Tabernacle was finished by Moses, and the Temple by Solomon, there was a "cloud," the "Shekinah Glory," but no smoke. Ex. 40:34-36. 1. Kings 8:10-11. The "cloud" means GRACE, the "smoke" means JUDGMENT. Isa. 6:1-4. Ex. 19:18.

FIRST VIAL.
(Boils.)
Rev. 16:1-2.

"And I heard a great voice out of the Temple saying to the 'Seven Angels,' Go your ways, and pour out the 'VIALS OF THE WRATH OF GOD' upon the earth. And the first went, and poured out his VIAL upon the earth: and there fell a noisome and grievous sore upon the men which had the 'MARK OF THE BEAST,' and upon them which WORSHIPPED HIS IMAGE."

These "VIALS" and their contents are LITERAL. One cannot imagine that such momentous things as are here described refer to historical events that are already past, as when some interpret the "First Vial" as the French Revolution in A. D. 1792, and the "sores" its infidelity; and the "Second Vial" as the naval wars of that Revolution; the "Third Vial" as the battles of Napoleon in Italy, and the rest of the Vials as historical events that happened in the Nineteenth Century. If this be true then we have been passing in the past 125 years through the period of the Great Tribulation without knowing it, and have been preaching "Grace" and not that "THE HOUR OF HIS JUDGMENT IS COME." This is supposition and not EXPOSITION, and requires the reader of the Book of Revelation to be versed in all the historical events of the Christian Era. No, these "Vial Judgments" are yet future, and will be literally fulfilled as here described, and this gives us the "KEY" to the LITERALNESS of the whole Book of Revelation. That these "Vial Judgments" are not figurative is clear from the fact that 4 of the 7 have actually happened before. They are simply repetitions of the "PLAGUES OF EGYPT." See the Chart on the "Seven Vials" and the "Egyptian Plagues" compared. This Plague of a "NOISOME AND GRIEVOUS SORE" that shall fall upon men, is a repetition of the "Plague of Boils" that fell upon the Egyptians at the time of the Exodus. Ex. 9:8-12. The "First Vial Judgment" then will be a repetition of the "Sixth Egyptian Plague." That that Plague actually happened no believer in the Bible doubts, then why should we try to explain away the literalness of the Plagues that shall follow the pouring out of each of these Vials.

Boils are caused by bad blood, and reveal corruption in the system. These "grievous sores" which will come upon MEN ONLY, and not upon the beasts also as in the time of Moses, will not only reveal corruption in the body, but in the heart of those whose sins will cause corruption in their bodies. That these "sores" are reserved for those who have the "MARK OF THE BEAST," and who worship his IMAGE is further proof that these "Vial Judgments" are still future. Here is the fulfillment of Rev. 14:9-11.

The effect of the Plague of Boils upon the Egyptians was to harden their hearts, and a like effect will be produced upon the followers of Antichrist by the Plagues that shall follow the pouring out of the "Vials," for we read in verse 9, that men will blaspheme God, and refuse to repent. From this we see that suffering alone does not lead to repentance.

THE SEVEN VIALS AND THE EGYPTIAN PLAGUES COMPARED

FIRST VIAL REV.16:1-2	SECOND VIAL REV.16:3	THIRD VIAL REV.16:4-7	FOURTH VIAL REV.16:8-9	FIFTH VIAL REV.16:10-11	SIXTH VIAL REV.16:12-16	SEVENTH VIAL REV.16:17-21
BOILS	BLOOD (SEA)	BLOOD (RIVERS)	GREAT HEAT	DARKNESS	EUPHRATES DRIED UP	GREAT HAIL

FIRST VIAL — BOILS:

AND I heard a great voice out of the temple saying to the seven angels, Go your ways, and pour out the vials of the wrath of God upon the earth.

2 And the first went, and poured out his vial upon the earth; and there fell a noisome and grievous sore upon the men which had the mark of the beast, and upon them which worshipped his image.

SECOND VIAL — BLOOD (SEA):

3 And the second angel poured out his vial upon the sea; and it became as the blood of a dead man: and every living soul died in the sea.

THIRD VIAL — BLOOD (RIVERS):

4 And the third angel poured out his vial upon the rivers and fountains of waters; and they became blood.

5 And I heard the angel of the waters say, Thou art righteous, O Lord, which art, and wast, and shalt be, because thou hast judged thus.

6 For they have shed the blood of saints and prophets, and thou hast given them blood to drink; for they are worthy.

7 And I heard another out of the altar say, Even so, Lord God Almighty, true and righteous are thy judgments.

FOURTH VIAL — GREAT HEAT:

8 And the fourth angel poured out his vial upon the sun; and power was given unto him to scorch men with fire.

9 And men were scorched with great heat, and blasphemed the name of God, which hath power over these plagues: and they repented not to give him glory

FIFTH VIAL — DARKNESS:

10 And the fifth angel poured out his vial upon the seat of the beast; and his kingdom was full of darkness; and they gnawed their tongues for pain,

11 And blasphemed the God of heaven because of their pains and their sores, and repented not of their deeds.

SIXTH VIAL — EUPHRATES DRIED UP:

12 And the sixth angel poured out his vial upon the great river Euphrates; and the water thereof was dried up, that the way of the kings of the east might be prepared.

13 And I saw three unclean spirits like frogs come out of the mouth of the dragon, and out of the mouth of the beast, and out of the mouth of the false prophet.

14 For they are the spirits of devils, working miracles, which go forth unto the kings of the earth and of the whole world, to gather them to the battle of that great day of God Almighty.

15 Behold, I come as a thief. Blessed is he that watcheth, and keepeth his garments, lest he walk naked, and they see his shame.

16 And he gathered them together into a place called in the Hebrew tongue Armageddon.

SEVENTH VIAL — GREAT HAIL:

17 And the seventh angel poured out his vial into the air; and there came a great voice out of the temple of heaven, from the throne, saying, It is done.

18 And there were voices, and thunders, and lightnings; and there was a great earthquake, such as was not since men were upon the earth, so mighty an earthquake, and so great.

19 And the great city was divided into three parts, and the cities of the nations fell: and great Babylon came in remembrance before God, to give unto her the cup of the wine of the fierceness of his wrath.

20 And every island fled away, and the mountains were not found.

21 And there fell upon men a great hail out of heaven, every stone about the weight of a talent: and men blasphemed God because of the plague of the hail; for the plague thereof was exceeding great.

SIXTH EGYPTIAN PLAGUE
Ex.9:8-12

8 ¶ And the LORD said unto Moses and unto Aaron, Take to you handfuls of ashes of the furnace, and let Moses sprinkle it toward the heaven in the sight of Pharaoh.

9 And it shall become small dust in all the land of Egypt, and shall be a boil breaking forth with blains upon man, and upon beast, throughout all the land of Egypt.

10 And they took ashes of the furnace, and stood before Pharaoh; and Moses sprinkled it up toward heaven; and it became a boil breaking forth with blains upon man, and upon beast.

11 And the magicians could not stand before Moses because of the boils; for the boil was upon the magicians, and upon all the Egyptians.

12 And the LORD hardened the heart of Pharaoh, and he hearkened not unto them; as the LORD had spoken unto Moses.

FIRST EGYPTIAN PLAGUE
Ex.7:19-21

19 ¶ And the LORD spake unto Moses, Say unto Aaron, Take thy rod, and stretch out thine hand upon the waters of Egypt, upon their streams, upon their rivers, and upon their ponds, and upon all their pools of water, that they may become blood; and that there may be blood throughout all the land of Egypt, both in vessels of wood, and in vessels of stone.

20 And Moses and Aaron did so, as the LORD commanded; and he lifted up the rod, and smote the waters that were in the river, in the sight of Pharaoh, and in the sight of his servants; and all the waters that were in the river were turned to blood.

21 And the fish that was in the river died; and the river stank, and the Egyptians could not drink of the water of the river; and there was blood throughout all the land of Egypt.

NINTH EGYPTIAN PLAGUE
Ex.10:21-23

21 ¶ And the LORD said unto Moses, Stretch out thine hand toward heaven, that there may be darkness over the land of Egypt, even darkness which may be felt.

22 And Moses stretched forth his hand toward heaven; and there was a thick darkness in all the land of Egypt, three days:

23 They saw not one another, neither rose any from his place for three days: but all the children of Israel had light in their dwellings.

SEVENTH EGYPTIAN PLAGUE
Ex.9:22-26

22 ¶ And the LORD said unto Moses, Stretch forth thine hand toward heaven, that there may be hail in all the land of Egypt, upon man, and upon beast, and upon every herb of the field, throughout the land of Egypt.

23 And Moses stretched forth his rod toward heaven: and the LORD sent thunder and hail, and the fire ran along upon the ground; and the LORD rained hail upon the land of Egypt.

24 So there was hail, and fire mingled with the hail, very grievous, such as there was none like it in all the land of Egypt since it became a nation.

25 And the hail smote throughout all the land of Egypt all that was in the field, both man and beast; and the hail smote every herb of the field, and brake every tree of the field.

26 Only in the land of Goshen, where the children of Israel were, was there no hail.

SECOND VIAL.
(Blood On the Sea.)
Rev. 16: 3.

"And the 'Second Angel' poured out his Vial **upon the sea:** and it became **as the blood of a dead man:** and **every living soul died in the sea.**"

We saw that at the sounding of the "Second Trumpet," that **the third part** of the sea became blood, and the third part of the creatures which were in the sea, and had life, died; and the third part of the ships were destroyed. Rev. 8:8-9. Here the whole of the sea **is** affected. This may mean only the Sea of Galilee, or the Mediterranean Sea, and not the oceans of the earth. It does not follow that this blood is that of men. It may be only of the living creatures that are in the sea. The Revised Version translates (in the margin) the word "soul" as the "soul of life," and we know that the word "soul" implies "self conscious life," and this is common to all animal life. The blood is certainly not the blood of sailors and marines caused by some great naval battle. The inference is that the creatures in the sea died, not because of the loss of their own blood, but because the waters of the sea became **"AS the blood of a dead man"** —that is, corrupt.

THIRD VIAL.
(Blood On the Rivers.)
Rev. 16:4-7.

"And the 'Third Angel' poured out his Vial upon the **rivers** and **fountains of waters;** and they **BECAME BLOOD.** And I heard the 'Angel of the Waters' say, Thou art righteous, O Lord, which art, and wast, and shalt be, because Thou hast judged thus. For they have shed the blood of saints and prophets, and Thou hast given them **BLOOD TO DRINK;** for they are worthy. And I heard another out of the Altar say, Even so, Lord God Almighty, true and righteous are Thy Judgments."

This is a repetition of the "First Egyptian Plague." Ex. 7: 19-24. When the waters of Egypt were turned into blood all the fish died, but here nothing is said about the inhabitants of the rivers and ponds. Then John heard the "Angel of the Waters" say— "Thou art righteous, O Lord, which art, and wast, and shall be, because Thou hast judged thus. For they have shed the blood of saints and prophets, and Thou hast given them **BLOOD TO DRINK;** for they are worthy," or deserve it. As a confirmation of the saying of the "Angel of the Waters," John heard another voice come from the Altar, saying, "Even so, Lord God Almighty, true and righteous are Thy Judgments." Those will be awful times when there will be nothing but **BLOOD** to quench the thirst. The expression "Angel of the Waters," reveals the fact that even certain divisions of nature are controlled by angels.

FOURTH VIAL.
(Great Heat.)
Rev. 16:8-9.

"And the 'Fourth Angel' poured out his Vial **UPON THE SUN**; and power was given unto him (the Sun) to **scorch men with fire.** And men were **scorched with GREAT HEAT,** and **blasphemed the name of God,** which hath power over these Plagues; and they repented not to give Him glory."

Under the "Fourth Trumpet" the **third part** of the Sun was smitten, and the **third part** of the Moon and of the Stars; so as the **third part of them was darkened,** and the day shone not for a **third part** of it, and the night likewise. Rev. 8:12. But it was only the light that was diminished, nothing is said about the **heat** of the Sun. This "Fourth Vial" is therefore not a recurrence of the "Fourth Trumpet." Here the **heat** of the Sun is intensified, and so great is the heat that men are **scorched** by it. How this will be done it is useless to conjecture. It is the time spoken of by Malachi. "Behold, the day cometh that shall **BURN AS AN OVEN**; and all the proud, yea, and all that do wickedly, shall be stubble; and the day that cometh shall burn them up, saith the Lord of Hosts, that it shall leave them neither root nor branch"; and the time is located as just before the **"SUN OF RIGHTEOUSNESS"** shall arise with healing in His wings. Mal. 4:1-2. The effect of this Plague will be not to make men repent, but to cause them to **blaspheme the name of God.** Blessed will those people be who do not live to see that day.

FIFTH VIAL.
(Darkness.)
Rev. 16:10-11.

"And the 'Fifth Angel' poured out his Vial upon the **SEAT** (Throne) **OF THE BEAST:** and his Kingdom was **full of darkness;** and they **GNAWED THEIR TONGUES FOR PAIN,** and **blasphemed the God of Heaven** because of their 'PAINS' and their 'SORES,' and repented not of their deeds."

Here we have a repetition of the "Ninth Egyptian Plague," that of **DARKNESS.** Ex. 10:21-23. This is the "day" spoken of by Joel. "A day of **darkness** and of **gloominess,** a day of **clouds** and of **thick darkness.**" Joel 2:1-2. Christ speaks of it in Mark 13:24, as the time when "the Sun shall be darkened, and the Moon shall not give her light."

Notice that this Plague immediately follows the Plague of "Scorching Heat," as if God in mercy would hide the Sun whose rays had been so hard to bear. The effect of the darkness was to make men **gnaw their tongues for PAIN** and for their **SORES,** showing that these Plagues overlapped each other, or followed in such rapid order that they were not over the sufferings of one before they were suffering from another, and that they were limited to a short period of a few months, and not distributed over a period of years as the Historical School of interpretation claims.

The notable feature is, that their sufferings brought no repentance, but caused them to blaspheme the God of Heaven. Some talk of conversion in Hell, and of the ultimate restoration of the wicked, but it is not revealed here. If Hell's torments will cause men to repent, why do not the torments of those under these plagues lead to repentance? No, it only causes them to blaspheme the more, and while sin and impenitence last, Hell lasts. This Plague extends over the whole Kingdom of the Beast.

SIXTH VIAL.
(The Euphrates Dried Up.)
Rev. 16: 12.

"And the 'Sixth Angel' poured out his Vial upon the **GREAT RIVER EUPHRATES;** and the water thereof was **DRIED UP,** that the way of the '**Kings of the East**' might be prepared."

This means the literal river Euphrates. The other Plagues will be real, and why does not this mean the drying up of the real Euphrates River. The opening up of a dry passage through the Red Sea that the Children of Israel might escape from Egypt, and the parting of the waters of the River Jordan that they might pass over into the Land of Canaan, are facts of history, why then shall not the River Euphrates be dried up that the Kings of the East and their armies may cross over and assemble for the Battle of Armageddon? The prophecy in Isa. 11: 15-16, where "the Lord shall utterly destroy the tongue of the Egyptian Sea (Red Sea), and . . . shake His hand over the River (Euphrates) and smite its seven streams, so men can go over 'DRY SHOD'," refers to this time. The Kings shall journey East from Africa, and West from Asia that they may meet in Palestine for the "Battle of Armageddon." The drying up of the Euphrates will serve a twofold purpose. It will permit the remnant of Israel from Assyria to return, and also allow the nations of the far East to be gathered for the "Judgment of Nations." Matt. 25: 31-46.

THE INTERVAL BETWEEN THE "SIXTH" AND "SEVENTH" VIALS.

THREE UNCLEAN SPIRITS.
Rev. 16: 13-16.

"And I saw **THREE UNCLEAN SPIRITS like frogs** come out of the mouth of the 'Dragon,' and out of the mouth of the 'Beast,' and out of the mouth of the 'False Prophet.' For they are the '**SPIRITS OF DEVILS**' (Demons), working miracles, which go forth unto the 'Kings of the Earth' and of the **whole world,** to gather them to the Battle of that 'Great Day of God Almighty' (Armageddon). Behold I come as a thief. Blessed is he that watcheth, and keepeth his garments, lest he walk naked, and they see his shame. And he (they R. V.) gathered them together into a place called in the Hebrew tongue Armageddon." (Har-Mageddon R. V.)

REV. 16:13-16

Here we are told how the "Kings of the Earth" and their armies are to be gathered for the "Battle of Armageddon." **"THREE UNCLEAN SPIRITS"** like frogs, John does not say they were frogs, will come one out of the mouth of the "Dragon," one out of the mouth of the "Beast," and one out of the mouth of the "False Prophet." That they are not real frogs is clear from their miracle working power. They are the **"SPIRITS OF DEMONS,"** working miracles, which go forth unto the "Kings of the Earth," and of the whole world, to gather them to the "Battle of that Great Day of God Almighty." They are the **"Seducing Spirits"** who go forth preaching the **"DOCTRINE OF DEVILS"** in the "latter times" of whom Paul warns Timothy. 1. Tim. 4:1. They are sent out by the **"SATANIC TRINITY,"** the "Dragon," the "Beast," and the "False Prophet," on a **miracle working ministry.**

They are **"frog-like"** in that they come forth out of the pestiferous quagmires of darkness, do their devilish work in the evening shadows of "Man's Day," and creep, and croak, and defile, and fill the ears of the nations with their noisy demonstrations, until they set the kings and armies of the nations in enthusiastic commotion and movement toward the Holy Land to crush out the effort to establish the Kingdom of Christ on earth. We have an illustration of their method and purpose in the story of the destruction of King Ahab. 1. Kings 22:20-38.

The power of a delusive and enthusiastic sentiment, however engendered, to lead to destruction great hosts of men is seen in the Crusades to recover the Holy Sepulchre at Jerusalem. If a religious fanatacism could, at 9 different times, cause hundreds of thousands of religious devotees to undergo unspeakable hardships for a religious purpose, what will not the **miracle working wonders** of the **"FROG-LIKE DEMONS"** of the last days of this Dispensation not be able to do in arousing whole nations, and creating vast armies to march in all directions from all countries, headed by their Kings, for the purpose of preventing the establishment of the Kingdom of the King of Kings in His own Land of Palestine?

SEVENTH VIAL.
(Great Hail.)
Rev. 16:17-21.

"And the 'Seventh Angel' poured out his Vial **INTO THE AIR:** and there came a great voice out of the Temple of Heaven, from the Throne, saying—**IT IS DONE.** And there were **VOICES,** and **THUNDERS,** and **LIGHTNINGS;** and there was a **GREAT EARTHQUAKE,** such as was not since men were upon the earth, so mighty an earthquake, and so great. And the Great City (Jerusalem) was divided into three parts, and the cities of the nations fell, and Great Babylon came in remembrance before God, to give unto her the cup of the wine of the fierceness of His wrath. And **every island fled away, and the mountains were not found** (they will be leveled). And there fell upon men a **GREAT HAIL** out of heaven, **every stone about the weight of a talent:** and men blasphemed God because of the Plague of the Hail; for the Plague thereof was exceeding great."

It is worthy of note that at the breaking of the "Seventh **SEAL,"** and the sounding of the "Seventh **TRUMPET,"** and the pouring out of the "Seventh **VIAL,"** that the same things occur. That is, **voices** and **thunderings** are heard, **great lightning** is seen, and there is a **GREAT EARTHQUAKE.** And at the sounding of the "Seventh **TRUMPET,"** and the pouring out of the "Seventh **VIAL"** there is a **GREAT HAIL STORM.** This only confirms what has been already stated that the **"SEVENTH SEAL"** includes the 'Trumpets' and "Vials," and that the **"SEVENTH TRUMPET"** includes the "Vials," and that what happens during the "Seventh **SEAL,"** and the "Seventh **TRUMPET,"** and the "Seventh **VIAL,"** all refers to the same period, the **"END OF THE WEEK."** In other words, the opening of the "Seventh **SEAL"** reveals the events that are about to happen; the blast of the "Seventh **TRUMPET"** announces the events as forth-coming, and the outpouring of the "Seventh **VIAL"** executes them.

When the "Seventh **SEAL"** was broken there was **"SILENCE"** in Heaven, but when the "Seventh **TRUMPET"** sounded, and the "Seventh **VIAL"** was poured out there were **"GREAT VOICES"** in Heaven. The "Great Voice" at the pouring out of the "Seventh Vial" was from the Throne, and cried—**"IT IS DONE."** When Christ expired on the Cross He cried—**"IT IS FINISHED,"** that is, the way and plan of Salvation was complete, and this voice from the Throne that cries "IT IS DONE" may be His voice, announcing that the pouring out of the "Seventh Vial" finishes the wrath of God.

The "Great Earthquake" that follows will be the greatest that this world has ever seen. It is foretold in Zech. 14:4-5. So great will it be, that it will level the mountains, and destroy islands, and so change the contour and shape of the Land of Palestine and the surrounding countries and seas, as to make new maps of that part of the world necessary; and it will raise the Dead Sea so that its waters shall flow again into the Red Sea. Ez. 47:1-12. It will divide the "Great City" (Jerusalem) into 3 parts, and the cities of the Nations (the "Ten Federated Nations"), and **"GREAT BABY-**

LON," whose destruction is described in chapter eighteen, will be destroyed in that "Great Earthquake." This reference to the "City of Babylon" is further incidental proof that the City of Babylon is to be rebuilt. Among the cities destroyed in that Earthquake will be Rome, Naples, London, Paris, and Constantinople.

At that time there will fall upon men a **"GREAT HAIL."** Each stone will weigh about a Talent, or 100 pounds. Here we have a repetition of the **"SEVENTH EGYPTIAN PLAGUE."** Ex. 9: 13-35. Hail has been one of God's engines of destruction. He used it to discomfit the enemies of Israel at Beth-horon in the days of Joshua. Josh. 10:11. The "Law" required that the "Blasphemer" should be **"STONED TO DEATH"** (Lev. 24:16), and here these Blasphemers of the "End Time" shall be **STONED FROM HEAVEN.**

It must not be forgotten that the "Seventh Vial" covers the whole period from the time the "Seventh Angel" pours out its contents until Christ returns to the Mount of Olives. For the earthquake that splits the Mount of Olives, upheaves the land of Palestine, levels mountains, submerges islands, and destroys the cities of the Nations, along with the City of Babylon, is caused by the touch of Christ's feet on the Mount of Olives at the Revelation stage of His Second Coming (Zech. 14:4), and the **"Great Hail"** in all probability will not fall until the time comes in the crisis of the Battle of Armageddon for the destruction of the Allied armies of Antichrist. Hailstones will be the missiles used by the Armies of Heaven.

In Rev. 19:15, we are told that out of the mouth of Christ, at His return, will go a **"SHARP SWORD,"** that with it He should smite the nations, and in 2 Thess. 2:8, we are told that Antichrist (that **WICKED**), shall be consumed by the **"SPIRIT OF THE LORD'S MOUTH."** Whether we take these statements as literal or not, it is clear that they stand for some **supernatural means of destruction,** and refer more to the followers of Antichrist, than to Antichrist himself, for he personally is not to be destroyed, but is to be cast **ALIVE** into the "Lake of Fire." Rev. 19:20.

As the pouring out of the "Seventh Vial" finishes the "Wrath of God," it is in harmony with the purposes of the Book of Revelation to foretell at this point what will then happen to the enemies of God. These we will now examine under the heading the "Seven Dooms."

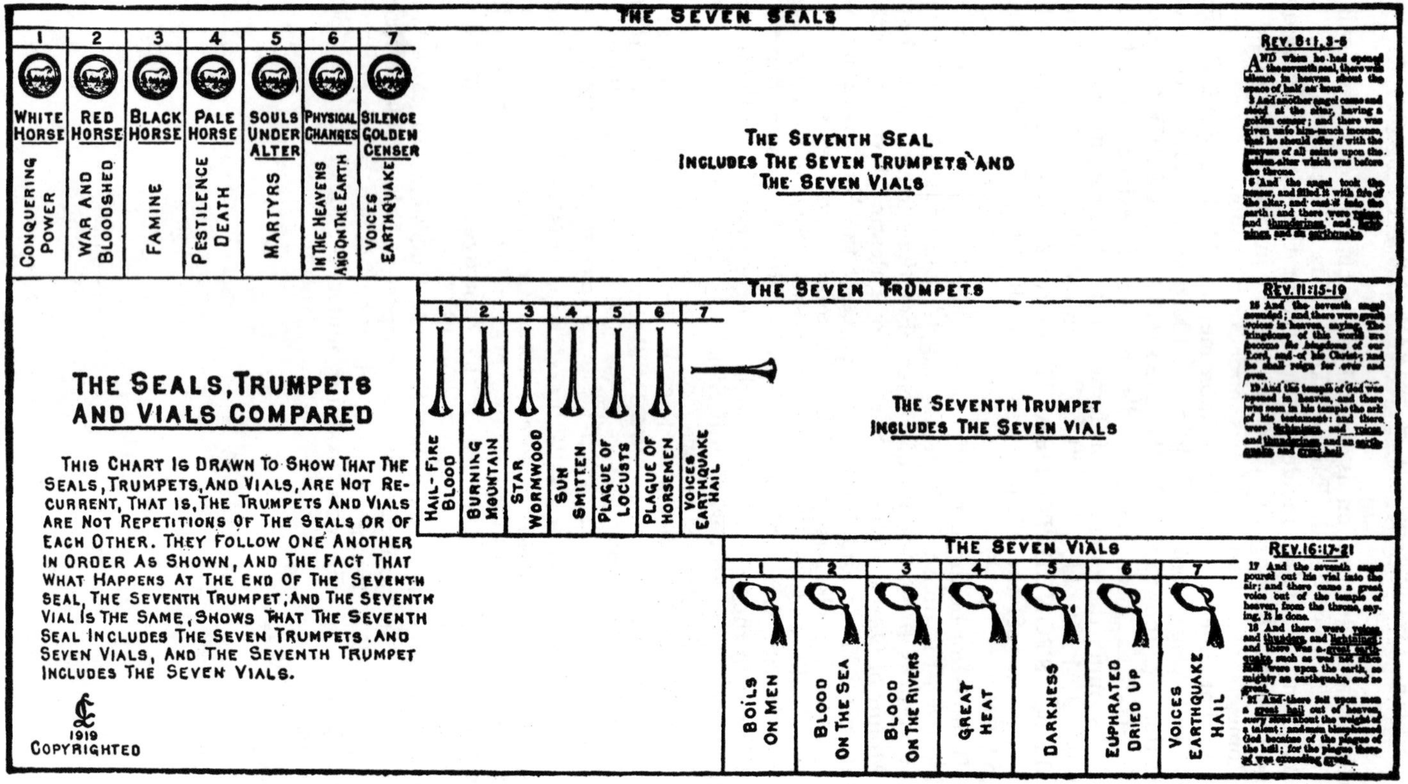
THE SEVEN SEALS
1 White Horse — Conquering Power
2 Red Horse — War and Bloodshed
3 Black Horse — Famine
4 Pale Horse — Pestilence Death
5 Souls Under Alter — Martyrs
6 Physical Changes — In The Heavens And On The Earth
7 Silence Golden Censer — Voices Earthquake
The Seventh Seal Includes The Seven Trumpets And The Seven Vials
Rev. 8:1, 3-5
THE SEVEN TRUMPETS
1 Hail-Fire Blood
2 Burning Mountain
3 Star Wormwood
4 Sun Smitten
5 Plague Of Locusts
6 Plague Of Horsemen
7 Voices Earthquake Hail
The Seventh Trumpet Includes The Seven Vials
Rev. 11:15-19
THE SEVEN VIALS
1 Boils On Men
2 Blood On The Sea
3 Blood On The Rivers
4 Great Heat
5 Darkness
6 Euphrated Dried Up
7 Voices Earthquake Hail
Rev. 16:17-21
THE SEALS, TRUMPETS AND VIALS COMPARED
This Chart Is Drawn To Show That The Seals, Trumpets, And Vials, Are Not Recurrent, That Is, The Trumpets And Vials Are Not Repetitions Of The Seals Or Of Each Other. They Follow One Another In Order As Shown, And The Fact That What Happens At The End Of The Seventh Seal, The Seventh Trumpet, And The Seventh Vial Is The Same, Shows That The Seventh Seal Includes The Seven Trumpets And Seven Vials, And The Seventh Trumpet Includes The Seven Vials.
1919
Copyrighted

The Seven Dooms.

FIRST DOOM.

ECCLESIASTICAL BABYLON.
"MYSTERY
BABYLON THE GREAT."
Rev. 17: 1-18.

"And there came one of the 'Seven Angels' which had the 'Seven Vials,' and talked with me, saying unto me, Come hither: I will shew unto thee the Judgment of the 'GREAT WHORE' that sitteth upon many waters; with whom the kings of the earth have committed fornication, and the inhabitants of the earth have been made drunk with the wine of her fornication. So he carried me away in the spirit into the wilderness; and I saw a 'WOMAN' sit upon a 'SCARLET COLORED BEAST,' full of names of blasphemy, having 'SEVEN HEADS' and 'TEN HORNS.' And the 'WOMAN' was arrayed in purple and scarlet color, and decked with gold and precious stones and pearls, having a 'GOLDEN CUP' in her hand full of abominations and filthiness of her fornication: and upon her forehead was a name written

MYSTERY,
BABYLON THE GREAT,
THE MOTHER OF HARLOTS AND
ABOMINATIONS OF THE EARTH.

And I saw the 'WOMAN' drunken with the blood of the saints, and with the blood of the martyrs of Jesus; and when I saw her, I wondered with great admiration. And the Angel said unto me, Wherefore didst thou marvel? I will tell thee the **MYSTERY** of the 'WOMAN,' and of the BEAST that carrieth her, which hath the SEVEN HEADS and TEN HORNS. The BEAST that thou sawest was, and is not; and shall ascend out of the BOTTOMLESS PIT, and go into PERDITION: and they that dwell on the earth shall wonder, whose names were not written in the 'Book of Life' from the foundation of the world, when they behold the **BEAST** that was, and is not, and yet is. And here is the mind which hath wisdom. The **SEVEN HEADS** are seven mountains, on which the '**WOMAN**' sitteth. And there (they, the mountains R. V.) are **SEVEN KINGS: five are fallen, and one is, and the other is not yet come:** and when he cometh, he must continue a short space. And the **BEAST** that was, and is not, even he is the **EIGHTH,** and is **OF THE SEVENTH,** and goeth into Perdition. And the **TEN HORNS** which thou sawest are **TEN KINGS,** which have received no kingdoms as yet; but receive power as kings one hour with the **BEAST.** These have one mind, and shall give their power and strength unto the **BEAST.** These shall make war with the **LAMB,** and the **LAMB** shall overcome them: for he is **LORD OF LORDS,** and **KING OF KINGS:** and they that are with Him are called, and chosen, and faithful. And he saith unto me, the waters which thou sawest, where the **WHORE** sitteth, are peoples, and multitudes, and nations, and tongues. And the **TEN HORNS** which thou sawest upon the **BEAST,** these shall hate the **WHORE,** and shall make her desolate and naked, and shall eat her flesh, and burn her with fire. For God hath put in their hearts to fulfil His will, and to agree, and give their kingdom unto the **BEAST,** until the words of God shall be fulfilled. And the **WOMAN** which thou sawest is that great city, which reigneth over the kings of the earth."

That the ancient city of Babylon restored is to play an important part in the startling events of the last days of this Dispensation, is very clear. This is seen from what is said of it in the seventeenth and eighteenth chapters of the Book of Revelation. At first sight the two chapters, which contain some things in common, are difficult to reconcile, but when we get the "Key" the reconciliation is easy.

The seventeenth chapter speaks of a "**Woman,**" and this "**Woman**" is called

"**MYSTERY,**
Babylon the Great,
The Mother of Harlots
And
Abominations of the Earth."

The eighteenth chapter speaks of a "City," a literal city, called "Babylon the Great." That the "**Woman**" and the "**City**" do not symbolize the same thing is clear, for what is said of the "Woman" does not apply to a city, and what is said of the "**City**" does not apply to a woman. The "**Woman**" is destroyed by the "**Ten Kings,**" while the "Kings of the Earth" in the next chapter, "bewail and lament" the destruction of the "City," which is not destroyed by them, but by a mighty earthquake and fire. Again the "**Woman**" is destroyed **Three and a Half Years BEFORE THE CITY**; and the fact that the first verse of chapter eighteen says—"after these things," that is after the destruction of the "**Woman,**" what happens to the "**City**" occurs, shows that the "Woman" and the "City" are not one and the same. The "**Woman's**" name is—

"**MYSTERY, Babylon the Great.**"

"**Mystery!**" Where have we heard that word before, and in what connection? Paul calls the Church a "Mystery" because it was not known to the Old Testament Patriarchs and Prophets. Eph. 3: 1-21.

That Christ was to have a "Bride" was first revealed to Paul (Eph. 5:23-32), and the "Mystery" that Antichrist is to have a "bride" was first revealed to John on the Isle of Patmos. The name of Antichrist's "bride" is "Babylon the Great." Some one may ask why give to a "bride" the name of a "City"? The answer is that it is not unusual in the Scriptures. When the same angel that showed John in this chapter "Mystery, Babylon the Great," came to him in chapter 21:9-10 and said—"Come hither, I will shew thee the Bride—'The Lamb's Wife'," he showed John, instead of a woman, that great City, the "Holy Jerusalem" descending out of Heaven from God. Here we see that a "city" is called a "bride" because its inhabitants, and not the city itself, are the bride. "Mystery, Babylon the Great," the "bride" of Antichrist, then, is not a literal city, but a "System," a religious and apostate "System." As the Church, the Bride of Christ, is composed of regenerated followers of Christ, so "Mystery, Babylon the Great," the bride of Antichrist, will be composed of the followers of all **False Religions.**

The river Euphrates, on which the city of Babylon was built, was one of the four branches into which the river that flowed through the Garden of Eden was divided, and Satan doubtless chose the site of Babylon as his headquarters from which to sally forth to tempt Adam and Eve. It was doubtless here that the Antediluvian Apostasy had its source that ended in the Flood. To this centre the "forces of Evil" gravitated after the Flood, and **"Babel"** was the result. This was the origin of nations, but the nations were not scattered abroad over the earth until Satan had implanted in them the **"Virus"** of a doctrine that has been the **source** of every false religion the world has ever known.

Babel, or Babylon, was built by Nimrod. Gen. 10:8-10. It was the seat of the first great Apostasy. Here the **"Babylonian Cult"** was invented. A system claiming to possess the highest wisdom and to reveal the divinest secrets. Before a member could be initiated he had to "confess" to the Priest. The Priest then had him in his power. This is the secret of the power of the Priests of the Roman Catholic Church today.

Once admitted into this order men were no longer Babylonians, Assyrians, or Egyptians, but members of a

Mystical Brotherhood,

over whom was placed a Pontiff or "High Priest," whose word was law. The city of Babylon continued to be the seat of Satan until the fall of the Babylonian and Medo-Persian Empires, when he shifted his Capital to Pergamos in Asia Minor, where it was in John's day. Rev. 2:12, 13.

When Attalus, the Pontiff and King of Pergamos, died in B. C. 133, he bequeathed the Headship of the "Babylonian Priesthood" to Rome. When the Etruscans came to Italy from Lydia (the region of Pergamos), they brought with them the Babylonian religion and rites. They set up a Pontiff who was head of the Priesthood. Later the Romans accepted this Pontiff as their civil ruler. Julius Caesar was made Pontiff of the Etruscan Order in B. C. 74. In B. C. 63 he was made "Supreme Pontiff" of the "Babylonian Order," thus becoming heir to the rights and titles of Attalus, Pontiff of Pergamos, who had made Rome his heir by will. Thus the first Roman Emperor became the Head of the "Babylonian Priesthood," and Rome the successor of Babylon. The Emperors of Rome continued to exercise the office of "Supreme Pontiff" until A. D. 376, when the Emperor Gratian, for Christian reasons, refused it. The Bishop of the Church at Rome, Damasus, was elected to the position. He had been Bishop 12 years, having been made Bishop in A. D. 366, through the influence of the monks of Mt. Carmel, a college of Babylonian religion originally founded by the priests of Jezebel. So in A. D. 378 the Head of the "Babylonian Order" became the Ruler of the "Roman Church." Thus Satan united

Rome and Babylon
In One Religious System.

Soon after Damasus was made "supreme Pontiff" the "rites" of Babylon began to come to the front. The worship of the Virgin Mary was set up in A. D. 381. All the outstanding festivals of the Roman Catholic Church are of Babylonian origin. Easter is not a Christian name. It means "Ishtar," one of the titles of the Babylonian Queen of Heaven, whose worship by the Children of Israel was such an abomination in the sight of God. The decree for the observance of Easter and Lent was given in A. D. 519. The "Rosary" is of Pagan origin. There is no warrant in the Word of God for the use of the "Sign of the Cross." It had its origin in the mystic "Tau" of the Chaldeans and Egyptians. It came from the letter "T," the initial name of "Tammuz," and was used in the "Babylonian Mysteries" for the same magic purposes as the Romish church now employs it.   Celibacy, the Tonsure, and the Order of Monks and Nuns, have no warrant or authority from Scripture. The Nuns are nothing more than an imitation of the "Vestal Virgins" of Pagan Rome.

As to the word "Mystery," the Papal Church has always shrouded herself in mystery. The mystery of "Baptismal Regeneration"; the mystery of "Miracle and Magic" whereby the simple memorials of the Lord's Supper are changed by the mysterious word "Transubstantiation," from simple bread and wine into the literal Body and Blood of Christ; the mystery of the "Holy Water"; the mystery of "Lights on the Altar," the "Mystery Plays," and other superstitious rites and ceremonies mumbled in a language that tends to mystery, and tends to confusion which is the meaning of the word Babylon.

All this was a "Mystery" in John's day, because the "Papal Church" had not as yet developed; though the "Mystery of Iniquity" was already at work (2. Thess. 2:7), but it is no longer a "Mystery" for it is now easy to identify the "Woman"—"Mystery, Babylon the Great," which John described, as the "Papal Church."

In Rev. 17:4 we read that the "Woman" "was arrayed in purple and scarlet color, and decked with gold and precious stones and pearls, having a 'Golden Cup' in her hand full of abominations and filthiness of her fornications."

Now who does not know that **scarlet** and **purple** are the **colors** of the Papacy? Of the different articles of attire specified for the Pope to wear when he is installed into office **five** are **scarlet**. A vest covered with **pearls**, and a mitre, adorned with **gold and precious stones** was also to be worn. How completely this answers the description of the Woman's dress as she sits upon the **Scarlet Colored Beast.**

We are also told that the Woman was "**drunken** with the **blood of the Saints,** and with the **blood of the Martyrs of Jesus.**" While this refers more particularly to the martyrs of the time of Antichrist, yet who does not know, who has studied the history of the Christian Church for the past nineteen centuries, that this is true of the Papal Church during those centuries? One has only to read the history of the persecutions of the early Christians and more particularly the story of the "Inquisition" in Papal lands, to see that the Papal Church has been "drunk" with the **blood of the Saints.**

The fact that the Woman sits on a "Scarlet Colored Beast" reveals the fact that at that time the Beast (Antichrist) will support the Woman in her ecclesiastical pretensions, or in other words, the Woman, as a "State Church," will control and rule the State, and her long dream of world-wide Ecclesiastical Supremacy will at last be realized, for John tells us that "the waters which thou sawest, where the '**Whore**' sitteth, are **Peoples,** and **Multitudes,** and **Nations** and **Tongues.**" That means that after the "**True Church**" (the Bride of Christ) is taken out of the world the "**False**" or "**Papal Church**" (the bride of Antichrist) will remain, and the professing body of Christians (having the "form of Godliness without the power") left behind. will largely enter the Papal Church, and it will become the **Universal Church.** But this will continue for only a short time for the "Ten Kings" of the "Federated Kingdom," finding their power curtailed by the "Papal System" will "hate The Whore," and strip her of her gorgeous apparel, confiscate her wealth (eat her flesh) and burn her churches and cathedrals with fire. Rev. 17: 16.

This will occur at the time the worship of the Beast is set up, for Antichrist in his jealous hate will not permit any worship that does not centre in himself.

The Beast upon which the Woman sits is introduced to show from whom the Woman (the Papal Church) gets her power and support after the True Church has been "caught out," and also to show that the Beast (Antichrist) and the Woman (the Papal Church) are not one and the same, but separate. Therefore the Papacy is not Antichrist. For a description of the "Scarlet Colored Beast" see the description of the "Beast out of the Sea" of chapter 13: 1-10.

From this foreview of the Papacy we see that the Papal Church is not a **dying** "System." That she is to be revived and become a "**Universal Church,**" and in doing so is to commit fornication with the kings of the earth, and that she shall again be "drunk with the blood" of the martyrs of the Tribulation Period. The meaning of chapter seventeen of the Book of Revelation is no longer a Mystery; the prophetic portrait of the Woman there given corresponds too closely with the history of the Papal Church to be a mere coincidence.

SECOND DOOM.
COMMERCIAL BABYLON.
Rev. 18:1-24.

"And after these things (the destruction of "Mystical Baby-lon") I saw ANOTHER ANGEL come down from Heaven, having great power; and the earth was lightened with his glory. And he cried mightily with a strong voice, saying BABYLON THE GREAT IS FALLEN, IS FALLEN, and is become the habitation of devils, and the hold of every foul spirit, and a cage of every unclean and hateful bird. For all nations have drunk of the wine of the wrath of her fornication, and the kings of the earth have committed fornication with her, and the merchants of the earth are waxed rich through the abundance of her delicacies. And I heard another voice from Heaven, saying, COME OUT OF HER, MY PEOPLE, THAT YE BE NOT PARTAKERS OF HER SINS, AND THAT YE RECEIVE NOT OF HER PLAGUES. For her sins have reached unto Heaven, and God hath remembered her iniquities. Reward her even as she re-warded you, and double unto her double according to her works: in the cup which she hath filled fill to her double. How much she hath glorified herself and lived deliciously. So much tor-ment and sorrow give her: for she saith in her heart, I sit a Queen, and am no widow, and shall see no sorrow. Therefore shall her Plagues come in one day, death, and mourning, and famine; and she shall be utterly BURNED WITH FIRE: for strong is the Lord God who judgeth her. And the kings of the earth, who have committed fornication and lived deliciously with her, shall bewail her, and lament for her, when they shall see the smoke of her burning. Standing afar off for the fear of her torment, saying, "Alas, alas, that Great City Babylon, that Mighty City! for in ONE HOUR is thy Judgment come. And the mer-chants of the earth shall weep and mourn over her; for no man buyeth their merchandise any more: the merchandise of gold and silver, and precious stones, and of pearls, and fine linen, and pur-ple, and silk, and scarlet, and all-thyme wood, and all manner vessels of most precious wood, and of brass, and iron, and mar-ble, and cinnamon, and odors, and ointments, and frankincense, and wine, and oil, and fine flour, and wheat, and beasts, and sheep, and horses, and chariots, and slaves, and SOULS OF MEN. And the fruits that thy soul lusted after are departed from thee, and all things which were dainty and goodly are de-parted from thee, and thou shalt find them no more at all. The merchants of these things, which were made rich by her, shall stand afar off for the fear of her torment, weeping and wailing, and saying, Alas, alas, that GREAT CITY, that was clothed in fine linen, and purple, and scarlet, and decked with gold, and precious stones, and pearls! For in ONE HOUR so great riches is come to nought. And every shipmaster, and all the company in ships (travellers), and sailors, and as many as trade by sea, stood afar off, and cried (wept) when they saw the smoke of her burning, saying What CITY is like unto this Great CITY. And they cast dust on their heads, and cried, weeping and wailing, saying, Alas, alas, that GREAT CITY, wherein were made rich all that had ships in the sea by reason of her costliness! for in ONE HOUR is she made desolate. Rejoice over her, thou Heaven, and ye Holy Apostles, and Prophets; for God hath avenged you on her. And a Mighty Angel took up a STONE like a GREAT MILLSTONE, and cast it into the sea, saying, THUS WITH VIOLENCE SHALL THAT GREAT CITY BABYLON BE THROWN DOWN, AND SHALL BE FOUND NO MORE AT ALL. And the voice of Harpers, and

Musicians, and of **Pipers** and **Trumpeters,** shall be heard no more at all in thee; and no **craftsman,** of whatsoever craft he be, shall be found any more in thee; and the **sound of a millstone** shall be heard no more at all in thee; and the **light of a candle** shall shine no more at all in thee; and the **voice of the bridegroom** and of the **bride** shall be heard no more at all in thee; for thy merchants were the great men of the earth; for by thy sorceries were all nations deceived. And in her was found the blood of Prophets, and of Saints, and of all that were slain upon the earth."

This chapter begins with the words "after these things." What things? The things recorded in the previous chapter, the **destruction of "Mystical Babylon."**

If "Mystical Babylon" was destroyed in the previous chapter then she cannot appear in this chapter, and the "City" here described must be a literal city called Babylon, and as there is no city of that name on the earth today, nor has been since the ancient city of Babylon was destroyed, it must refer to some future city of Babylon. That the two chapters refer to different things is further verified by the fact that they are announced by different angels. The events of chapter seventeen are announced by one of the "Vial" Angels, while those of the eighteenth are announced by "another" angel; probably the "Second Angel Messenger," who by way of anticipation, announced in chapter 14:8, the "Fall of Babylon," that is there called— **"That Great City."**

The ancient city of Babylon from the days of Nimrod (Gen. 10: 10), grew in size and importance century after century until it reached its greatest glory in the reign of Nebuchadnezzar B. C. 604-562. As described by Herodotus it was an exact square of 15 miles on a side, or 60 miles around, and was surrounded by a brick wall 87 feet thick, and 350 feet high, though probably that is a mistake, 100 feet being nearer the height. On the wall were 250 towers, and the top of the wall was wide enough to allow 6 chariots to drive abreast. Outside this wall was a vast ditch surrounding the city, kept filled with water from the river Euphrates; and inside the wall, and not far from it, was another wall, not much inferior, but narrower, extending around the city.

Twenty-five magnificent avenues, 150 feet wide, ran across the city from North to South, and the same number crossed them at right angles from East to West, making 676 great squares, each nearly three-fifths of a mile on a side, and the city was divided into two equal parts by the river Euphrates, that flowed diagonally through it, and whose banks, within the city, were walled up, and pierced with brazen gates, with steps leading down to the river. At the ends of the main avenues, on each side of the city, were gates, whose leaves were of brass, and that shone as they were opened or closed in the rising or setting sun, like "leaves of flame."

The Euphrates within the city was spanned by a bridge, at each end of which was a palace, and these palaces were connected by a subterranean passageway, or tube, underneath the bed of the river, in which at different points were located sumptuous banqueting rooms constructed entirely of brass.

Near one of these palaces stood the
"Tower of Bel,"

or Babel, consisting of 8 towers, each 75 feet high, rising one upon the other, with an outside winding stairway to its summit, which towers, with the Chapel on the top, made a height of 660 feet. This Chapel contained the most expensive furniture of any place of worship in the world. One golden image alone, 45 feet high, was valued at $17,500,000, and the whole of the sacred utensils were reckoned to be worth $200,000,000.

Babylon also contained one of the "Seven Wonders" of the world, the famous Hanging Gardens.

These Gardens were 400 feet square, and were raised in terraces one above the other to the height of 350 feet, and were reached by stairways 10 feet wide. The top of each terrace was covered with large stones, on which was laid a bed of rushes, then a thick layer of asphalt, next two courses of brick, cemented together, and finally plates of lead to prevent leakage; the whole was then covered with earth and planted with shrubbery and large trees. The whole had the appearance from a distance of a forest-covered mountain, which would be a remarkable sight in the level plain of the Euphrates. These Gardens were built by Nebuchadnezzar simply to please his wife, who came from the mountainous country of Media, and who was thus made contented with her surroundings. The rest of the city was, in its glory and magnificence, in keeping with these palaces, towers, and "Hanging Gardens." The character of its inhabitants and of its official life is seen in the description of "Belshazzar's Feast" in Dan. 5: 1-31.

Babylon was probably the most magnificent city the world has ever seen and its fall reveals what a city may become when it forsakes God and He sends His judgment upon it. It is so intimately connected with the history of God's people that the Scriptures have much to say about it. A large part of the Book of Daniel and of the prophecy of Jeremiah relate to it, and it is mentioned in 11 other books of the Old Testament, and in 4 of the New Testament. And that the Book of Revelation is a continuation of the Book of Daniel is further proven by the fact that the city of Babylon is again spoken of in it, and its prominence in the affairs of the world at the "End Time" disclosed, and its final destruction foretold.

THE CITY OF BABYLON TO BE REBUILT.

That the ancient city of Babylon was destroyed there can be no question, but when we affirm that it is to be rebuilt and again destroyed we are met with two objections.

1. That all the Old Testament prophecies in reference to its destruction have been literally fulfilled, and that it cannot be rebuilt.

2. As there is no city of Babylon now in existence the references in the Book of Revelation to the destruction of such a city must be symbolical and not refer to a literal city.

Let us take up the first objection. For a description of Babylon and her destruction we must turn to Isaiah, chapters 13 and 14, and Jeremiah, chapters 50 and 51. In these two prophecies we find much that has not as yet been fulfilled in regard to the city of Babylon.

The city of Babylon was captured in B. C. 541 by Cyrus, who was mentioned "by name" in prophecy 125 years before he was born. Isa. 44:28; 45:4, B. C. 712. So quietly and quickly was the city taken on the night of Belshazzar's Feast by draining the river that flowed through the city, and entering by the river bed, and the gates that surmounted its banks, that the Babylonian guards had forgotten to lock that night, that some of the inhabitants did not know until the "third" day that the king had been slain and the city taken. There was no destruction of the city at that time.

Some years after it revolted against Darius Hystaspis, and after a fruitless siege of nearly 20 months was taken by strategy. This was in B. C. 516. About B. C. 478 Xerxes, on his return from Greece plundered and injured, if he did not destroy, the great "Temple of Bel."

In B. C. 331 Alexander the Great approached the city which was then so powerful and flourishing that he made preparation for bringing all his forces into action in case it should offer resistance, but the citizens threw open the gates and received him with acclamations. After sacrificing to "Bel," he gave out that he would rebuild the vast Temple of that god, and for weeks he kept 10,000 men employed in clearing away the ruins from the foundations, doubtless intending to revive the glory of Babylon and make it his capital, when his purpose was defeated by his sudden death of marsh-fever and intemperance in his thirty-third year.

During the subsequent wars of his generals Babylon suffered much and finally came under the power of Seleucus, who, prompted by ambition to build a Capital for himself, founded Seleucia in its neighborhood about B. C. 293. This rival city gradually drew off the inhabitants of Babylon, so that Strabo, who died in A. D. 25, speaks of the latter as being to a great extent deserted. Nevertheless the Jews left from the Captivity still resided there in large numbers, and in A. D. 60 we find the Apostle Peter working among them, for it was from Babylon that Peter wrote his Epistle (1. Pet. 5:13), addressed "to the strangers scattered throughout Pontus, Galatia, Cappadocia, Asia and Bithynia."

About the middle of the 5th century Theodoret speaks of Babylon as being inhabited only by Jews, who had still three Jewish Universities, and in the last year of the same century the "Babylonian Talmud" was issued, and recognized as authoritative by the Jews of the whole world.

In A. D. 917 Ibu Hankel mentions Babylon as an insignificant village, but still in existence. About A. D. 1100 it seems to have again grown into a town of some importance, for it was then known as the "Two Mosques." Shortly afterwards it was enlarged and fortified and received the name of Hillah, or "Rest." In A. D. 1898 Hillah contained about 10,000 inhabitants, and was surrounded by fertile lands, and abundant date groves stretched along the banks of the Euphrates. Certainly it has never been true that "neither shall the **Arabian** pitch tent there, neither shall the **shepherds make their fold there."** Isa. 13:20. Nor can it be said of Babylon—"Her cities are a desolation, a dry land, and a wilderness, a land **wherein no man dwelleth,** neither doth any son of man pass thereby." Jer. 51:43. Nor can it be said—"And they shall not take of thee a **stone for a corner,** nor a **stone for foundations,** but thou shalt be desolate forever, saith the Lord" (Jer. 51:26), for many towns and cities have been built from the ruins of Babylon, among them **Four Capital Cities,** Seleucia, built by the Greeks; Ctesiphon, by the Parthians; Al Maiden, by the Persians; and Kufa, by the Caliphs. Hillah was entirely constructed from the debris, and even in the houses of Bagdad, Babylonian stamped bricks may be frequently noticed.

But Isaiah is still more specific for he locates the **Time** when his prophecy will be fulfilled. He calls it the **"Day of the Lord."** Isa. 13:9. That is the Millennium. And he locates it at the **beginning** of the Millennium, or during the events that usher in the Millennium, for he says—

"The **stars of heaven** and the **constellations thereof shall not give their light; the sun shall be darkened** in his going forth, and the **moon shall not cause her light to shine."** Isa. 13:10 (Luke 21:25-27).

Surely nothing like this happened when Babylon was taken by Cyrus.

In the description of the destruction of the city of Babylon given in Rev. 18, we read that her judgment will come in **one hour** (vs. 10), and that in **one hour** she shall be made **desolate** (vs. 19), and as an illustration of the **suddenness** and **completeness** of her destruction, a mighty angel took up a stone like a **Great Millstone,** and cast it into the sea, saying—"Thus with **Violence** shall that great city Babylon be thrown down and shall be **found no more at all."** Rev. 18:21.

We are also told in the same chapter that she is to be destroyed by **FIRE** (Rev. 18: 8, 9, 18), and this is in exact harmony with the words of Isa. 13:19.

"And **Babylon,** the glory of kingdoms, the beauty of the Chaldees' excellency, shall be as when God overthrew **Sodom and Gomorrah;"**

and the Prophet Jeremiah makes the same statement. Jer. 50:40.

The destruction of Sodom and Gomorrah was not protracted through many centuries, their glory disappeared in a few hours (Gen. 19:24-28), and as ancient Babylon was not thus destroyed, the prophecies of Isaiah and Jeremiah cannot be fulfilled unless there is to be a future Babylon that shall be thus destroyed.

In Rev. 16:17-19, we are told that Babylon shall be destroyed by an Earthquake, attended with most vivid and incessant lightning and awful thunder. It would appear then, that as Sodom and Gomorrah were first set on fire and then swallowed up by an earthquake, that the rebuilt city of Babylon will be set on fire, and as the site of ancient Babylon is underlaid with **Bitumen** (Asphalt), that an earthquake will break up the crust of the earth, and precipitate the burning city into a **"Lake of Fire,"** and the city like a **"Millstone"** (Rev. 18:21) sink below the surface of the earth as into the sea, and be swallowed up so that it will be impossible to ever take of her stones for building purposes, and the land shall become a **Wilderness** where no man shall ever dwell.

The fact that in her will be found the blood of the Prophets, and Holy Apostles and Saints (verses 20, 24), shows that the Papal Church is not in view in this eighteenth chapter, for there was no Papal Church in Old Testament times, or in the days of the Apostles. It is the ancient as well as the revived **City of Babylon** that is meant. For in Old Testament days the blood of the Prophets was shed by the "Babylonish System" of false religions as visualized in the City of Babylor   So that it can truthfully be said that the blood of Prophets and Apostles of all ages has been shed by her.

THE EPHAH OF COMMERCE.

There is a remarkable Prophetic Vision recorded by the Prophet Zechariah, that has mystified the Commentators. "Then the Angel that talked with me went forth, and said unto me, Lift up now thine eyes, and see what is this that goeth forth.   And I said, What is it? And he said, This is an **EPHAH** that goeth forth.   He said moreover: This is their resemblance through all the earth.   And, behold, there was lifted up a 'Talent of Lead': and this is a **WOMAN** that sitteth in the midst of the **EPHAH**.   And he said, This is **WICKEDNESS**.   And he cast it (her down R. V.) into the midst of the **EPHAH**: and he cast the **weight of lead** upon the mouth thereof. Then lifted I up mine eyes, and looked, and, behold, there came out **TWO WOMEN**, and the **wind was in their wings**; for they had wings like the **wings of a Stork**: and they lifted up the **EPHAH** between the earth, and the heaven.   Then said I to the Angel that talketh with me, Whither do these bear the **EPHAH**?   And he said unto me, To build it (her R. V.) an house in the **LAND OF SHINAR**: and (when it is prepared, she shall be set there in her own place R. V.)."   Zech. 5: 5-11.

The "**EPHAH**" which the Prophet saw go forth, is the largest of Hebrew dry measures, and is often used as a symbol of **Commerce**, and its "**resemblance**," or going forth through all the earth, doubtless refers to **UNIVERSAL COMMERCIALISM**.   In this "Ephah" sat a "**WOMAN**" who was called "**WICKEDNESS**."   This "**WOMAN**" attempted to rise but the Angel thrust her back, and replaced the lid made of a "**Talent of Lead**."   Then "**Two Women**," with the wings of a Stork, came, and lifted the "Ephah" high in the air and carried it with the swiftness of the wind to the "**LAND OF SHINAR**" to build it (her R. V.) a **HOUSE**.   Now the "**LAND OF SHINAR**" was the place where they built the Tower of Babel (Gen. 11: 1-9), on whose site ancient **BABYLON** was located.   As this vision of the Prophet occurred many years after the Fall of ancient Babylon, the **HOUSE** that is to be built for this "Ephah," or the "**WOMAN**" who was transported in it, must be built in some **future** City of Babylon.

As we have seen the "Ephah" stands for **COMMERCE**, and as the **occupant** of the "Ephah" is called "**WICKEDNESS**," it reveals the fact that the "**Commercialism**" of the time of the Vision's fulfilment will be characterized by all manner of dishonest schemes and methods.   And the fact that the "**WOMAN**" is thrust back into

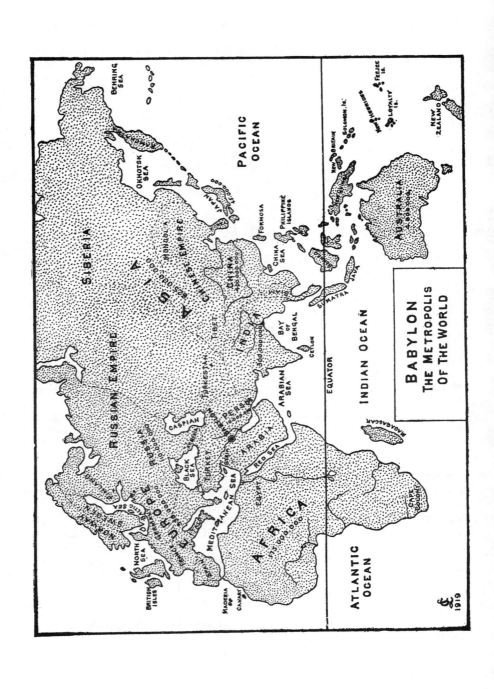

BABYLON
THE METROPOLIS
OF THE WORLD

DESIGNED AND DRAWN
BY CLARENCE LARKIN
FOX CHASE, PHILA, PA.
COPYRIGHTED

1/3/1918

MAP OF THE
LD ROMAN EMPIRE
WITH MODERN APPLICATION

AD RAILROAD
JILT
BE BUILT

THE DOTTED PORTION INDICATES
THE EXTENT OF THE OLD ROMAN EMPIRE

Moscow

RUSSIAN EMPIRE

RUSSIA

CASPIAN SEA

OXUS

BLACK SEA

ARMENIA

OUMANIA
BER R
BULGARIA
ROUMELIA

TREBIZOND
LAKE VAN
M.T ARARAT
LAKE URUMIAH

Constantinople
BOSPHORUS
Scutari
MARMORA SEA
ANGORA

TURKEY

MEDIA

AEGEAN SEA
SMYRNA
IONIA
KARAMAN
MESSINA

ASSYRIA

M.T ORONTES
EGBATANA

ATHENS
Patmos
CYPRUS
HAMATH
ALEPPO
BAGDAD R.R

TRIPOLI
BEIRUT
BAALBEK
DAMASCUS

KING OF THE NORTH
DAN.8.1.12

BAGDAD

OAN.T.S

CRETE

TYRE
ACRE
HAIFA
JAFFA
JERUSALEM
BOSRA

BABYLON
EL-AMARA

SHUSHAN

SEA

ALEXANDRIA
CAIRO

BEERSHEBA

CHALDEA
BACHT

PERSIA

KUWEIT

PERSIAN GULF

NAICA
LIBYA

KING OF THE SOUTH
DAN.11.1-45

SINAI PENINSULA
SINAI

ARABIA

EGYPT

RED SEA

THEBES

MEDINA

the "Ephah" and covered with a "**Talent of Lead,**" indicates that those dishonest schemes and methods are to be kept out of sight. The further fact that the "Ephah" is borne to the "**LAND OF SHI-NAR**" by two "**Stork Winged Women**" is not without significance. The Stork, according to the Mosaic Law, is an **unclean** bird. The name "**Chasid**" by which it was known, signified the "**PIOUS BIRD,**" and may well stand for the pursuit of wealth under the guise of religion. That will doubtless be a characteristic of those Babylonian days.

This vision of the "Ephah" by the Prophet Zechariah is still further confirmatory proof that the ancient City of Babylon is to be rebuilt and become the **COMMERCIAL CENTRE OF THE WORLD.** Every influence political and commercial will favor this, and as the "Stork Winged Women" will be favored by the "**wings of the wind,**" the tendency of Commercialism to that part of the world, when the time comes to carry the "Ephah" to the "Land of Shinar," we can readily see that it will not take long, with the wealth of the world at the command of the Capitalists of that day, to re-build Babylon and make it the great Commercial Centre of the world. Once however Commerce is firmly established in Babylon, the occupant of the "Ephah"—"**WICKEDNESS,**" will lift the lid and reveal herself, and no one will be able to buy or sell but he who has the "**MARK OF THE BEAST.**"

As to the probability of the ancient city of Babylon being rebuilt we have only to consider the events that in recent years have been happening in that part of the world looking to just such a thing.

In the Department of War of France, at Paris, there is to be seen the records of valuable surveys and maps made by order of Napoleon I, in Babylonia, and among them is a plan for a **New City of Babylon,** thus showing that the vast schemes of Napoleon comprehended the **Rebuilding of the Ancient City of Babylon,** and the making it his Capital, as his ambition was to conquer the whole of Europe and Asia, and he recognized to that end the strategical position of ancient Babylon as a governmental and commercial centre.

It is a fact that the whole country of Mesopotamia, Assyria and Babylonia, only needs a system of irrigation to make it again the most fertile country in the world, and steps have already been taken in that direction. In 1850 the British Government sent out a military officer with his command to survey and explore the river Euphrates at a cost of $150,000, and when the European war broke out, the great English Engineer who built the Assouam dam in Egypt, was engaged in making surveys in the Euphratean valley for the purpose of constructing a series of irrigation canals that would restore the country and make it again the great grain producing country it once was. As a result towns and cities would spring up and railroads would be built. What is needed in that part of the world is a "**Trans-European-Asiatic-Indian Air Line**" that will connect Europe with India, and China. Such a line was the dream of ex-Emperor William of Germany. It was that desire that made him and Abdul Hamid, of Turkey, the closest of political friends, and he secured from Abdul Hamid a concession to build a railway from the

Asiatic side of the Bosphorus, by way of Aleppo, to the Tigris river, and from there to Bagdad, and from Bagdad via Babylon (via Babylon, mark that) to Koweit on the Persian Gulf, and most of the road has been built to Bagdad.

With these facts in mind it can readily be seen that it is the purpose of European capitalists to revive the country of Babylonia and rebuild its cities, and when once the time comes the city of Babylon will be rebuilt almost in a night and on a scale of magnificence such as the world has never seen.

The rapid growth of modern cities is one of the remarkable phenomena of the times. Since 1880 more than 500 cities have been built in America. Less than 100 years ago the site of the City of Chicago was but a swampy expanse at the mouth of the Chicago river. Now it has been transformed into a beautiful Metropolis, stretching 25 miles along the shore of Lake Michigan, with 5000 miles of streets, many of them beautiful boulevards 120 feet wide. In 1840 Chicago had only 4470 inhabitants, today the population is over 3,000,000. Once the Capitalists of the world are ready the revived City of Babylon will spring up in a few years.

But I hear a protest. How you say can we be expecting Jesus to come at "any moment," if the city of Babylon must be rebuilt before He can come? There is not a word in Scripture that says that Jesus cannot come and take away His Church until Babylon is rebuilt. The Church may be taken out of the world 25 or even 50 years before that.

Babylon the Great will be an immense city, the greatest in every respect the world has ever seen. It will be a typical city, the London, the Paris, the Berlin, the Petrograd, the New York, the Chicago of its day. It will be the greatest commercial city of the world. Its merchandise will be of gold and silver, and precious stones and pearls, of purple, and silk, and scarlet and costly wools. Its fashionable society will be clothed in the most costly raiment and decked with the most costly jewels. Their homes will be filled with the most costly furniture of precious woods, brass, iron and marble, with the richest of draperies, mats and rugs. They will use the most costly of perfumes, cinnamon, fragrant odors, ointments and frankincense. Their banquets will be supplied with the sweetest of wines, the richest of pastry, and the most delicious of meats. They will have horses and chariots and the swiftest of fast moving vehicles on earth and in the air. They will have their slaves, and they will traffic in the "souls of men." That is women will sell their bodies, and men their souls, to gratify their lusts.

The markets will be crowded with cattle, sheep and horses. The wharves will be piled with goods from all climes. The manufactories will turn out the richest of fabrics, and all that genius can invent for the comfort and convenience of men will be found on the market. It will be a city given over to pleasure and business. Business men and promoters will give their days and nights to scheming how to make money fast, and the pleasure loving will be constantly planning new pleasures. There will be riotous joy and ceaseless feasting. As it was in the days of Noah and of Lot, they will be marrying and giving in marriage, buying and selling, building and planting.

The blood will run hot in their veins. Money will be their god, pleasure their high-priest, and unbridled passion the ritual of their worship.

It will be a city of music. Amid the noise and bustle of its commercial life will be heard the music of its pleasure resorts and theatres. There will be the sound of "harpers and musicians, of pipers and trumpeters" (vs. 22). The world's best singers and players will be there. Its theatres and places of music will be going day and night. In fact there will be no night, for the electric illumination of the city by night will make the night as bright and shadowless as the day, and its stores and places of business will never close, night or day, or Sunday, for the mad whirl of pleasure and the absorbing desire for riches will keep the wheels of business constantly moving. And all this will be easy because the "God of this World"—Satan, will possess the minds and bodies of men, for we read in verse 2, that Babylon at that time will be "the Habitation of Devils, and the Hold of Every Foul Spirit, and the Cage of Every Unclean and Hateful Bird." The city will be the seat of the most imposing "OCCULT-ISM," and mediums, and those desiring to communicate with the other world, will then go to Babylon, as men and women now go to Paris for fashions and sensuous pleasures. In that day demons, disembodied souls, and unclean spirits will find at Babylon the opportunity of their lives to materialize themselves in human bodies, and from the atmospheric heavens above, and from the Abyss below they will come in countless legions until Babylon shall be full of demon possessed men and women, and at the height of its glory, and just before its fall, Babylon will be ruled by SATAN HIMSELF, incarnate in the "Beast"—ANTICHRIST.

But before its destruction God will mercifully deliver His own people, for a voice from heaven will cry—

"Come Out of Her, My People, That Ye be Not Partakers of Her Sins, and that Ye Receive Not of Her Plagues."

As Sodom and Gomorrah could not be destroyed until righteous Lot had escaped, so Babylon cannot be destroyed until all the righteous people in it have fled.

The destruction of the city will be sudden and without warning. A fearful storm will sweep over the city. The lightning and thunder will be incessant. The city will be set on fire and a great earthquake will shake it from centre to circumference. The tall office buildings, the "Hanging Gardens" and the great towers will totter and fall, the crust of the earth will crack and open, and the whole city with its inhabitants will sink like a "Millstone" (vs. 21), into a lake of burning bitumen, and the smoke will ascend as of a burning fiery furnace, and the horror of the scene will be intensified by vast clouds of steam, generated by the waters of the Euphrates pouring into that lake of fiery asphalt, and when night comes on those clouds of steam will reflect the light of the burning city so it can be seen for miles in all directions in that level country. And the kings of the earth, and the merchants, and the shipmasters, and sailors, and all who have profited by her merchandise, will stand afar off and cry **and** wail because of her destruction, but the heavens will rejoice for God will have rewarded her **Double** according to her works, and **BABYLON WILL BE NO MORE.**

THE INTERVAL BETWEEN THE SECOND AND THIRD DOOMS

THE HALLELUJAH CHORUS.
Rev. 19:1-7.

"And **after these things** I heard a great voice of much people in Heaven, saying, **Alleluia; Salvation,** and **Glory,** and **Honor,** and **Power,** unto the Lord our God: for true and righteous are His Judgments; for He hath Judged the **'GREAT WHORE,'** which did corrupt the earth with her fornication, and hath avenged the blood of His Servants at her hand. And again they said, **Alleluia.** And her smoke rose up for ever and ever. And the 'Four and Twenty Elders' and the 'Four Beasts' **fell down** and worshipped God that sat on the Throne, saying, Amen; **Alleluia.** And a voice came out of the Throne, saying, Praise our God, all ye His Servants, and ye that fear Him, both small and great. And I heard as it were the voice of a great multitude, and as the voice of many waters, and as the voice of mighty thunderings, saying **Alleluia: for the Lord God omnipotent reigneth.** Let us be glad and rejoice and give honor to Him: for the **MARRIAGE OF THE LAMB IS COME, AND HIS WIFE HATH MADE HERSELF READY."**

After these things. What things? The destruction of **"MYSTICAL BABYLON"** and the restored **CITY OF BABYLON.** The first **"Alleluia"** is for the destruction of the **"GREAT WHORE"**—**"Mystical Babylon."** The second **"Alleluia"** is for the destruction of the **"CITY OF BABYLON"** whose smoke rose up for ever and ever, which could not be said of "Mystical Babylon" but only of a **CITY.** In the preceding chapter, verse 20, at the destruction of the "City of Babylon," we read—"Rejoice over her, thou Heaven, and ye Holy Apostles and Prophets; for God hath avenged you on her." Here we **hear** the rejoicing. What the merchants, and shipmasters, and sailors, and traders, weep and wail and mourn over, the—"Fall of Babylon," Heaven rejoices over. Here we see the difference between Heaven and Earth's opinion of the these Divine Judgments. Here we have the first occurrence in the New Testament of the word "HALLELUJAH." It is a compound Hebrew word "HALLELU-JAH" ("Praise-Ye-Jah"). It occurs **24** times in the Old Testament, and **4** times in the New Testament. In the Old Testament the word is always translated—"**Praise ye the Lord,**" in the New Testament the Greek word "ALLELUIA" is left untranslated, but in the New Version the word "HALLELUJAH" is substituted for "Alleluia." Four times the word "Hallelujah" is uttered in this chapter, not only by a great multitude, but by the "Four Beasts," and by the "Four and Twenty Elders." It is the "**cry of victory**" in which praise is ascribed to God. They also sang "Hallelujah" because the time had come for the **"MARRIAGE OF THE LAMB."**

2. THE MARRIAGE OF THE LAMB.

Rev. 19:8-10.

"And to **HER** (The Bride) was granted that she should be arrayed in fine linen, clean and white: for the fine linen is the righteousness of saints. And he said unto me, Write, **BLESSED ARE THEY WHICH ARE CALLED UNTO THE MARRIAGE SUPPER OF THE LAMB.** And he saith unto me, These are the true sayings of God."

It is marvellous how the Holy Spirit hath enshrined in the Scriptures the Bridal relation of the Church and her Lord. It is revealed to the spiritual mind in the most unexpected places. It is foreshadowed in the Old Testament in the story of Isaac and Rebekah. Doubtless many readers of the Bible have wondered why the "SONG OF SOLOMON" was ever included among the books of the Old Testament. Upon the first reading it appears as only a love song of Solomon for one of the many women that he loved. But a careful study of the Song reveals the fact that it is an inspired song of the love of the Church of Christ during His absence in the Heavenlies. The Song describes a maiden of Shulam, a Galilean town some 5 miles south of Mt. Tabor, who was taken from her home to one of Solomon's palaces, probably in the Lebanon district, where Solomon tries to win her love. She had lived with her mother, but her brothers had treated her cruelly and made her the keeper of the vineyards until her skin was so tanned that she spoke of herself as "BLACK BUT COMELY," and had not kept the vineyard of her own beauty, and her brothers even went so far as to speak disparagingly of her character. But there was one, a shepherd, who loved and believed in her, and whose love she returned with the most intense passion. At times Solomon visited her and sought to win her away from her beloved, but she would not listen to him. During the day she would talk to herself of her lover and imagine she heard his voice calling, and during the night she dreamt of him and imagined she was walking the streets of the city hunting for him. At times she bursts out in rapturous praise of her lover's beauty, then she calls him in loving tones. At last she escapes and finds her lover and they are seen approaching from the meadows happy in each other's love.

What a beautiful picture we have here of the love of the True Church for her absent Lord. The Church is held captive in this world and is being constantly solicited by the offers of wealth and splendor to withdraw her love from Immanuel, her Shepherd Lover, who is feeding His flock in Paradise, and give her heart to her Solomonic lovers, and consort with the kings and governments of the world, as does her sister the Harlot Church. But she cannot give her Heavenly Lover up. At times she is sorely tempted, then she sees Him with the eye of faith, and dreams of Him as spiritually present, and she is ravished by the vision of His beauty. Then suddenly He vanishes, and she is alone again carrying on the conflict with the world that tries to cast its spell upon her, and offers her its glories if she will only forsake her Shepherd Lover. But while the temptation is great her love never wavers, for she sees

the time approaching when she shall be caught away from the earth
to meet her Shepherd Lover on the plains of Paradise.

The "Marriage of the Lamb" was one of the themes that Jesus
loved to dwell on.   In the Parable of the "Ten Virgins" He tells
how the Virgins went out to meet the Bridegroom, and the unpre-
paredness of some of them to meet Him.   And in the Parable of
the "Marriage of the King's Son" (Matt. 22:1-14), He prophetically
refers to it, and gives us a foreview of it, and in the verses now
under consideration He describes its consummation, saying—"Let us
be glad and rejoice and give honor to Him, for the 'MARRIAGE
OF THE LAMB' is come, and His wife hath made herself ready.
And to her was granted that she should be arrayed in fine linen,
clean and white, for the fine linen is the righteousness of saints. And
he saith unto me, write—"BLESSED ARE THEY WHICH ARE
CALLED UNTO THE MARRIAGE SUPPER OF THE LAMB."

Notice that it does not say the "Marriage of the BRIDE," but
the "Marriage of the LAMB."   That grand event will be not so
much the consummation of the hopes of the Bride, as it will be the
consummation of the PLAN OF GOD FOR HIS SON, arranged
for before the Foundation of the World.   Eph. 1:4.

The "Marriage of the Lamb" is the consummation of the joy of
Christ AS A MAN.   It would not have been possible if Christ had
not been born IN THE FLESH.   Otherwise it would have been
the union of dissimilar natures, for the Bride is of human origin.
This is why Jesus took His HUMAN NATURE back with Him
to glory, and today we have in Heaven the MAN Christ Jesus.
1. Tim. 2:5.

While the Bride was chosen for Him before the Foundation of
the World, the "Espousal" could not take place until after Christ
assumed humanity, and so it was not until after Christ's incarnation
that Paul could say—"I am jealous over you with godly jealousy:
for I have ESPOUSED you to one husband, that I may present you
as a CHASTE VIRGIN to Christ. 2. Cor. 11:2.   There have been
many long betrothals in which the betrothed have been faithful to
their vows until the long wait has ended in a happy marriage, but
the longest this world has ever heard of is that of Christ waiting for
His Bride the Church.   He has been waiting now for nearly 1900
years, but He will not have to wait much longer.   Soon the sleeping
Church shall hear the cry—"BEHOLD THE BRIDEGROOM
COMETH, GO YE OUT TO MEET HIM," and Heaven will re-
sound with the cry—"Let us be glad and rejoice, and give honor to
Him, for the MARRIAGE OF THE LAMB IS COME." Rev. 19:7.
Ordinarily the most interest in a wedding clusters around the bride,
but the intimation in Scripture is, that the most interest at the "Marriage of the Lamb" will centre around the BRIDEGROOM.   If
there is joy in Heaven in the presence of the angels of God over one
sinner that repenteth, and that joy is the joy of the FATHER, how
much greater will be the joy of the FATHER when He shall behold
the consummation of His plan for His Son in His Marriage to His
Bride the Church.   There have been many royal weddings of inter-
national interest where the invited guests and spectators witnessed

a spectacle magnificent in its appointments, and rejoiced in a union that bound together different nations. But the Wedding of the Lamb and His Bride will surpass them all, for it shall unite Heaven and Earth in a bond that shall never be broken.

Let us now look at the "Marriage of the Lamb" more in detail. Let us ask and try to answer some of the questions that relate to it. Most Biblical Expositors take it for granted that the subject is so familiar to Bible students that it needs no explanation, and so they do not dwell upon it, but this is not so. These difficulties will appear as we try to answer them.

1. WHERE AND WHEN SHALL THIS MARRIAGE TAKE PLACE?

The Marriage takes place in Heaven **after** the "Judgment of Reward," and before the appearing of Christ with His Saints at the Revelation.

The character of the ceremony or who shall perform it (though doubtless it will be God the Father Himself), and what vows the Bridegroom and Bride will take, is not disclosed, but that there will be a ceremony of some kind that no divorce or separation can break, cannot be questioned, for there never was a legal marriage without some ceremony. Of one thing we are certain that there is no one to give away the Bride, for Christ **presents her to Himself** a "GLORIOUS CHURCH, not having SPOT, or WRINKLE, or any SUCH THING." Eph. 5: 25-27.

2. WHO IS THE BRIDEGROOM?

To this question there can be but one answer. The "Bridegroom" is the **King's SON** of the Parable of the "Marriage of the King's Son" (Matt. 22: 1-14), or **JESUS,** spoken of here as the **LAMB.** John the Baptist spoke of Christ as the **"BRIDEGROOM,"** and of himself as the **"Friend"** of the Bridegroom who rejoiced to hear His voice. John 3: 29. Jesus also represented **Himself** as the "Bridegroom," saying—"Can the 'Children of the Bride-chamber' mourn as long as the **Bridegroom is with them."** Matt. 9: 15. And in the Parable of the "Ten Virgins" Jesus refers to Himself as the "Bridegroom." Matt. 25: 1-10. The Bridegroom then is Christ.

3. WHO IS THE BRIDE?

Here there is a difference of opinion. Some claim that the "Bride," because she is called "WIFE" in Rev. 19:7, is ISRAEL, because in the Old Testament God calls Himself the HUSBAND of Israel. Isa. 54: 5. Those who advocate this view claim that **"Wife"** is the earthly name of Israel, and **"Bride"** the Heavenly. Some hold that because Isaac's bride was taken from his own kin, that, therefore, to complete the type, Jesus' Bride must be Israel, His own kin, and not the Church composed mainly of Gentiles. But we must not forget that while Abraham was the first Hebrew his kin were **Gentiles.** Abraham was not, strictly speaking, a Jew, for the Jews are the descendants of Judah, the fourth son of Jacob or Israel. So we see that Rebekah was not an Israelite, but a Gentile, so the type holds good.

We must not forget that there are "Two Brides" mentioned in the Scriptures. One in the Old Testament, and the other in the New. The one in the Old Testament is Israel, the Bride of Jehovah; the one in the New Testament is the Church, the Bride of Christ. Of Israel it is said—"Thy Maker is Thine husband." Isa. 54: 5-8. Because of her Whoredoms, Israel is a cast off WIFE, but God, her husband, promises to take her back when she ceases from her adulteries. Jer. 3: 1-18; Ez. 16: 1-63; Hosea 2: 1-23; 3: 1-5. She will not be taken back as a Virgin, but as a WIFE. But it is a VIRGIN that the Lamb (Christ) is to marry. So the Wife (Israel) of the Old Testament cannot be the BRIDE (Virgin) of the New Testament. Again the Wife (Israel) is to reside in the earthly Jerusalem during the Millennium, while the BRIDE (the Church) will reside in the New Jerusalem. These distinctions make it clear that Israel cannot be the "Bride" of Christ. We must remember that John did not call the bride—WIFE, until Rev. 21:9, which was after the marriage, when she was no longer Bride but WIFE.

The Bride of the Lamb is from a disowned and outcast race, made so by the disobedience of the head of that race in the Garden of Eden, but the Bridegroom saw her and loved her. To redeem her He came from His own lovely home in Heaven to her sin-cursed home on earth, where He was rejected by members of her family, and seized and subjected to a mock trial and nailed to a cross as a malefactor, where He laid down voluntarily His life for her, thus demonstrating His love, and opening up the way for her redemption from the Law that held her in bondage. He then left her to return to His Father's House to prepare a home for her, and during the period of her betrothal He has left her with her own family, simply sending the Holy Spirit to teach and protect her, and fit her for the day of her marriage, when He will descend into midair to meet her on her way to the BRIDAL HALLS OF HEAVEN. 1. Thess. 4: 16-17.

Many assume that the "Bride" is composed of all the saints from Abel down to the time of the taking out of the Church, but this cannot be so, for the Church did not exist until the Day of Pentecost, and only those who live and die in Christ between Pentecost and the taking out of the Church belong to the Church.

4.   WHAT IS MEANT BY HER MAKING HERSELF READY?

We are told in verse 7, that she hath "made herself ready," and in verse 8, that it was permitted her to be "arrayed in fine linen, clean and white; which is the righteousness of saints," and in chapter 21:2, she is described as—"prepared as a bride adorned for her husband." The fact that the "fine linen" in which the Bride is clothed is called not the "righteousness of Christ," but the "righteousness-es (plural) of SAINTS, makes it clear that it is not the "imputed righteousness" of Christ that is meant, and that the "Wedding Garment" in the Parable of the "Marriage of the King's Son" stands for, but the righteous acts and works of the saints themselves.

Where does the Church thus clothe herself and when? It is certain that she does not thus clothe herself on earth, for we must not forget that the Bride does not put on her wedding robes until after she has been tried at the Judgment Seat of Christ, where all her "false works" will have been consumed by fire (1. Cor. 3:11-15), and it is this "Fiery Judgment" that Peter refers to as the "TRIAL OF FAITH" which—"being much more precious than of gold that perisheth, though it be tried with fire, might be found unto praise and honor and glory at the APPEARING OF JESUS CHRIST." 1. Pet. 1:7. The "righteousnesses" then of the Saints will be their righteous acts and works that will come out of the "fiery test" of the Judgment of Reward, and be found unto PRAISE and HONOR and GLORY at the "APPEARING" of Jesus Christ; and these shall make up the beautiful wedding garments in which the Saints shall be clothed. What a contrast there will be between the purple and scarlet colored dress, and jewel bedecked person of the "Harlot Wife" of Antichrist, and the spotless white robe of fine linen of the "Bride" of the Lamb.

5. WHAT IS THE MARRIAGE SUPPER?

It is not the wedding itself. The "Marriage Feast" is the supper that follows after the Marriage has been solemnized. There is one thing about this Feast it will be such an honor to receive an invitation, and to be present, that the angel said to John, "WRITE," put it down in black and white lest you forget, do not trust to tradition lest the world never hear about it, but—"WRITE, BLESSED ARE THEY WHICH ARE CALLED UNTO THE MARRIAGE SUPPER OF THE LAMB." What a supper it will be. As a Feast, the Feasts of Belshazzar and Ahasuerus will be but a poor meal in comparison. It is called a "Supper" in contrast with the supper mentioned in the seventeenth verse of the same chapter, where the fowls of the air are invited to gather themselves together unto the "SUPPER OF THE GREAT GOD, that they may eat the flesh of kings, and the flesh of mighty men, and the flesh of horses, and of them that sit upon them, and the flesh of all men, both free and bond, both small and great." Rev. 19:17-18.

6. WHO ARE THE GUESTS?

Here again there is a difference of opinion. It is clear that the Guests are not the Bride, at least this is true as to earthly weddings. The Bride would not be "called" or "invited" to the Wedding, she has a place there of her own right and there could be no wedding without her. Some hold that the "Virgins" in the Parable of the "Ten Virgins" are not the "Bride" but simply "Bridesmaids"; and that those invited to the "Marriage Supper" of the King's Son, are simply "Guests" and do not constitute the "Bride." But as both of these Parables do not mention the Bride, and are "Kingdom of Heaven" Parables, which describe the character of this Gospel Dispensation, and have a double significance, we are led to believe that the "Wise Virgins" and the Guests who possessed a "Wedding Garment" are intended to represent the BRIDE, because they represent true believers, and true believers constitute the Church, and the Church and the Bride are one and the same.

But there will be "Guests," for as all the dead in Christ shall rise and be present at the "Marriage of The Lamb," and as only those who are saved from Pentecost to the taking out of the Church, belong to the Church (The Bride), there will be present as **"GUESTS"** the Old Testament Saints, such as Abel, Seth, Enoch, Noah, Abraham, Job, Moses, David, the Prophets, and even John the Baptist who claimed to be only the "Friend" of the Bridegroom. Then there will be the "Blood Washed Multitude" that come out of the Tribulation **after** the Church has been caught out. Thus we see that the righteous of all the past Ages and Dispensations, and all the Saints of God who shall be worthy, and who are not included in the Bride (The Church), will be "Guests" at the "Marriage Supper of the Lamb." Angels will be "spectators" of the scene but they cannot be **"Guests,"** for that honor is reserved for only those who have been redeemed by the "Blood of the Lamb."

7. WHAT HAPPENS AFTER THE MARRIAGE SUPPER?

What happens at earthly weddings after the supper? The guests make merry among themselves. Often there is music and dancing, and then the Bridegroom and the Bride change their wedding garments for a travelling dress, and steal away on their wedding trip. Generally this is to some pleasure resort or place that they have never seen. Often it is a trip across the ocean to some distant land. Sometimes it is a visit to the old home of the Bridegroom or the Bride. So after the "Marriage of the Lamb" the Heavenly Bridegroom will take His Bride on a wedding trip, and to what more suitable place can they go than back to the old home of the Bride, this earth. The place where the Bridegroom suffered and died to purchase her redemption with His own precious blood. The place where her people rejected Him, and despised His Royal claims. Then He will show them that He was no imposter, that He was what He claimed to be, the Son of God. He will then set up His Earthly Kingdom, and the Lord God shall give unto Him the **"THRONE OF DAVID,"** and His Bride (The Church) shall reign with Him for a **THOUSAND YEARS.** Oh what a sweet and delightful **"HONEY-MOON"** that will be, when, during that long "Millennial Reign" the earth shall be blessed with the presence of the King of Kings and His Consort—**THE CHURCH.** But that long "Honey-Moon" will end, not for the Bridegroom and the Bride, but for the Earth, by the return of the Bridegroom and the Bride to the Father's House. Then after the Earth has had its "Baptism of Fire," they will return with the descent of the "Holy City" to abide on the "New Earth" forever. So enraptured was John by the Revelation that he says—"I fell at his (the angel's) feet to worship him. And he said unto me, See thou do it not: I am thy fellow servant, and of thy brethren that have the testimony of Jesus: worship God: for the Testimony of Jesus is the **SPIRIT OF PROPHECY."** That is, all prophecy testifies of Jesus.

3. THE BATTLE OF ARMAGEDDON.
Rev. 19:11-19.

"And I saw Heaven opened, and behold a **WHITE HORSE:** and He that sat upon him was called '**Faithful and True**,' and in righteousness He doth judge and make war. His eyes were as a **flame of fire,** and on His head were **many crowns;** and He had a name written, that no man knew, but He Himself. And He was clothed with a vesture **dipped in blood:** and His name is called **THE WORD OF GOD.** And the armies which were in Heaven followed Him upon White Horses clothed in fine linen, white and clean. And **out of His mouth goeth a SHARP SWORD,** that with it He should smite the nations; and He shall rule them with a '**ROD OF IRON**': and He treadeth the **WINEPRESS OF THE FIERCENESS AND WRATH OF ALMIGHTY GOD.** And He hath on His vesture and on His Thigh a name written, **KING OF KINGS, AND LORD OF LORDS.** And I saw an angel standing in the sun; and he cried with a loud voice, saying to all the fowls that fly in the midst of heaven, **Come and gather yourselves together unto the SUPPER OF THE GREAT GOD;** that ye may eat the flesh of kings, and the flesh of captains, and the flesh of mighty men, and the **flesh of horses,** and of **them that sit on them,** and the **flesh of all men,** both free and bond, both small and great. And I saw the 'Beast,' and the kings of the earth, and their armies, gathered together to make war against Him that sat on the 'Horse,' and against His Army."

In chapter 6:2, a "White Horse Rider" was seen, who had a bow in his hand, and a crown was given him, and he went forth conquering and to conquer. That "Rider" we saw was **"ANTICHRIST,"** but this "Rider" has **eyes like a flame of fire,** and on His head were **many crowns,** and out of His mouth went a **sharp sword.** This identifies Him as the Person John saw standing in the midst of the "Seven Candlesticks" of chapter one, and whom we saw to be the **"SON OF MAN."** The name of the first "White Horse Rider" is not given, but this "White Horse Rider" is called

"THE WORD OF GOD,"

and on His Vesture, and on His thigh, a name was written "KING OF KINGS AND LORD OF LORDS."

Many stumble at the "White HORSE" and his **RIDER;** and ask, in amazement, if we believe it? Yes! Why not? We believe it, just as we believe the prophecy of Zech. 9:9, where the Prophet, speaking of the First Coming of Christ, said—"Behold, thy King cometh unto thee . . . lowly and riding upon an ass, and upon a colt the foal of an ass," which we know was literally fulfilled as recorded in Matt. 21:4-11. Jesus, as far as we know, rode but once in the days of His Humiliation, and then upon an humble animal, an ass, but when He comes again in His Glory, as "King of Kings," He shall sit astride a magnificent **WHITE CHARGER.** Oh, you say that is figurative, who ever heard of **horses** in Heaven? We answer **"horses and chariots of fire"** were seen in the heavens in the days of Elijah and Elisha, and why not again? 2. Kings 2:11 6:13-17.

The riders upon these "White Horses" were clothed in fine linen, white and clean. As this is the dress of the Saints that compose the

Bride, it is clear that Christ's Bride will accompany Him back to the earth, and here we have the fulfilment of the prophecy of Enoch, the seventh from Adam, recorded in Jude 14—"Behold, the Lord cometh with **10,000 OF HIS SAINTS.**" But they doubtless will be but one division of that great army, for we are told that Christ shall be accompanied by the **ARMIES** of Heaven.

"Lo, He comes! from Heaven descending,
Once for favored sinners slain:
Thousand thousand saints attending,
Swell the Triumph of His Train!
Hallelujah!
Jesus comes, and comes to reign."

But He does not come unarmed. "Out of His mouth goeth a **SHARP SWORD,** that with it He should smite the nations: and He shall rule them with a **ROD OF IRON.**" Here we have the fulfilment of the Second Psalm. "Why do the heathen rage, and the people imagine a vain thing? The **'KINGS OF THE EARTH'** set themselves and the **Rulers** take counsel together **AGAINST THE LORD,** and against His Anointed, saying, Let us break their bands asunder, and cast away their cords from us." These "Kings" are the "Ten Federated Kings" under Antichrist. But the Lord shall have them in **derision,** and then Christ shall do as the Psalmist says He is directed to do—"Ask of me, and I shall give thee **the heathen for thine inheritance, and the uttermost parts of the earth for thy possession.** Thou shalt break them with a **'ROD OF IRON,'** Thou shalt **dash them in pieces like a potter's vessel.**"

With Christ at this time shall be the "Overcomers" of the "Thyatiran Church Period" (A. D. 606-1520), to whom He promised to give power over the nations that they should rule them with a "**ROD OF IRON,**" and to them shall be given some official position of a ruling character.

We have here fulfilled the prophecy of Isa. 11:1-4, where a colon (:) in verse 4, makes a break or gap that covers this Present Dispensation from the First to the Second Coming of Christ—"And He shall smite the earth with the **'ROD OF HIS MOUTH,** and with the **BREATH OF HIS LIPS** shall He slay—THE WICKED (the **ANTICHRIST**)." 2. Thess. 2:7-8. The "**SHARP SWORD**" that goeth out of the mouth of the "White Horse Rider" is not the "**SWORD OF THE SPIRIT,**" for that bringeth "**Salvation,**" not destruction, but stands for some supernatural form of destruction, called in the above passage the—"**ROD OF HIS MOUTH.**"

But probably the most remarkable thing about this "White Horse Rider" is, that John saw His **VESTURE** had been **dipped in BLOOD.** Whose is this blood? His own blood that He shed on Calvary, or the blood of His enemies? We must turn to the Prophet Isaiah for the answer. Isa. 63:1-6.

"Who is this that cometh from Edom, with **dyed garments** from Bozrah? this that is glorious in his apparel, travelling in the greatness of his strength?" And the answer comes back—"I that speak in righteousness, mighty to save." Then the Prophet asks, "Wherefore art thou red in thine apparel, and thy garments like him that treadeth in the **Winefat?**" And the re-

sponse is—"I have trodden the wine-press **alone**; and of the people there was none with me; for I will tread them in mine anger,
and trample them in my fury; and their **blood** shall be sprinkled
upon **my garments**, and I will **stain all My Raiment."** Isa. 63: 1-6.

That this does not refer to Christ's atonement on the Cross is
clear, for the Prophet adds—

> "For the **'Day of Vengeance'** is in mine heart, and the year
> of my redeemed is come."

There was no "vengeance" in Christ's heart on the Cross. It was
"Father 'forgive them' for they know not what they do." The time
the Prophet foretells, is the "Day of Christ's Vengeance" on His
enemies, and the day when He shall redeem His chosen people the
Jews from the power of Antichrist. It is the time when He shall
tread—

"THE 'WINEPRESS'
Of the Fierceness and Wrath of
Almighty God."

The Apostle John had a vision of this "Winepress" in **chapter
fourteen**, verses 14 to 20. That was before the pouring out of the
"Vials," and was a prophetic foreview of what should happen in chapter nineteen.

In verses 18 to 20, an angel with a sharp sickle is told to—

> "Thrust in thy **Sharp Sickle**, and gather the clusters of the
> **'Vine of the Earth,'** for her grapes are **fully ripe.** And the angel
> thrust in his **Sickle** into the earth, and gathered the **'Vine of
> the Earth,'** and cast it into the **Great Winepress** of the wrath of
> God." And we read that "The Winepress was trodden **Without
> the City,** and blood (not wine), came out of the Winepress, even
> unto the **horses' bridles,** by the space of a **Thousand and Six
> Hundred Furlongs."**

From this we see that the "Allied Armies" of Antichrist **will**
cover the whole of Palestine, and so great shall be the slaughter, **that,**
in the valleys and hollows, all over the whole of Palestine, for the
length of Palestine as far south as Bozrah is 1600 furlongs or 200
miles, the **blood** shall be up to the **horses' bridles.**

It will be the time of which Isaiah speaks, when the land shall be
"Soaked With Blood." Isa. 34: 1-8.

The "Tribulation Period" will close with the great "Battle of
Armageddon." As we have seen the armies of the East and the West
will be assembled in the Holy Land by the "Demon Spirits" that
shall be sent forth from the mouths of the "Satanic Trinity." The
field of battle will be the "Valley of Megiddo," located in the heart
of Palestine, the battlefield of the great battles of the Old Testament.
The forces engaged will be the "Allied Armies" of Antichrist on the
one side, and the "Heavenly Army" of Christ on the other. The
"time" will be when the **Harvest of the Earth" IS RIPE** (Rev. 14:
15), and at the "Psychological Moment" when the "Allied Armies" of
Antichrist are about to take the city of Jerusalem.

The Prophet Zechariah says—

> "Behold the **'Day of the Lord' cometh."** (The "Day of the
> Lord" is the Millennial Day.) When—"I will **Gather All Nations
> Against Jerusalem to Battle . . . Then shall the Lord Go
> Forth and Fight Against Those Nations."** Zech. 14: 1-3.

THIRD DOOM.
"THE BEAST" AND "FALSE PROPHET."
Rev. 19:20.

"And the 'BEAST' was taken, and with him the 'FALSE PROPHET' that wrought miracles before him, with which he deceived them that had received the 'Mark of the Beast,' and them that worshipped his 'Image.' These both were cast **ALIVE** into a 'Lake of Fire' burning with brimstone."

The issue of the "Battle of Armageddon" will never be in doubt. The previous summoning of the birds and beasts of prey, prove this. Before the destruction of the army of Antichrist, he and the False Prophet will be cast "alive" into the "Lake of Fire." This shows that they are not "Systems" but "Persons," and as Enoch and Elijah were taken to Heaven **without dying**, so Antichrist and the False Prophet will be cast into the "Lake of Fire" **without dying**, and will be still there and alive when Satan is cast in a 1000 years later.

Before Antichrist is seized and cast into the "Lake of Fire," Satan will make his exit from his person, and after the battle is over, Satan will be bound and cast into the "Bottomless Pit," where he will be "sealed up" for 1000 years. This is the culminating act of the "Tribulation Period."

FOURTH DOOM.
THE ANTICHRISTIAN NATIONS.
Rev. 19:21.

"And the remnant were slain with the **SWORD** of Him that sat upon the Horse, which sword proceeded out of His mouth: and all the fowls were filled with their flesh."

So great will be the destruction of human life in the Battle of Armageddon, that God will prepare for it in advance less the stench of the unburied dead should breed pestilence.

"And I saw an angel standing in the sun; and he cried with a loud voice, saying to all the **fowls that fly in the midst of Heaven** (Buzzards, Vultures, Eagles, etc.), Come and gather yourselves together unto the

SUPPER OF THE GREAT GOD,

that ye may eat the flesh of Kings . . . **Captains . . Mighty Men,** and the flesh of horses and of them that sit on them (common soldiers), and the flesh of all men, both free and bond, both small and great." Rev. 19:17, 18.

This "Feast" is described in the Old Testament.

"And, thou son of man, thus saith the Lord God, Speak unto every **feathered fowl,** and to every **beast of the field,** Assemble yourselves, and come, gather yourselves on every side to **My Sacrifice,** that I do sacrifice for you, even a great sacrifice upon the **Mountains of Israel,** that ye may eat flesh, and drink blood. Ye shall eat the flesh of the **Mighty,** and drink the blood of the **Princes of the Earth,** of rams, of lambs, and of goats, of bullocks, all of them fatlings of Bashan. And ye shall eat **fat till ye be full,** and drink blood till ye be drunken. . . . Thus ye shall be filled 'at **My Table,'** with horses and **chariots** (their occupants), with **Mighty Men,** and with all **Men of War, said the Lord God."** Ez. 39:1-22.

And in the same chapter we are told that the "House of Israel," the occupants of Palestine in that day, shall be **seven months** burying the bones of the dead, the flesh having been eaten by the birds and beasts of prey, and the wood from the weapons of warfare, army wagons, spears, etc., shall last the inhabitants of the land for fuel **seven years,** so that they will not have to take wood out of the field, nor cut down any out of the forests.

The words in Rev. 19:21, "and all the **fowls were filled with their flesh,**" declare that those "**Fowl Guests**" will be GORGED WITH CARRION.

Then will be fulfilled the words of Jesus—"For wheresoever the **carcase** is, there will the **Eagles** (birds of prey) be gathered together." Matt. 24:27, 28. The eagle feeds mainly on fresh meat. The Hebrews classed the eagle among the birds of prey, such as the vulture.

The destruction of this great army will be brought about by supernatural means, and as there is to be a "**GREAT HAIL**" to fall from heaven upon the enemies of God when the "Seventh Vial" is poured out, which includes this period, that may be the means God will use, for it was in that way that the enemies of Israel were destroyed on the same battlefield in the "Battle of Beth-Horon" in the days of Joshua. Josh. 10:1-11.

THE INTERVAL BETWEEN THE "FOURTH" AND "FIFTH" DOOMS.

1. SATAN BOUND FOR A THOUSAND YEARS.
Rev. 20:1-3.

"And I saw an Angel come down from Heaven, having the Key of the 'BOTTOMLESS PIT' and a GREAT CHAIN in his hand. And he laid hold on the DRAGON, that OLD SERPENT, which is the DEVIL, and SATAN, and bound him a 1000 YEARS, and cast him into the 'BOTTOMLESS PIT,' and shut him up, and set a seal upon him, that he should deceive the nations no more, till the 1000 YEARS should be fulfilled: and after that he shall be loosed a little season."

Here Satan is called by four different names—"Dragon," "Serpent," "Devil," and "Satan." From these and from the fact that he can be **bound,** we see that he is a "**PERSON,**" because you cannot bind an "influence" or a "principle of evil." While Satan is the "Prince of the Powers of the Air" (Eph. 2:2), and the "God of this Age" (2. Cor. 4:4), and the "Ruler of the Powers of Darkness" (Eph. 6:11-12), and whose position is so exalted that even Michael the Archangel dare not insult him (Jude 9), and while he has great power and influence, yet he is not **omnipotent,** for **ONE** Angel and he is not called a strong angel, is able to seize and bind him. This Angel, who has the "Key" of the "BOTTOMLESS PIT," is the same "STAR Angel" that is seen by John when the "Fifth Trumpet" sounded (Rev. 9:1-2), who seems to be the custodian of the "Key" of the "Bottomless Pit."

The objection has been raised to the possibility of binding a "spirit" with an IRON chain. But the word "iron" is not used, it is simply a "great chain," and we are told in other scriptures that "Spirit" beings can be chained. In 2. Pet. 2:4, and Jude 6, we read of the angels who sinned and kept not their "First Estate," and who are now "reserved in CHAINS," in darkness, unto the Judgment of the Great Day (The Great "White Throne" Judgment). What interests us most is, not the character of the chain, but the fact that Satan can and will be bound and confined in a place where he cannot get out for a 1000 years, and while nothing is said of the binding and confining of his angels and other evil agents, as demons and the "evil powers of the air," the inference is that they too will be powerless during that period.

The Binding of Satan reveals the fact that God can stop his evil work when He is ready, and that without sending the armies of Heaven to do so. When the time has come, God will empower and command a single Angel to seize, handcuff, and imprison him, just as an officer of the law with a warrant arrests and locks up a criminal. Satan is not cast at this time into the "Lake of Fire," to keep company with the "Beast" and "False Prophet," because God has further use for him at the end of the 1000 years for which period he is bound.

2. THE FIRST RESURRECTION.
Rev. 20:4-6.

"And I saw Thrones, and they sat upon them, and Judgment was given unto them.

"And I saw the SOULS of them that were beheaded for the witness of Jesus, and for the word of God, and which had not worshipped the 'Beast,' neither his 'Image,' neither had received his 'Mark' upon their foreheads, or in their hands. (These are the Tribulation Saints.) And they (the 'Throne Sitters' and 'Tribulation Saints') lived and reigned with Christ a thousand years. But the rest of the dead (Wicked Dead) lived not again until the thousand years were finished. This (the resurrection of the 'Throne Sitters,' and 'Tribulation Saints') is the FIRST RESURRECTION.

"Blessed and holy is he that hath part in the 'FIRST RESURRECTION': on such the 'SECOND DEATH' hath no power, but they shall be priests of God and of Christ, and shall reign with Him a THOUSAND YEARS."

In this passage we meet for the first time the expression—"THE FIRST RESURRECTION." In 1. Thess. 4:16, we read that the dead IN CHRIST shall rise FIRST, but as no wicked are mentioned it is simply a relative statement to show that the living Christians shall not be caught away before the "Dead in Christ" shall be raised. This passage speaks of two separate "Companies of Believers" who are to be raised, each in their own order, at the "First Resurrection."

(1). The First Company is described by the words—"I saw Thrones, and they sat upon them, and Judgment was given unto them." Now the only "Company of Believers" that we see sitting on Thrones are the "Four and Twenty Elders" of chapter 4:4-5. These as we have seen stand for the Church, and were resurrected or caught

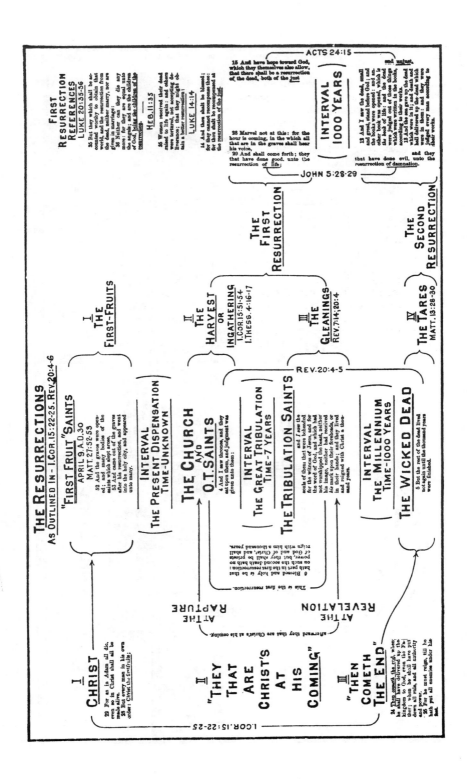

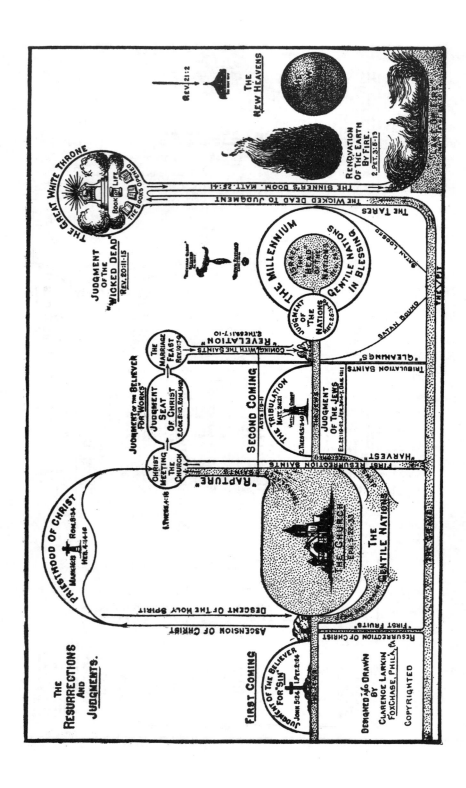

out before "The Tribulation," and are the "Harvest" of which Christ and those who rose at the time of His Resurrection were the "First Fruits." See the Chart on "The Resurrections."

(2). The Second Company is described by the words—"And I saw the SOULS of them that were beheaded for the witness of Jesus, and for the word of God, and which had not worshipped the 'Beast,' neither his 'Image,' neither had received his 'Mark' upon their foreheads, or in their hands." This Company is made up of those who were slain for refusing to worship the "Beast" or his "Image," and represent the "Tribulation Saints," or those who perish as martyrs after the Church has been caught out, and during the "Tribulation Period," and are the "Gleanings" of the "Harvest."

Now we read that these Two Companies "lived," that is, they were dead but lived again, that is, had been raised from the dead, for John saw the Tribulation Saints in their disembodied or SOUL-ISH state between death and the resurrection of the body. This clearly teaches that both these Companies were resurrected and lived and were to reign with Christ for a 1000 YEARS, and not that only the Tribulation Saints lived and would reign with Him during the 1000 Years. Thus both Companies make up the FIRST RESUR-RECTION SAINTS.

In the next verse (5) we have another class or Company of persons mentioned, called the "REST OF THE DEAD," who are not to live again (that is, raised from the dead) until the 1000 Years are finished. Who these dead are we are told in verse 12, where they are referred to as the "WICKED DEAD." It is clear then that there are to be TWO Resurrections of the dead, the first of the "RIGHT-EOUS," and the second of the "WICKED," and that these two Resurrections are to be 1000 YEARS APART.

But some object to the statement that there are to be Two Resurrections, and say that we are not justified in basing such a doctrine on a single statement in a symbolical book. But if we are to reject the statements of the Word of God simply because they are mentioned only once, then we must reject the doctrine of the "Virgin Birth," for that was only mentioned once in the Old Testament before it was fulfilled, but of the resurrection of the "Righteous" a 1000 years before the "Wicked" we are told in this Book of Revelation three times.

But we do not have to depend on this passage to prove that the "Righteous" shall rise before the "Wicked," its value lies in the fact that it gives us the LENGTH OF TIME (1000 years) between the Two Resurrections. The Scriptures, while they speak of the Resurrection of the "JUST" and the "UNJUST" (the Justified and the Unjustified), Acts 24:15, and a Resurrection of "LIFE," and a Resurrection of "DAMNATION" (John 5:28-29), also speak of an "OUT" Resurrection "FROM AMONG" the dead, called in Luke 14:13-14, the Resurrection of the "JUST." In Luke 20:35-36 a Resurrection is spoken of called a Resurrection "FROM (out from) THE DEAD," and is an "OUT" Resurrection, because those who rise are called the "CHILDREN OF GOD," being the children of "THE (First or "out from") RESURRECTION." Again in Heb. 11:35, we read of a "BETTER RESURRECTION," and all these references to a "SPECIAL" Resurrection are made clear, and the "time element" and its "length" (1000 years) between the Resurrection of the "JUST" and "UNJUST" revealed in the passage we are considering.

There could be no statement more clear than—"THE REST OF THE DEAD LIVED NOT AGAIN UNTIL THE THOUSAND YEARS WERE FINISHED," to show that the "Unrighteous Dead" will not be raised until the end of the Millennium. This at one stroke does away with the argument of those who claim that all the dead will be raised at the beginning of the Millennium, and shall have another chance to accept the Gospel and be saved.

We read—"Blessed and holy is he that hath part in the 'FIRST Resurrection'; on such the 'SECOND DEATH' hath no power." What is the "SECOND DEATH"? First, what is DEATH? It is the separation of the "soul" and "spirit" from the "body." That is the "FIRST DEATH." At the Resurrection the "soul" and "spirit" are reunited to the "body." This is true of both the Righteous and the Wicked. But the Wicked after they have been raised are to be Judged at the Great White Throne Judgment, and because their names are not found written in the "Book of Life," they are sentenced to die again, that is, their "soul" and "spirit" are again separated from their "body," and they go to the "LAKE OF FIRE" without a material body, and as "soul" and "spirit" are incombustible they can remain in the flames of a literal fire for all eternity without being consumed. This is the doom of the Wicked dead. The Rich Man in Hell (Luke 16:19-31) was conscious and tormented in the flame after his death, and he shall remain so until his body shall be raised from the dead at the Resurrection of the Wicked, and when he shall be Judged and condemned at the Great White Throne Judgment, and sentenced to die again, his "soul" and "spirit" will descend to the "Lake of Fire" (the Final Hell), where they will exist in a conscious state and in torment for all eternity. But the "Second Death" has no terror for the Righteous, for the promise is that it shall have no power over them.

3. THE MILLENNIUM.
Rev. 20:4.

"And they lived and reigned with Christ a THOUSAND YEARS."

That there is to be a period of a 1000 years during which Satan shall be bound and Christ shall reign on this earth, is plainly stated in the New Testament. This period is mentioned 6 times in Rev. 20: 1-7, and is generally called

"The Millennium,"
from the Latin words "Mille" (1000) and "Annum" (year). It is to be regretted, however, that the word "Millennium" ever supplanted the Biblical word "Kingdom," for it is this period that Christ taught His Disciples to pray for in the petition—"Thy Kingdom Come."

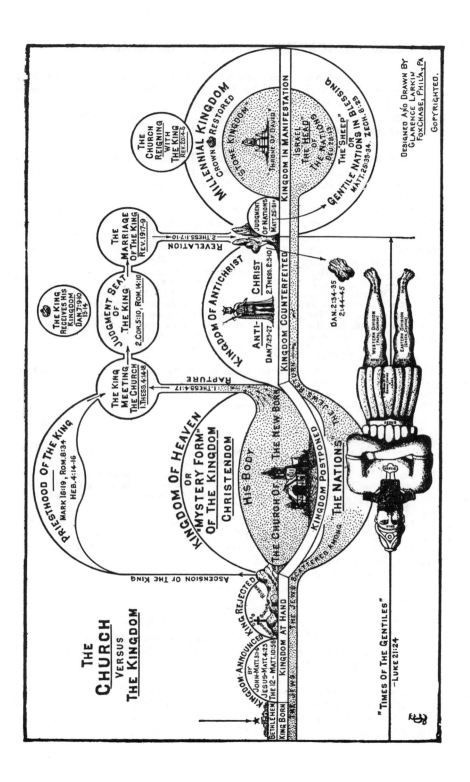

Let us drop then for the present the word "Millennium" and look at the word "Kingdom." In the Book of Daniel we learn that there were to be "Four World-wide Kingdoms" that were to succeed each other on the earth and that they were to be destroyed in turn by a Kingdom called the

"Stone Kingdom."

As those "Four Kingdoms" were "literal" Kingdoms it follows that the "Stone Kingdom" must be a "literal" Kingdom, for it takes the place of those Kingdoms and "fills the whole earth." This "Stone Kingdom" is the "Millennial Kingdom of Christ."

The time when this "Stone Kingdom" shall be set up is at the "Revelation of Christ," when He shall come with the "armies of Heaven" and destroy Antichrist (Rev. 19:11-21) and judge the Nations.

> "When the Son of Man shall come in His glory, and all the holy angels with Him, then shall He sit upon the
> ### 'Throne of His Glory';
> and before Him shall be gathered all nations; and He shall separate them one from another as a shepherd divideth his sheep from the goats, and He shall set the Sheep (Sheep Nations) on His right hand, but the Goats (Goat Nations) on the left. Then shall the King say unto them on His right hand, Come, ye blessed of my Father, inherit the Kingdom Prepared for You From the Foundation of the World." Matt. 25: 31-34.

This Kingdom is an earthly, visible Kingdom, and is the "Millennial Kingdom" of the Lord Jesus Christ.

1. The Form of Government.

It will be a "Theocracy." God will rule in the person of the Lord Jesus Christ.

> "And the angel said unto Mary, thou shalt bring forth a son and shalt call His name Jesus. He shall be great and shall be called the 'Son of the Highest,' and the Lord God shall give unto Him the Throne of His Father David; and He shall reign over the House of Jacob FOREVER, and of His Kingdom There Shall Be NO END." Luke 1: 30-33.

There are 7 of God's "shalls" in this passage. Four of them have been fulfilled, for Mary did bring forth a "son," He was called "Jesus," He was "great," and was called the "Son of the Highest"; the other three must and will be fulfilled.

Daniel the Prophet describes the event.

> "I saw in the night visions, and, behold, one like the 'Son of Man' came with the clouds of heaven, and came to the 'Ancient of Days' (God), and they brought Him near before Him. And there was given Him Dominion, and Glory and a KINGDOM that all people, nations, and languages, should serve Him; His Dominion is an Everlasting Dominion, Which Shall Not Pass Away, and His KINGDOM that which Shall Not Be Destroyed."

Whether Christ shall sit in person on the Throne at Jerusalem, or whether He shall rule through another is not so clear. There are several passages of Scripture that seem to teach that King David will be raised and placed on the throne again, and that the Children of Israel will seek him, or it may mean that the new King shall be named David.

"Afterward shall the Children of Israel return, and seek the Lord their God, and **David Their King;** and shall fear the Lord and His goodness in the **Latter Days.**" Hosea 3:5.

"They shall serve the Lord their God, and **David Their King,** whom I will **Raise Up Unto Them.**" Jer. 30:9.

"And **David,** my servant, shall be **King Over Them.**" Ezek. 37:24.

"I Jehovah will be their God, and my servant **David a Prince in Their Midst.**" Ezek. 34:24.

"My servant **David** shall be their **Prince Forever.**" Ezek. 37:25.

As the "Lord of Hosts" shall reign in Mt. Zion, and in Jerusalem, and before His ancients "gloriously" (Isa. 24:23), the inference is that King David will reign simply as "Regent," and will be called "King" or "Prince" as circumstances may require. It is very clear from Ezekiel that the "Prince," whoever he may be, is not perfect, and has to offer sacrifices for himself. Ezek. 45:22.

We have a hint of the manner of government in the Parable of the Pounds. That Parable was spoken to show what Jesus will do to His servants (the Jews) when He shall have "received the Kingdom and returned." The man whose Pound shall have gained "Ten Pounds" will be rewarded by being placed in authority over "ten cities." The man whose Pound shall have gained "Five Pounds" will have authority over "five cities." The man who failed to use his Pound is simply deprived of it and loses all opportunity of authority. Luke 19:11-26.

The promise that Jesus made to His Disciples that

"In the **Regeneration** when the Son of Man shall sit on the **Throne of His Glory,** ye also shall sit upon **Twelve Thrones, Judging the Twelve Tribes of Israel.**" Matt. 19:28.

in all probability does not refer to the "Millennial Age," but to the "Perfect Age," the "Age" that is to follow the renovation of the Earth by fire. The use of the word "regeneration" suggests this, as it refers to the time when the present earth is to be "re-created" and made "new." It has occurred to the writer that we have not as yet the proper perspective as to all the Old Testament prophecies, and that we are putting in the "Millennial Age" some things that belong to the "Perfect Age." The one just mentioned for example.

Some object to the "visible reign" of King David, or the Disciples on the earth during the Millennium because it involves the anomaly of intercourse between men in the flesh and those who are clad in resurrected and glorified bodies. But why should this be an objection? Did not Jesus appear "eleven" times "after His resurrection," during a period of "forty days," to His disciples? Did He not "eat" and "drink" with them during that period? Did they not "walk" with Him to the Mount of Olives and see Him go up in that **Same Resurrection Body?** Did not angels appear in human form and "eat" and "drink" with men in Old Testament times? Gen. 18:1-8.

We must not forget that they who shall be accounted worthy to obtain "**That Age,**" and the "**Resurrection From Among the Dead,**" shall be "**Angel like**" (Luke 20:35, 36), and like the angels can mingle with earth's inhabitants, having visible bodily forms, can eat and drink, and there is probably more truth than poetry in the Prophet's utterance that in those days,

> "They that wait upon the Lord (as messengers) shall renew their strength; they shall mount up with wings as eagles (Angels); they shall run and not be weary; and they shall walk and not faint." Isa. 40: 31.

This can be said of only those who have been "Raised in Power." 1. Cor. 15: 42, 43.

2. The Seat of Government.

The Seat of Government will be at Jerusalem. Jerusalem is to be trodden down of the Gentiles, until the "Times of the Gentiles be fulfilled." Luke 21: 24. Then it will be rebuilt. The Prophet Ezekiel gives us a detailed description of the restored Land and City in Ezek. 48: 1-35. See Chart of the Millennial Land.

The "Royal Grant" of land that God gave to Abraham and his descendants extended from the "River of Egypt" unto the "Great River," the river Euphrates. Gen. 15: 18. Ezekiel fixes the Northern boundary at Hamath, about 100 miles north of Damascus (Ezek. 48: 1), and the Southern boundary at Kadesh, about 100 miles south of Jerusalem. Ezek. 48: 28. This "Royal Grant" was not conditional and was never revoked. It is 8 times as large as that formerly occupied by the Twelve Tribes. See Map of the "Royal Grant" to Abraham.

This "Royal Grant" is to be divided among the restored Twelve Tribes in parallel horizontal sections, beginning at Hamath on the North with a section for Dan, next comes Asher, then Naphtali, Manassah, Ephraim, Reuben, Judah. Then comes the

"Holy Oblation,"

a square tract on the west of Jordan, 25,000 reeds, or 50 miles on a side. A "Reed," according to Ezek. 40: 5, is 6 cubits long, the cubit being an ordinary cubit 18 inches long plus a hand-breadth, 3 inches, making the "reed cubit" 21 inches. Six of such cubits make the "reed" 10½ feet long. South of the "Holy Oblation" will be the Tribes of Benjamin, Simeon, Issachar, Zebulon and Gad.

The "Holy Oblation" is divided into three horizontal sections. The Northen section is 25,000 reeds long, from East to West, and 10,000 reeds wide. It is called the "Levites' Portion." South of it is the "Priests' Portions" of equal size. South of the "Priests' Portion" is the section for the "City" with its suburbs and farming sections. This section is 25,000 reeds long, from East to West, and 5000 reeds wide. Ezek. 48: 15-19.

In the centre of this section the City (Jerusalem) is located. This helps us to map out the whole of the "Holy Oblation," as the 'New City" is to be located on the site of the Old. The "New City," however, is to be much larger than the Old. It is to be 9 miles square, and with its suburbs, ½ mile on a side, 10 miles square. It will have a wall around it with 3 gates on each side like the New Jerusalem (Ezek. 48: 15-18, 30-35), these gates being named after the 12 sons of Jacob.

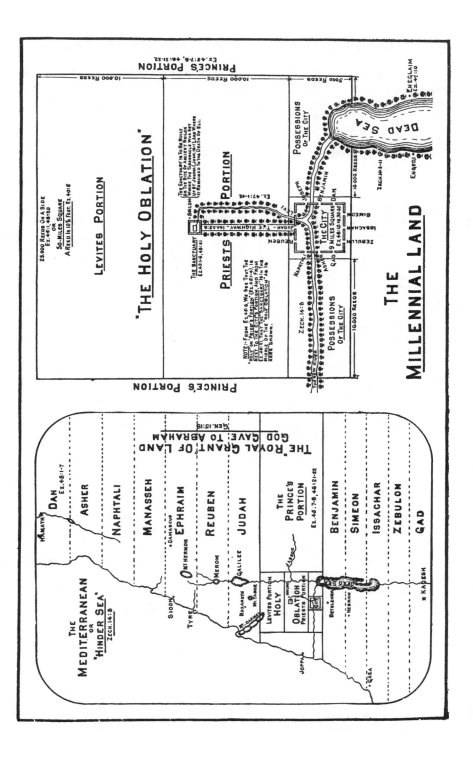

PRINCE'S PORTION Ez. 45:7-8, 46:21-22

10,000 Reeds | 10,000 Reeds | 5000 Reeds

"THE HOLY OBLATION"

LEVITES PORTION

25,000 Reeds On A Side
Ez. 48:1, 48:20
OR
50-Miles Square
A Reed 10½ Feet. Ez. 40:5

PRIESTS PORTION
Ez. 1:1-12

The Sanctuary Is To Be Built On The Site Of Ancient Shiloh Where The Tabernacle Was Set Up By Joshua. (Josh. 18:1) And Where It Remained To The Death Of Eli.

SHILOH

THE SANCTUARY
Ez. 43:1-4, 48:21

NOTE:- From Ez. 48:6, We See That The "Holy" Or "Priest's Portion" (Ez. 4:61:0), Is Next To The City's Portion And From Ez. 48:10, That We See "Sanction" Is In The Middle Of The "Holy Oblation." 48:16 Here Shown.

POSSESSIONS Of The City

DEAD SEA

EN-EGLAIM Ez. 47:10

EN-GEDI Ez. 47:10

10,000 Reeds

JOSEPH
BENJAMIN
LEVI
SIMEON
ISSACHAR
ZEBULUN

THE CITY
Ez. 48:15-19, 30-35
9 MILES SQUARE

JUDAH - THE HIGHWAY - ISA.35:8

REUBEN
NAPHTALI
ASHER
GAD
DAN

Zech. 14:8

THE NEW RIVER

POSSESSIONS Of The City

10,000 Reeds

Zech. 14:8

PRINCE'S PORTION

THE MILLENNIAL LAND

THE MEDITERRANEAN OR "HINDER SEA" Zech. 14:8

THE "ROYAL" GRANT OF LAND GOD GAVE TO ABRAHAM GEN. 13:18

HAMATH

DAN
ASHER
NAPHTALI
MANASSEH
EPHRAIM
REUBEN
JUDAH

THE PRINCE'S PORTION
Ez. 46:7-8, 48:21-22

BENJAMIN
SIMEON
ISSACHAR
ZEBULUN
GAD

Ez. 48:1-7

DAMASCUS
Mt. HERMON
MEROM
GALILEE
NAZARETH
Mt. TABOR
SIDON
TYRE
Mt. CARMEL
JOPPA

LEVITES PORTION

HOLY
OBLATION
Priests Portion

SHILOH
JORDAN
JERICHO
DEAD SEA
JERUSALEM
BETHLEHEM
HEBRON
CAEA
× KADESH

The "Temple," or "Sanctuary," will not be rebuilt in the "New City," but in the "midst" or middle of the "Holy Oblation." Ezek. 48:10, 20, 21. This will locate it at or near Shiloh, where the Tabernacle rested after the Children of Israel conquered the Land, and where it remained until the Temple of Solomon was finished. A "Highway" shall lead from the "Sanctuary" to the "New City." Isa. 35:8. It will be a magnificent boulevard, 12 miles long, lined with beautiful shade trees.

The "New Temple" or "Sanctuary" will occupy a space of 500 reeds on a side, or nearly a mile square. Ezek. 42:15-20. The old Temple was not a mile in circuit.

The Prophet Zechariah tells us (Zech. 14:8), that in "That Day" (the Millennial Day)—

> "Living Waters Shall Go Out From Jerusalem," half of them toward the Former Sea (Red Sea) and half of them toward the Hinder Sea (Mediterranean); in summer and in winter shall it be."

But those "Living Waters" will not have their "source" in Jerusalem. The life-giving spring from which they flow will be located under the "Sanctuary." Ezekiel tells us how he saw in vision the "New Temple" or "Sanctuary" and how the Lord took him to the eastern door of the "House" or "Sanctuary," where he saw the waters come forth from under the Threshold of the door, and flow past the "Altar of Burnt Offering" on the south side eastward until the stream was deep enough to swim in.

> "Then said he unto me, These waters . . . go down into the desert (by way of Jerusalem) and go into the sea (Dead Sea), which being brought forth into the sea, the waters (of the Dead Sea) shall be healed (lose their saltness). . . . And everything shall live whither the river cometh. And it shall come to pass that the fishers shall stand upon it (Dead Sea), from Engedi (on the west shore) even unto Eneglaim (on the east shore); they shall be a place to spread forth nets; their fish shall be according to their kinds, as the fish of the Great Sea (Mediterranean) exceeding many. . . . And by the River upon the banks thereof, on this side and on that side, shall grow all trees for meat, whose leaf shall not fade, neither shall the fruit thereof be consumed; it shall bring forth new fruit according to its months, because the waters they issued out of the 'Sanctuary'; and the 'Fruit' thereof shall be for meat and the 'Leaf' thereof for medicine." Ezek. 47: 8-12. Compare Rev. 22: 1, 2.

The size of the "New City," the location of the "New Sanctuary" and the elevation of the Dead Sea, which is now 1200 feet below the level of the Mediterranean Sea, call for great physical changes in the land surface of Palestine. How are these changes to come about?

When Christ comes back it will be to the Mount of Olives from whence He went up. Acts 1:9-12. The Prophet Zechariah describes what will then happen.

> "His (Christ's) feet shall stand in That Day (the day of His return) upon the Mount of Olives, which is before Jerusalem on the east and the Mount of Olives shall Cleave in the midst Thereof Toward the East and Toward the West, and There Shall Be a Very Great Valley; and Half of the Mountain Shall Remove Toward the North and Half of It Toward the South. . . "All the Land Shall Be Turned as a Plain From Geba to Rimmon South of Jerusalem; and it shall be LIFTED UP AND INHABITED." Zech. 14:4, 10, 11.

These great changes will probably be brought about by earthquakes or volcanic action.

"Behold, the Lord cometh forth out of His place, and will come down, and tread upon the high places of the earth. And the mountains shall be **Molten Under Him**, and the valleys shall be **Cleft as Wax Before the Fire, and as the Waters That Are Poured Down a Steep Place**." Micah 1: 3, 4.

These great physical changes will level the land surface of Palestine, and make room for the "New City," and raise the Dead Sea, so its waters can flow into both the Red and Mediterranean Seas. Ezekiel tells us that the name of Jerusalem in that day shall be "**Jehovah-Shammah**," the **Lord Is There**. Ezek. 48: 35.

3. The Temple and Its Worship.

As we have seen the Temple or Sanctuary will be located in the centre of the "Holy Oblation." A full description of the Temple and its courts is given in Ezek. 40: 1; 44: 31. No such building as Ezekiel so minutely describes has ever yet been built, and so the prophecy cannot refer to either Zerubbabel's or Herod's Temple, and as there is to be no Temple in the New Jerusalem, it must be a description of the Temple that is to be on the earth during the Millennium. That it does not belong to the New Earth is also clear, for the land in which it is located is bounded by the Sea, and the waters that flow from it, flow "into the Sea," but in the New Earth there is "no more sea." Rev. 21: 1. This is still further confirmed by the Prophet's mention of the "desert," the "River Jordan," the "Mediterranean Sea," and other localities that will not be found on the New Earth after its renovation by fire.

The "Aaronic Priesthood" will be re-established, and the sons of Zadok shall officiate and offer sacrifices. Ezek. 44: 15-31. The New Temple, however, will lack many things that were the features of the old Temple. There will be no "Ark of the Covenant," no "Pot of Manna," no "Aaron's Rod" to bud, no "Tables of the Law," no "Cherubim," no "Mercy Seat," no "Golden Candlestick," no "Shew Bread," no "Altar of Incense," no "Veil," no unapproachable "Holy of Holies" where the High Priest alone might enter, nor is there any "High Priest" to offer atonement for sin, or to make intercession for the people, unless a rather obscure passage in Zech. 6: 12, 13 means that Christ (The Branch, Jer. 23: 5, 6) shall be a "King-Priest," and perform the duties of High Priest conjointly with His Kingly office.

While the Levites as a class shall perform Temple service they shall be barred from Priestly duties for their past sins. Ezek. 44: 10-14. There shall be a daily "morning" sacrifice, but no evening sacrifice. Ezek. 46: 13-15. The offerings will be the "Burnt," the "Meat," the "Drink," the "Sin," the "Peace" (Ezek. 45: 17), and the "Trespass" offering. Ezek. 42: 13. Two Feasts are to be observed, "The Passover," but no Passover Lamb will be offered as Jesus fulfilled that Type (Ezek. 45: 21-24), and the "Feast of Tabernacles," Zech. 14: 16-19. This Feast is to be observed by all the nations under penalty of "Drought" or "Plague."

The "Feast of Pentecost" will be done away with on account of its fulfillment. The "Day of Pentecost," recorded in Acts 2: 1-4, was only a partial fulfillment of the prophecy of Joel 2:28-32. No such wonders in the heavens and the earth as "blood," and "fire" and "pillars of smoke," the "Sun turned to darkness," and the "Moon into blood," occurred at Pentecost. But all those things will happen before "The Great and Terrible Day of the Lord."

The conversion of the Jewish Nation will be sealed with a great outpouring of the Holy Spirit. Whether this shall be universal, or only upon Israel is not clear. The original prophecy in Joel was given to Israel, and its partial fulfillment at Pentecost seems to have been limited to them. The knowledge of the Lord, however, will be world-wide, and "it shall come to pass that ten men of all languages and nations shall take hold of the skirt of him that is a **Jew**, saying, **We will go with you; for we have heard that God is with you.**" Zech. 8:22, 23. There will be one "universal religion" in that day. Malachi 1:11. The "Shekinah Glory" that departed from the Temple at the time of the Babylonian Captivity (Ezek. 10:18-20; 11:22, 23), will again take up its residence in the "New Temple." Ezek. 43:1-5.

4. The Character of the Millennium.

(1.) Satan Bound. Rev. 20:1-3.

That man may be "without excuse" God is going to subject him to a final test under the most favorable circumstances. Man has charged his fall and continuance in sin to Satan. "Take him away," he cries, "paralyze his power; cripple his malignant activity; bind and imprison him and deliver us from his dominating influence, and then you will see that man is radically good and virtuous and is simply the victim of an unfavorable environment."

God answers it shall be done. Satan shall be bound and imprisoned so that he can no longer deceive men, and lest man shall say that sinful habits are too deeply rooted to be soon eradicated the test shall last for a **Thousand Years,** and man shall have during that period of probation all the blessed influences of the **Holy Spirit** and the presence of **Christ Himself.**

Man has never known and therefore cannot conceive what this world would be like free from Satanic influence. It would certainly be a marvelously different world. There would be no one to stir up hate and passion, and engender strife and turmoil. True, man would still have an evil heart of unbelief to contend against, but it would be like a magazine of gunpowder without a spark to ignite it. That the evil heart of man has not been eradicated will be evident when at the close of the Millennium Satan is loosed and finds no difficulty in deceiving the nations. Rev. 20:8.

During the Millennium the "Prince of the Powers of the Air" will be "dethroned" and the "Prince of Peace" "enthroned." When the "Great Red Dragon" (Satan) is cast out of the Heavenlies there will be cast out with him all the "Principalities and Powers" and "Age Rulers of Darkness" (Eph. 6:12), and the Heavens which now are "not clean" in His sight (Job. 15:15), will be "cleansed" of all Evil Powers.

There will be no universal peace until the Lord comes back. Then the nations will beat their swords into "plow-shares" and their spears into "pruning-hooks" (Mich. 4:3, 4), and shall be no longer impoverished by the enormous tax on their revenues for the support of armies and navies and the building of "Dreadnoughts." Then ships of war and armorclad vessels will rust and rot in the navy yards and guns and cannon will be recast into implements of agriculture. The great armies of earth will be disbanded, and in the pursuits of peace and the tilling of the soil, the depleted treasuries of the world will be replenished. There will be little if any political graft. Corporations and combines will not be run in restraint of trade, and there will be no entailed estates if the law of the "Year of Jubilee" is re-established. Lev. 25:8-17. Num. 36:4.

(2.) The Revival of the Land of Palestine.

The Land of Palestine when it was first occupied by the Children of Israel under Joshua, was a land of "milk" and "honey" and of "all manner of fruits," and its soil brought forth "abundantly," and this continued as long as the Children of Israel kept its Sabbaths. But God had warned them that if they did not obey Him and turned aside to worship other Gods He would shut up the heavens and the harvests would fail. Deut. 11:13-17. Palestine today has the same fertile soil it had in Joshua's time, but it lacks rain and irrigation. God has withheld the "early" and "latter" rain, but they are now becoming more frequent and copious. The "early" rain falls in October and November, and prepares the land for ploughing and sowing; the "latter" rain falls in April and May and insures a good crop.

In the Millennium the Land of Palestine will be restored to its former fertility. This will be aided not only by the rains, but by numerous rivers and streams that shall flow from the "New River" that shall have its source in the Sanctuary.

> "It shall come to pass in **That Day** (Millennium) that the **mountains shall drop new wine**, and the **hills shall flow with milk**, and all the **Rivers of Judah** (where the New River will be) shall **flow with waters**, and a **fountain shall come forth of the House of the Lord**, and shall water the **Valley of Shittim**," the country about the Dead Sea. Joel 3:18.

The "mountains dropping new wine," and the "hills flowing with milk," are figures of speech declaring that the mountain sides will be covered with vineyards from which an abundance of wine shall be obtained, and that the pasture lands will be so productive that they will sustain vast herds of milk cattle.

The harvests will be so great and abundant that the ploughman will "overtake the reaper," and the treader of grapes him that "soweth seed." Amos 9:13.

> "The wilderness and the solitary place shall be glad for them; and the desert shall rejoice, and blossom as the rose." Isa. 35:1.
>
> "Instead of the thorn shall come up the fir-tree, and instead of the briar shall come up the myrtle tree; and it shall be to the Lord for a name, for an everlasting sign that shall not be cut off." Isa. 55:13.
>
> "**Then** shall the earth yield her increase." Psa. 67:6.
>
> "And the floors shall be **full of wheat**, and the vats shall **overflow with wine and oil**. And I will **restore to you the years that the locust hath eaten**, the cankerworm and the caterpillar, and the

palmerworm, my great army which I sent among you. And ye shall **eat in plenty** and be **satisfied,** and praise the name of the Lord your God that hath dealt wondrously with you; and **My People** (the Jews) shall never be ashamed." Joel 2: 24-26.

(3.) There Will Be Changes in the Animal Kingdom.

"The wolf also shall dwell with the lamb, and the leopard shall lie down with the kid; and the calf and the young lion and the fatling together; and a little child shall lead them. And the cow and the bear shall feed; their young ones shall lie down together, and the lion shall eat straw like the ox. And the sucking child shall play on the hole of the asp and the weaned child shall put his hand on the cockatrice's den. They shall not hurt nor destroy in all my holy mountain (Jerusalem), for the earth shall be full of the knowledge of the Lord, as the waters cover the sea." Isa. 11: 6-9.

We cannot spiritualize these words. This was the character of these animals in Eden before the Fall, and in the Ark. The ferocity of the brute creation is the outcome of the "Fall of Man." While the context seems to imply that this change in the brute creation has reference to the "Millennial Earth," where it may be partially true, yet the fact that the Edenic condition of the earth is not to be restored until the appearance of the New Earth may postpone the fulfillment of this prophecy until then.

The Apostle Paul says—

"We know that the **Whole Creation** groaneth and travaileth in pain together until now. . . . Waiting for the adoption, to wit, the **Redemption of Our Body.**" Rom. 8: 23.

That is, until the human race is redeemed from the results of the "Fall, and fitted to occupy the New Earth, Creation must wait for its restoration to 'Edenic conditions'."

(4.) Human Life Will Be Prolonged.

"There shall be no more thence an **infant of days,** . . . for the child shall die a **hundred years old.**" Isa. 65: 20.

That is, a person dying 100 years old shall be considered only a child. Therefore a man, to be called a man, must live for several hundred years.

"For as the days of a **Tree** (oak tree) are the days of my people." Isa. 65: 22.

"Thus saith the Lord of Hosts: There shall yet **Old Men** and **Old Women** dwell in the streets of Jerusalem, and every man with his staff in his hand **For Very Age.**" Zech. 8: 4.

Patriarchal Years will be restored, and men shall live as long as they did before the Flood. This may be due to some climatic or atmospheric change, or to the healing or life-giving qualities of the water of the "New River" that shall flow from the "Sanctuary," and the leaves of the trees that line the banks of the River, which shall be for "Medicine." Ezek. 47: 12.

(5.) There Will Be a Sevenfold Increase of Light.

"Moreover the light of the moon shall be as the light of the sun, and the light of the sun shall be **SEVENFOLD** as the light of **seven days,** in the day that the Lord bindeth up the breach of His people, and healeth the stroke of their wound." Isa. 30: 26.

The "atmosphere" of the Millennial Earth will be of such a character as to make moonlight nights as bright as day, and the days seven times as bright.

"The sun shall be no more thy light by day: neither for brightness shall the moon give light unto; but the Lord Shall Be Unto Thee An Everlasting Light, and Thy God Thy Glory." Isa. 60: 19-20.

This may refer to that part of the Holy Land that shall be illuminated by the "Shekinah Glory," where it will make no difference whether the sun shines or not. It will have its complete fulfillment when the nations of the New Earth shall walk in the Light of the New Jerusalem. Rev. 21: 23-24.

Israel's Mission during the "Millennial Age" will be that of "blessing" to the Gentile nations. Of the nation of Israel, that has never as yet been a leading nation. God says—

"I will make thee the Head, and not the Tail." Deu. 28: 13.

The nations today are a "Headless" body. There is no "Chief Nation" today. In that day Israel shall be the "Chief Nation," and the nation that will not serve her shall perish. Isa. 60: 12.

But those nations will only be kept in subjection by the "Iron Rule" of Christ. This is brought out in the "Messianic Psalm," Psa. 2: 6-9. It is very clear that during the "Millennial Age" the "will of God" will not be done on earth as it is done in heaven. The peace among the nations will be more superficial than real. It will only be feigned obedience, more the result of fear than of love. As the "afternoon" of that long "Millennial Day" draws to a close the shadows deepen.

4. SATAN LOOSED.
Rev. 20: 7-8.

"And when the Thousand Years are expired, Satan shall be loosed out of his prison, and shall go out to deceive the nations which are in the four quarters of the earth, Gog and Magog, to gather them together to battle: the number of whom is as the sand of the sea. And they went up on the breadth of the earth, and compassed the 'Camp of the Saints' about, and the Beloved City (Jerusalem): and fire came down from God out of heaven, and devoured them."

As the evening shadows of the Millennial Day fall, the Angel who imprisoned Satan will unlock the "prison house" of the "Bottomless Pit," and Satan will come forth embittered by his forced confinement to vent his anger upon the people of God, a refutation of the claim that the miseries of perdition will lead to repentance. Satan will still be the same malignant being after his 1000 years of confinement that he was before. His hatred against God and His people will be unquenched.

FIFTH DOOM.
GOG AND MAGOG.

As soon as Satan is loosed from his prison in the "Bottomless Pit," he will find a vast multitude ready to believe his lie, and to serve and obey him. He will gather them from the "Four Quarters of the

Earth" to battle. They will be in number as the "sand of the sea." Rev. 20:8-9. The revolt will be **Worldwide,** and will mean the **Mobilizing of Vast Armies.** Satan will conduct them across the "Breadth of the Earth" until they compass the "Camp of the Saints" (the Holy Land), and lay siege once more to the "Beloved City." From this we see that the unregenerate heart is like a powder magazine, all it needs is a match to set it off, and Satan when freed will be that match. This the **"last war"** that this world shall ever see, will be bloodless, for the vast armies of Satan shall be destroyed by **FIRE.**

From this we see that the "Millennial Dispensation," like all the six Dispensations before it, will end in **failure.** God will have tested man in "Innocence," under "Conscience," under "Self-Government," under the "Headship of the Family," under "Law," under "Grace," and finally under the influence of the "Holy Spirit," free from Satanic influences, and under them all he will prove himself to be hopelessly, incurably and incorrigibly bad.

If after a 1000 years of the **Presence of the King,** and of universal peace and blessing, man still persists in rebelling against his Maker, what will there be left for God to do? Humanly speaking, there will seem to be nothing for God to do but destroy the human race. To send another Flood and wipe out mankind. But this He cannot do, for He promised Noah that He would never again destroy the earth with a flood of waters. Gen. 9:11. But do something He must, so He is going to purge the earth with **Fire.** 2. Pet. 3:7.

SIXTH DOOM.

SATAN.

Rev. 20:10.

"And the 'Devil' that deceived them was cast into the 'LAKE OF FIRE AND BRIMSTONE,' where the 'Beast' and the False Prophet are, and shall be **tormented day and night for ever and ever.**"

As punishment for his final act of Rebellion, Satan shall be seized, probably by the same Angel that chained him, and hurled into the "LAKE OF FIRE," where he will find alive and waiting for him the "Beast" and the "False Prophet" who were cast therein a 1000 years before. This shows that there is no such thing as annihilation. The "Lake of Fire" was prepared for the Devil and his angels (Matt. 25:41), not to consume them in, for God could do that with **fire from heaven,** but to **PUNISH THEM IN;** and all those whose names are not written in the "Book of Life" will go to the same place to spend eternity. The reason why Satan does not want people to read and study the Book of Revelation is, because he does not want the world to know that there is an end to his power.

Only the **"bodies"** of those who perish in this last great war will be destroyed by fire, their **"souls"** and **"spirits"** will go to the "Hell Compartment" of the "Underworld" to come out at the Resurrection

of the Wicked dead and appear at the "Great White Throne Judgment," and be sentenced to the "SECOND DEATH," which, as we
have seen, means that they must spend eternity without a material
body in the "Lake of Fire." See Chart of "The Underworld."

SEVENTH DOOM.

THE WICKED DEAD.
"THE GREAT WHITE THRONE JUDGMENT."
Rev. 20: 11-15.

"And I saw a GREAT WHITE THRONE, and Him that
sat on it, from whose face the earth and the heaven (atmosphere
of our earth) fled away; and there was found no place for them.
And I saw the dead, small and great, stand before God: and the
Books were opened: and another Book was opened, which is the
'BOOK OF LIFE': and the dead were judged out of those things
which were written in the Books, according to their works. And
the sea gave up the dead which were in it: and 'Death' and 'Hell'
delivered up the dead which were in them: and they were judged
every man according to their works. And 'Death' and 'Hell'
were cast into the 'LAKE OF FIRE.' This is the 'SECOND
DEATH.' And whosoever was not found written in the 'BOOK
OF LIFE' was cast into the 'LAKE OF FIRE'."

This is not a "General Judgment," for there is no such thing in
the Scriptures. The Church is not in this Judgment, nor is Israel,
for both have been already judged. The Church was Judged at the
"Judgment Seat of Christ," and Israel was Judged during the "Tribulation Period." This is a Judgment of the DEAD ONLY, and is an
entirely different Judgment from that of "The Nations" recorded in
Matt. 25: 31-46. That is on the earth, this is in Heaven. That is
of the "Living Nations," as Nations, this is of the DEAD. That is
for the Nations' treatment of Christ's brethren, the Jews, this is for
WORKS. There no "books" are opened, here they are. No "Book
of Life" is mentioned there, here there is. That Judgment was before
the Millennium, when Christ shall sit on the "Throne of His Glory,"
and is to find out what Nations shall have a right to enter into the
"Millennial Kingdom," this is after the Millennium when Christ shall
sit on the "Great White Throne." The two Judgments are entirely
separate as to time, place, basis of judgment and result. See Chart
of the Resurrections and Judgments.

In this Judgment "Death" and "Hell" are personified. By
"Death" we are to understand the "Grave" which holds the "body"
until the Resurrection; by "Hell," the Compartment of the "Underworld" or "HADES," where the "souls" of the Wicked Dead remain
until the Resurrection of the Wicked. That both "Death" and "Hell"
are cast into the "LAKE OF FIRE" signifies that Death and Sin
will not be found on the New Earth.

The "Great White Throne" will not be on the earth, for the
"Great White Throne Judgment" will take place during the "Renovation of the Earth By Fire," for the "Renovation of the Earth" is
reserved or kept until the time of that Judgment, which Peter calls
"The Day of Judgment and Perdition of Ungodly Men" (2. Pet. 3:7),

because the Judgment of the "Great White Throne" is the Judgment of the **WICKED DEAD.** All the Righteous dead arose at the "First Resurrection." If any Righteous die between the "First Resurrection" and the "Resurrection of the Wicked," or "Second Resurrection," they will rise with the **Wicked dead** at that Resurrection. The words—"Whosoever was not found written in the '**Book of Life**'," implies that there will be **some,** probably very few in comparison, Righteous at the "Second Resurrection." At the close of the Millennium, and just before the "Renovation of the Earth By Fire," the living Righteous will probably be translated, and the living Wicked or Ungodly will be destroyed in the flames that will consume the Earth's atmosphere and exterior surface.

The Wicked or Ungodly will not be judged to see whether they are **entitled** to "Eternal Life," but to ascertain the "**degree**" of their punishment. The sad feature of this Judgment will be that there will be many kind and lovable people there who were not saved, and who will be classed among the "**ungodly**" because they rejected Christ as a Saviour. The "**Books**" will be opened in which the "Recording Angel" has kept a **record** of every person's life, and they will be Judged every man **according to his** "**Works.**" Some will be sentenced to a more severe punishment than others, but none will escape. The worst of all is, that those who were not so bad must spend Eternity with the ungodly, and that in the "Lake of Fire." Their punishment includes the "**Second Death,**" which means, as we have seen, that they shall lose their resurrection body, in which they were Judged and become "**disembodied spirits**" again, and so exist in the "**Lake of Fire**" FOREVER.

What a Judgment Scene that will be. There will be Cain and the wicked Antediluvians; the inhabitants of Sodom and Gomorrah; Pharoah, Ahab, Jezebel, Judas and all those Scribes and Pharisees and Chief Priests who caused the Crucifixion of our Lord, and did not repent, and Ananias and Sapphira, and the great host of the wicked and rejectors of Christ of all nations and ages.

The "**Fallen Angels**" (not the Devil's angels) who are "**reserved in everlasting chains under darkness,**" will be Judged at this time, which Jude calls the "**Judgment of the GREAT DAY.**" Jude 6. When this Judgment is over the Devil and his angels, and all the ungodly, will have been consigned to the "Lake of Fire," and the Universe purged of all evil, and righteousness shall **reign supreme** on the New Earth.

The Seven New Things

1. THE NEW HEAVEN.
Rev. 21:1.

"And I saw a **NEW HEAVEN**."

As the word **HEAVEN** is here, and in Gen. 1:1, in the singular number, it will clarify matters to limit this creative act to our own planet, rather than the whole of the sidereal heavens, or the starry spaces of the Universe. By a new **heaven** then we are to understand a new atmosphere for the new earth."

2. THE NEW EARTH.
Rev. 21:1.

"And I saw a new Heaven and a **NEW EARTH**: for the first heaven and the first earth were passed away; and there was **no more sea.**"

The first heaven and the first earth were created in the dateless past. The Scriptures begin with the sublime declaration—"In the **beginning** God **CREATED** the heaven and the earth." Gen. 1:1. The second verse of Gen. 1, records that "the earth was **without form and void**; and **darkness was upon the face of the deep.**" That this earth was not originally created **"formless and void"** is clear from Isa. 45:18 (R. V.). "Thus saith the Lord that created the heavens; He is God; that formed the earth and made it; He established it, He created it **not a waste**, He formed it to be inhabited." See also Jer. 4:23-26. What caused the earth to become a **waste** after its original creation is not expressly stated. Some awful catastrophe must have befallen it. It is clear from the account of the Fall of Adam and Eve that sin existed before man was created. The inference is from Ezek. 28:12-19, and Isa. 14:12-14, that when the earth was originally created that Satan was placed in charge of it, and that he and his angels rebelled and led astray the inhabitants of the Original Earth, and that the Pre-Adamite race are now the demons who as they are permitted liberty seek to re-embody themselves in human beings that they may again dwell on the earth. It is clear that the Original Earth was inhabited, or God would not have blessed Adam and Eve and said—"Be fruitful and multiply and **REPLENISH the Earth.**" Gen. 1:28. It does not follow however that those inhabitants were human beings like ourselves. No human remains have been found ante-dating the creation of man.

Peter speaks of the Original Earth as the—"World that then **WAS**, that, being **OVERFLOWED WITH WATER, perished.**" 2. Pet. 3:6. It is clear that Peter does not refer here to Noah's Flood, for the world of Noah's day did **not perish**, and Peter goes on to add that—"The heavens and the earth **WHICH ARE NOW** (that is, have been in existence since the restoration of the earth as described in Gen. 1:3-31), by the same word are kept in store, **RESERVED UNTO FIRE**" (2 Pet. 3:7), nevertheless he adds, "we look for a

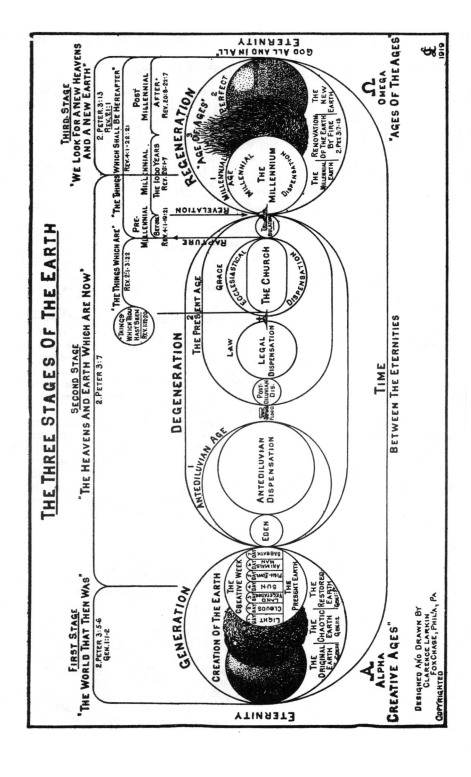

THE THREE STAGES OF THE EARTH

FIRST STAGE
"THE WORLD THAT THEN WAS"
2.Peter 3:5-6
Gen.1:1-2

SECOND STAGE
"THE HEAVENS AND EARTH WHICH ARE NOW"
2.Peter 3:7

THIRD STAGE
"WE LOOK FOR A NEW HEAVENS AND A NEW EARTH"
2.Peter.3:13

GOD ALL AND IN ALL
ETERNITY

REGENERATION

"AGE OF THE AGES"
PERFECT

2.Peter.3:13 Rev.21:1
"The Things Which Shall Be Hereafter"
Rev.4:1-22:21
POST MILLENNIAL
AFTER
Rev.20:6-22:7

THE NEW EARTH

THE RENOVATION, MILLENNIAL OF THE EARTH BY FIRE
2.Pet.3:7-13

MILLENNIAL AGE
MILLENNIAL DISPENSATION
THE MILLENNIUM
The 1000 Years Rev.20:1-7
MILLENNIAL
Rev.4:1-22:21

PRE-MILLENNIAL
"The Things Which Are"
Rev.2:1-3:22
Before Rev.4:1-19:21

REVELATION
RAPTURE
TRIBULATION

THE PRESENT AGE

GRACE
ECCLESIASTICAL DISPENSATION
THE CHURCH

LAW
LEGAL DISPENSATION

"THE THINGS WHICH ARE"
Rev.2:1-3:22

THINGS WHICH THOU HAST SEEN Rev.1:1-20

Post-Diluvian Dis.
Flood

DEGENERATION

ANTEDILUVIAN AGE
ANTEDILUVIAN DISPENSATION

EDEN

GENERATION
CREATION OF THE EARTH

THE CREATIVE WEEK
SABBATH
MAN
ANIMALS
FISH-FOWL
LAND VEGETATION
SUN
CLOUDS
LIGHT
Gen.1:1

THE PRESENT EARTH

THE ORIGINAL EARTH Gen.1:1
THE CHAOTIC EARTH Gen.1:2
THE RESTORED EARTH Gen.1:2

ALPHA
CREATIVE AGES

TIME
BETWEEN THE ETERNITIES

ETERNITY

OMEGA
"AGES OF THE AGES"

DESIGNED AND DRAWN BY
CLARENCE LARKIN
FOX CHASE, PHILA., PA.
COPYRIGHTED

1919

NEW HEAVEN AND A NEW EARTH." 2. Pet. 3:13. These words of Peter reveal the fact that this Earth is to pass through 3 stages. First the Original Earth that "perished" by WATER. Second the Earth that is now, that is to be renovated or cleansed by FIRE. And the New Earth that is to exist forever. See the Chart "The Three Stages of the Earth."

There can be no question but what the Earth in its original formation required millions of years. There is ample time in the statement of Gen. 1:1 that—"In the BEGINNING God 'created' the heaven and the earth," for all the "Geologic Ages" that science declares were necessary for the creation of the Earth. There is no conflict between the Bible and Science as to the time occupied in the formation of the Earth.

How long a period elapsed between the Creation of the Earth and its becoming "formless and void" we do not know, neither do we know how long it continued in that condition, but when the time came in the purpose of God to restore it to a habitable state, and make it fit for the abode of the human race, He did it in six periods of longer or shorter duration. These "Periods" were six in number, and with the seventh or Sabbatic Period, are called the "Creative Week."

These "Six Periods" do not describe or include the original creation. The word "CREATE" is not mentioned after Gen. 1:1 until verse 21, which describes the work of the Fifth Day. God did not "create light" on the First Day. He simply said—"let there be light," as one would say "turn on the light."

On the Second Day God simply divided the waters by providing clouds to hold the moisture of the atmosphere.

The work of the Third Day is "twofold," the emergence of the land from the sea, and the reappearance of vegetable life. This was not a new creation but a RESURRECTION. The earth rises up out of the "Waters of Death," and seeds, and the roots of plants and herbs are called upon to germinate and sprout and grow as they did before the catastrophe that submerged the Primeval Earth. If that catastrophe was what we know as the "Glacial Period" the resurrection of plant life no more required a "creative act" than vegetation does in the spring of the year after the winter is over. That this is what really happened is clear from Gen. 1:11-12, where it says, "Let the earth bring forth grass, the herb yielding seed, and the fruit tree yielding fruit after his kind, whose seed is IN ITSELF, UPON (in) THE EARTH." That is, the seed was already in the earth, having been buried by the flood that swept over the Primeval Earth, and, being indestructible, it only needed the proper condition to spring up and cover the earth with verdure. This reveals the fact that the Primeval Earth was clothed with verdure, and covered with plants and trees.

The appearance of the Sun and Moon on the Fourth Day was not a new creation. They had existed in connection with the Primeval Earth and had not been destroyed when it was made waste. The word translated "made" in the 16th verse is not the same word as is translated "created" in verse one, and does not imply a "creative act." What is meant is that the clouds broke away that up to this time had shrouded the earth and permitted the Sun and Moon to be seen, and that from that time they were appointed to measure the days, and years, and seasons as we have them today. In other words, on the Fourth Day "Time" in contrast with "eternity" began.

The work of the Fifth Day was the "CREATION" of fish and fowl. Here is the first time we come across the word "create" since we read of the original creation of the Earth in verse one. This shows that all "animal life" was destroyed in the catastrophe that overtook the Primeval Earth. We have traces of this animal life in the fossil remains of birds and animals found in the earth. If scientists will relegate fossils and the remains of mammoth animals, etc., to the period of the Primeval Earth there will be no conflict between Science and the Genesis account of Creation. The remains of man are never found in a "fossil state," showing that man did not exist on the Primeval Earth. Man was made for this present earth and is a "NEW" Creation.

The creative work of the Sixth Day was "twofold," that of land animals and man. These land animals were probably the same that we have today. The fact that they were created "after their kind," which expression is six times repeated, shows that they were not "evolved" from one common species. That man also was "CREATED" as man, shows that he has not descended from an "ape." Man was made in the "IMAGE OF GOD," not in the image of an "ape," and was not formed from a brute, but of the "Dust of the Earth." The fact is, there is an "IMPASSABLE GULF" between the lowest order of man and the highest type of beast that science has failed to bridge. The "Missing Link" has never been found.

That all the different species of animals were created "separately" is proven from the fact that when species are crossed their offspring are sterile. The crossing of the jackass and a mare is the mule, and a mule is a hybrid and is sterile. That the whole human race is of "one species" and had a common origin (Acts 17:26) is clear from the fact that, when the different races of the earth's inhabitants marry their offspring are not sterile but fertile. This nullifies the argument that the white race alone is the Adamic race.

Neither was Adam created a baby or a primitive savage, but a full grown man perfect in intellect and knowledge, else he could not have named the beasts of the field and the fowls of the air. And the fact that his descendants had such skill in the invention of musical instruments and mechanical devices and could build cities and towers and such a vessel as the Ark, proves that the men of Antediluvian times were men of gigantic intellect and attainments, and that instead of man having "evolved upward" he has "degenerated downward."

THE FLOOD VERSUS THE SECOND COMING.

While the Earth has had its "Baptism of Water," and is to have its "Baptism of Fire," it is worth noting that between these two Great Events there are two Minor Events that affect the structure of the Earth. The first was "the flood." At that time there were great "cataclysmic" and "climatic" changes, for the "FOUNTAINS OF THE GREAT DEEP WERE BROKEN UP." Gen. 7:11. That is, there was a subsidence of the land, that resulted in great physical changes that affected the climate of the earth, and divested the atmosphere of some of its life sustaining properties, so that the length of life was reduced from 900 to 100 years, and later to three-score years and ten.   The second "Minor Event" will be caused by the Return of the Lord Jesus Christ to the earth to set up His Millennial Kingdom.   Then the Mt. of Olives will be divided in twain, the mountains and valleys of Palestine will be leveled, the Dead Sea will be raised, and the whole contour of that part of the world will be changed. Zech. 14:4-10. Ez. 47:1-12. As a result of the "cataclysmic" and "climatic" changes thus produced, the effects of the Flood will be reversed and the life-sustaining power of the atmosphere will be restored, and human life will again be prolonged, and men shall live as long as did the people before the Flood. Isa. 65:20.

THE NEW HEAVEN AND THE NEW EARTH.

Immediately after the destruction of Satan and his armies, John says,

"I saw a 'Great White Throne' and Him that sat on it, from whose face the Earth and the Heaven (atmosphere of the earth) fled away; and there was no place for them." Rev. 20:11.

John then describes the Judgment of the "Great White Throne," and then adds—

"I saw a New Heaven; and a New Earth; for the first heaven and the first earth were passed away; and there was no more sea." Rev. 21:1.

Of such a change in this earth we are not ignorant, but John does not tell us how it is to come to pass. But the Apostle Peter does.

"But the heavens and the earth which are now, by the same word are kept in store, RESERVED UNTO FIRE against the Day of Judgment and Perdition of Ungodly Men. (The Great White Throne Judgment)—The 'Day of the Lord' will come as a thief in the night; in the which the Heavens Shall Pass Away With a Great Noise, and the Elements Shall Melt With Fervent Heat, the Earth Also and the Works That Are Therein Shall be Burned Up.

"Nevertheless we, according to His Promise (Isa. 65:17; 66:22), look for a New Heavens and a New Earth, wherein dwelleth righteousness." 2. Pet. 3:7-13.

It is clear that Peter is referring to the same event as John, for he says it is to be at the "Day of Judgment and Perdition of Ungodly Men," and that is the "Great White Throne Judgment" of the Wicked Dead.

A surface reading of the above passage would lead one to believe that the earth as a planet, and the sidereal heavens, are to be destroyed by fire and pass away. But a careful study of the Scriptures will show us that this is not so, that what is to happen is, that this present earth, and the atmosphere surrounding it, is to be Renovated by Fire, so that its exterior surface shall be completely changed, and all that sin has brought into existence, such as thorns and thistles, disease germs, insect pests, etc., shall be destroyed, and the atmosphere purified and forever freed from evil spirits and destructive agencies.

That this is the correct view of the passage is clear from Peter's words in verses 5 and 6.

"By the word of God the heavens were of old, and the earth standing out of the water and in the water; whereby the world that then was, being overflowed with water, PERISHED."

As we have seen the Apostle Peter was referring here not to the Flood, but to the Primeval Earth, which was made "formless and void" by a "Baptism of Water" that completely submerged it and destroyed all animal life.

Now as the **Framework** of the "Primeval Earth" was not destroyed by its "Watery Bath," so the Framework of the "Present Earth" is not to be destroyed by its "Baptism of Fire."

This is confirmed by the Apostle's use of the Greek word "Cosmos," which means the "land surface," the inhabitableness of the earth and not the earth as a planet. It is the exterior surface of the earth then that is to "Melt With Fervent Heat" and the "Works Therein Burnt Up." The intense heat will cause the gases in the atmosphere to explode, which the Apostle describes as the "heavens (the atmosphere) passing away with a great noise." The result will be the destruction of all animal and vegetable life, and the alteration of the earth's surface.

The Greek word "Parerchomai," translated "pass away," does not mean "termination of existence" or "annihilation," but means to pass from "one condition of existence to another." The Apostle Paul in his letter to Titus (Titus 3:5), speaking of the "Regeneration" of men, uses the same word that Jesus used when, in Matt. 19:28, He promised His Disciples that in the "Regeneration," that is in the "New Earth," they should sit on "Twelve Thrones" judging the "Twelve Tribes" of Israel. Now no one supposes that the "Regeneration of a man is his Annihilation." It is simply a **Renewing Process** by which he is brought back to the condition of man spiritually as before the Fall. The word "Restitution" in Acts 3:21, means the same thing. The "Dissolving" of which Peter speaks (2 Pet. 3:11), is the same word Jesus used when He said of the colt—"Loose him and let him go." The teaching of the Scriptures is, that "Creation" is at present in a "State of Captivity," waiting to be **Loosed from the Bondage** that sin has caused. Rom. 8:19-23.

As to the "Departing as a Scroll" of the heavens, and the "Flying Away" of the earth and heavens, of which John speaks, (Rev. 6:14; 20:11), a total disappearance of all the material worlds is not at all the idea, for he tells us that afterwards he saw—the New Jerusalem coming down out of Heaven, and nations living and walking in the Light of it on the earth, and the Kings of the Earth bringing their Glory and Honor Into It." Rev. 21:2, 24.

The Holy Spirit by Solomon said,

"One generation passeth away, and another generation cometh, but the **Earth Abideth Forever.**" Ecc. 1:4.

It is specifically promised that "the Meek shall Inherit the Earth," (Matt. 5:5), and that the Children of Israel shall dwell in it forever, (Isa. 60:21; 66:22), and if God's people are to inhabit it forever, it must EXIST FOREVER. It is clear then that this earth as a planet is not to be annihilated, but that it is to be Cleansed and Purified by Fire and made fit for the home of those peoples and nations that are to occupy it after its renovation.

This earth that has been consecrated by the Presence of the Son of God, where the costliest sacrifice that the Universe could furnish was offered up on Calvary to redeem a race, for which God has a great future, is too sacred a place to ever be blotted out or cease to exist, for it is the most cherished orb in the mind of God of all His great creation.

With the "Renovation of the Earth by Fire," Time does not end and Eternity begin, for we read in the New Testament of a

"Perfect Kingdom"

that Christ shall surrender to the Father, so that God may be "All in All." 1 Cor. 15:24-28. A Kingdom in which—

"At the name of Jesus every knee shall bow, of things in Heaven, and things in Earth, and things Under the Earth, and that every tongue shall confess that Jesus Christ IS LORD." Phil. 2:9-11.

This describes a Kingdom in which all things Celestial, Terrestrial and Infernal are to be subject to the SON OF MAN.

Now this "Perfect Kingdom" cannot be the "Millennial Kingdom," for that, as we have seen, ends in Apostasy and Rebellion. It must therefore mean another Kingdom on the Other Side of the "Millennial Kingdom," and as there is to be no other Kingdom between the "Millennial Kingdom" and the "Renovation of the Earth by Fire," it must mean a Kingdom that is to follow the "Renovation of the Earth by Fire," and that Kingdom is the Kingdom of the "New Heaven and the New Earth," which we call on the "Rightly Dividing the Word" Chart, the "Perfect Kingdom."

If, as some hold, the "Seventh Day" of the "Creative Week" corresponds to the Millennium, then we have a prophecy of the Dispensation that follows the "Renovation of the Earth" in the "Morrow After the Sabbath." Lev. 23:36.

The Seventh day of Genesis had to do with the "Old Creation," which was imperfect, but the "Eighth Day" has to do with the "New Creation," which is perfect, for it was on the "Eighth Day," or the "First Day of the week," that our Lord arose from the dead, and 50 days later, on the "Eighth Day," that the Holy Spirit was given at Pentecost. The "Eighth Day" cannot point to the Millennium, for that is represented by the "Seventh Day," neither can it point to Eternity, for a day is a Period of Time, while Eternity is Timeless. The "Eighth Day" must then point to a "period of time" between the "Renovation of the Earth" and Eternity, or what we are pleased to call the "Perfect Age."

It is also a Dispensation, called in Eph. 1:10—

"The Dispensation of the Fulness of Times."

That is, a "Full-Time Dispensation." The intimation is, that all the previous Dispensations were not "Full-Time" Dispensations, that God had to cut them short on account of sin.

As to the duration of this Dispensation of the "Fulness of Times" we are not in the dark. Israel is to have a large place in that Dispensation.

"For as the New Heavens and the New Earth, which I will make shall remain before me, saith the Lord, so shall your (Israel's) **Seed** and your **Name REMAIN.**" Isa. 66:22.

And as the duration of God's Covenant with Israel was **extended** in Deu. 7:9 to a "Thousand Generations" or 33,000 years, we have an intimation that the "Dispensation of the Fulness of Times" will last for at least that length of time.

Let us look at some of the characteristics of that Age or Dispensation.

There Will Be No Sin.

All the powers of Evil will have been expelled from the earth and imprisoned in the "Lake of Fire" forever.

The atmosphere of the New Earth will afford no lurking place for disease germs, for there shall be no more sickness or death, and health will be preserved by the use of the leaves of the "Tree of Life." The heavens shall not robe themselves in angry tempests and sombre blackness, nor flash with the thunderbolts of Divine wrath, nor cast plagues of hail on the earth, nor cause devouring floods of water or destructive wind storms. It may be that in that day "a **Mist** shall go up from the earth and water the whole face of the ground" as in Eden, for we read that there shall be—"**No More Sea,**" not that there shall not be large bodies of water, for the river that flows through the street of the New City must have an outlet, but that there shall be no great oceans.

The earth shall also put on its Edenic beauty and glory. There shall no longer be thorns and thistles, no parasites or destructive insects, and labor shall be a delight. No serpents shall hiss among its flowers, nor savage beasts lie in ambush to destroy and devour. Its sod shall not be heaped over newly made graves, nor its soil moistened with tears of sorrow and shame, or saturated with human blood in fratricidal strife. The meek shall inherit the earth, and from north to south, and from east to west, it shall blossom like the rose and be clothed with the verdure of Paradise Restored.

Rev. 21:2-8.

"And I John saw the Holy City, New Jerusalem, coming down from God out of Heaven, prepared as a bride adorned for her husband. And I heard a great voice out of Heaven saying: Behold the 'Tabernacle of God' is with men, and He will dwell with them, and they shall be His people, and God Himself shall be with them, and be their God. And God shall wipe away all tears from their eyes; and there shall be **no more death**, neither **sorrow**, nor **crying**, neither shall there be any more **pain**; for the **FORMER THINGS ARE PASSED AWAY.** And He that sat upon the Throne said, Behold, I make **all things NEW.** And He said unto me, Write: for these words are true and faithful. And He said unto me, **IT IS DONE.** I am Alpha and Omega, the beginning and the end. I will give unto him that is athirst of the Fountain of the 'Water of Life' freely. He that **overcometh** shall **inherit all things**; and I will be his God and he shall be My **son.**

But the fearful, and unbelieving, and the abominable, and murderers, and whoremongers, and socerers, and idolators, and all liars, shall have their part in the LAKE OF FIRE which burneth with FIRE and BRIMSTONE: which is the SECOND DEATH."

3. THE NEW CITY.
Rev. 21:9-23.

"And there came unto me one of the 'Seven Angels' which had the 'Seven Vials' full of the 'Seven Last Plagues,' and talked with me, saying, Come hither, I will shew thee the Bride, the LAMB'S WIFE. And he carried me away in the 'spirit' to a great and high mountain, and shewed me that Great City THE HOLY JERUSALEM, descending out of Heaven from God, having the Glory of God; and her light was like unto a stone most precious, even like a Jasper stone, clear as crystal; and had a wall great and high, and had twelve gates, and at the gates, twelve Angels, and names written thereon, which are the names of the 'Twelve Tribes' of the 'Children of Israel'; on the East three gates; on the North three gates; on the South three gates; and on the West three gates. And the wall of the City had twelve foundations, and in them the names of the 'Twelve Apostles of the Lamb.' And he that talked with me had a Golden Reed to measure the City, and the gates thereof, and the wall thereof. And the City lieth foursquare, and the length is as large as the breadth; and he measured the City with the Reed, 12,000 furlongs. The length and the breadth and the height of it are equal. And he measured the wall thereof, a 144 cubits, according to the measure of a man, that is, of the Angel. And the building of the wall of it was of Jasper; and the City was pure gold, like unto clear glass. And the foundations of the wall of the City were garnished with all manner of precious stones. The first foundation was Jasper; the second, Sapphire; the third, a Chalcedony; the fourth, an Emerald; the fifth, Sardonyx; the sixth, Sardius; the seventh, Chrysolite; the eighth, Beryl; the ninth, a Topaz; the tenth, a Chrysoprasus; the eleventh, a Jacinth; the twelfth, an Amethyst. And the twelve gates were twelve pearls; every several gate was of one pearl; and the street of the City was pure gold, as it were transparent glass. And I saw no Temple therein; for the Lord God Almighty and the Lamb are the Temple of it. And the City had no need of the Sun, neither of the Moon, to shine in it; for the Glory of God did lighten it, and the LAMB IS THE LIGHT THEREOF."

Rev. 22:5.

"And there shall be no night there: and they need no candle, neither light of the Sun: for the Lord God giveth them light; and they shall reign for ever and ever."

The Angel said to John—"Come hither, I will shew thee the Bride the LAMB'S WIFE." Some claim that because the word "WIFE" is used here, that Israel instead of the Church, is to be the Bride of Christ. But we must not forget that this offer to show John the Bride, was made after the Wedding of Christ to the Church, and at this time she was no longer the Bride but had become the WIFE of Christ, and should be thus spoken of. But instead of John being shown a Woman, he was shown a CITY, the Holy Jerusalem, and as what makes up a City is not its buildings and parks and business, but its inhabitants, it is clear that the Bride and the City are identical.

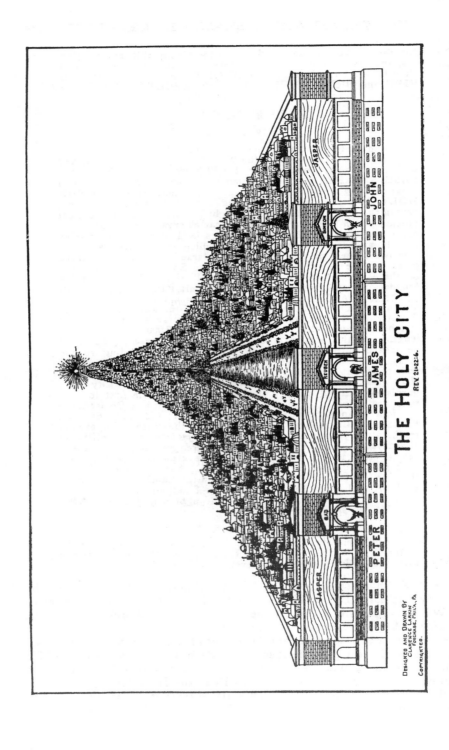

THE HOLY CITY

REV 21+22:6.

JASPER

JOHN

JAMES

PETER

JASPER

Designed and Drawn By
CLARENCE LARKIN
FOXCHASE, PHILA, PA.

Copyrighted.

That is, that the New Jerusalem is the home and residence of the Bride, that is, the same as the Bride.

From this we see that there is not only to be a **New Heaven** and a **New Earth,** there is also to be a **New City.** This City is the place Jesus said He was going back to Heaven to prepare for His Bride the Church. John 14:2-4. It is just such a place as we would expect the Divine Architect to design and build. The description of it is surpassingly grand. It is of Celestial origin. It is not Heaven itself, for it comes down "out of Heaven." No mortal hands are employed in its construction. It will take up its abode on the New Earth, and we see in this why this present Earth will have to be renovated by fire, and why there shall be "no more sea," for the New City is 12,000 furlongs, or 1500 miles square, and would reach from Maine to Florida, and from the Atlantic Seaboard 600 miles to the west of the Mississippi River. In other words would occupy more than one-half of the United States.

We are told that the length and breadth and the height of it are equal. This does not necessarily imply that it is a Cube, for there is another geometrical figure that has equal dimensions, and that is a— Pyramid. This is its probable form, for a wall 144 cubits, or 216 feet thick, could not support a wall 1500 miles high, and a wall that high would hide the pyramidal part of the City from view.

The 144 cubits (Rev. 21:17) then must refer to the "height" of the wall. In this wall are 12 gates, 3 on each side, each gate of one Pearl, and these gates are never closed.

The wall itself is of Jasper, and the foundations are garnished with all manner of precious stones. The foundations contain the names of the Twelve Apostles of the Lamb, and over the gates are the names of the Twelve Tribes of Israel.

What a magnificent spectacle such a city must present from a distance with its pyramidal top surmounted by the light of the

"Glory of God."

"For the city had no need of the sun, neither of the moon, to shine in it, for the 'Glory of God' did lighten it, and THE LAMB is THE LIGHT THEREOF." Rev. 21:23.

"And the gates of it shall not be shut at all by day, for there shall be **No Night There.**" Rev. 21:25.

This refers to the City only, and not to the outlying parts of the New Earth, for there will be day and night wherever the light of the City does not reach.

The Pyramidal part of the City will doubtless be in the centre of the City, and probably not occupy over one-half of the surface area, leaving the remainder to be divided up into boulevards and broad avenues, with numerous parks and residential sections. We are told that the City itself is of **Pure Gold, Like Unto Clear Glass.** Rev. 21:18. If this refers to the houses and homes of the inhabitants, then the redeemed are to live in palaces of **Transparent Gold,** and the streets are to be of the same material. Rev. 21:18, 21. We cannot imagine a city with such dwellings and streets to be unclean or lack beauty.

4. THE NEW NATIONS.

Rev. 21 : 24-27.

"And the **NATIONS OF THEM WHICH ARE SAVED** (the Saved Nations) shall walk in the light of it (the City): and the kings of the earth do bring their glory and honor into it. And the gates of it shall not be shut at all by day: for there shall be no night there. And they shall bring the glory and honor of the nations into it. And there shall in no wise enter into it anything that defileth, neither whatsoever worketh abomination, or maketh a lie: but they which are written in the Lamb's Book of Life."

This last verse does not imply that there will be sin on the New Earth to endanger the City, but to show that the City will never be contaminated by evil of any kind.

Outside the walls of this beautiful City, spread over the surface of the "New Earth," nations shall dwell, whose kings shall bring their glory and honor into it, but nothing that will defile or work abomination shall ever enter in through those "Gates of Pearl," for there will be no sin on that New Earth. Rev. 21 : 24-27.

Who Are to Be the Happy Inhabitants of This New Earth?

Where did the people who inhabited the earth **after the Flood** come from? They were the lineal descendants of Noah, how did they escape the Flood? They were saved in an Ark which **God Provided**. Gen. 6: 13-16. Shall not God then during the "Renovation of the Earth by Fire," in some manner, not as yet revealed, take off righteous representatives of the Millennial nations that He purposes to save, and when the earth is again fit to be the abode of men, place them back on the New Earth, that they may increase and multiply and replenish it, as Adam (Gen. 1: 27, 28), and Noah (Gen. 9: 1), were told to multiply and replenish the present earth.

If God could take off Elijah for the purpose of sending him back again to herald the Second Coming of the Lord, surely God can take off representative men from the nations and put them back again on the New Earth to repopulate it. If this is not God's plan then we have one type in the Scriptures that has no antitype, for Noah's Ark, which is a type, has no antitype unless it be this.

It is clear from the Scriptures that God does not purpose to create a new race for the New Earth. His promise as to Israel is that the descendants of Abraham shall inherit this earth for a "thousand generations," or 33,000 years; now this is not possible unless they are transplanted to the New Earth. And this is just what God has promised.

"For as the New Heavens and the New Earth, which I will make, shall remain before Me, saith the Lord, so shall Your 'Seed' and Your 'Name' REMAIN." Isa. 66: 22.

It seems clear from the presence of the Tree of Life in the Garden of Eden, that God intended the human race to populate the Earth, and when it became too thickly populated, to use the surplus population to colonize other spheres. Our "Solar System" is only in its infancy. The Earth is the only one of its planets as yet habitable. Where are the inhabitants for the other planets to come from? Think you that the planets of our Solar System, and the planets of other solar systems, of which the stars are the suns, were made simply to adorn the heavens for our little earth.   God does not plan things on a **Small Scale,** and it magnifies His power and wisdom to believe that He created man in His own likeness, a created being higher than the angels, and gifted with the power of **Procreation,** that He might by means of him populate the Universe.   This magnifies the Scheme of Redemption.   Think you that God gave His Son to die on Calvary just to redeem a **few** millions of the human race?   Why He could have blotted them out, as He probably did the Preadamite race, and created a new race, and Satan would have laughed because he had the second time blocked God's plan for the peopling of this earth.

No, God will not permit Satan to block His plan for peopling this earth with a **Sinless Human Race.**   The death of Christ was not merely to redeem a few millions of the human race, but to redeem the **Earth,** and the **Race Itself** from the curse of sin, and the dominion of Satan.

The Apostle James tells us that we are only the **"First Fruits"** of His **"Creatures."**   James 1: 18.   What then must the HARVEST BE?

The Universe is **young yet.**   We are only in the **beginning of** things, for

"Of the increase of His government and peace THERE SHALL BE NO END."   Isa. 9: 7.

When this Earth shall have gone through its "Baptism of Fire," and shall be again fit for the occupancy of man, the representatives of the "Saved Nations" (Rev. 21: 24) will be men and women in whom no taint of sin will remain, and who cannot therefore impart it to their offspring, who will be like the offspring of Adam and Eve would have been if they had not sinned.   This magnifies the whole scheme of redemption, and justifies God in the creation of the human race.

5.   THE NEW RIVER.
Rev. 22: 1.

"And he shewed me a pure 'RIVER OF WATER OF LIFE,' clear as crystal, proceeding out of the Throne of God, and of the Lamb."

The waters of earthly rivers are not crystal clear.   Many of them are muddy and contaminated with sewerage.   This wonderful river is called the River of the "Water of Life," because of its "life giving" properties.   Earthly streams have their source in some mountain spring, but the "River of Life" has its source in the Throne of God. Rev. 22: 1.

Somewhere on that "Pyramidal Mountain" in the centre of the City, probably on its summit, will rest

"The Throne of God,"

from under the seat of which shall flow down in cascades, from terrace to terrace, the crystal stream that shall feed that wonderful "River of Life."

6. THE NEW TREE OF LIFE.
Rev. 22:2.

"In the midst of the street of it, and on either side of the River, was there the 'TREE OF LIFE,' which bare twelve manner of fruits, and yielded her fruit every month: and the leaves of the Tree were for the healing of the nations."

The streets are to be lined with trees, as are also the banks of a wonderful river. These trees are not mere shade trees, but beautiful Fruit Trees, called the "TREE OF LIFE," that bear Twelve Kinds of Fruit, a different kind each month. The fruit of these trees is for Overcomers Only.

"To him that overcometh will I give to eat of the 'Tree of Life' which is in the midst of the Paradise of God." Rev. 2:7.

The leaves of the trees are for the Healing of the Nations that shall occupy the New Earth. Not that there will be any sickness, but to preserve them in health, as Adam would have been preserved in health if he had eaten of the Tree of Life in the Garden of Eden. Gen. 3:22-24.

7. THE NEW THRONE.
Rev. 22:3-4.

"And there shall be no more curse: but the THRONE OF GOD AND OF THE LAMB shall be in it; and His servants shall serve Him: and they shall see His FACE: and His NAME shall be in their foreheads."

Whoever heard of an earthly city without some place of worship, be it heathen or Christian, but the wonderful thing about the New Jerusalem is, that it has no Temple. Why need a Temple when the object of worship is present, for "The Lord God Almighty and the Lamb Are the Temple of It." In fact the whole City itself will be a Temple.

"Then the 'Tabernacle of God' shall be with men, and He will dwell with them, and they shall be His People, and God Himself shall be with them, and be their God. And God shall wipe away all tears from their eyes; and there shall be no more death, neither sorrow, nor crying, neither shall there be any more pain; for the FORMER THINGS ARE PASSED AWAY." Rev. 21:3, 4.

This means that Heaven shall have come down to Earth, and that this earth will become the RESIDENCE OF GOD.

The Great Abdication

The "Millennial Age" and the "Perfect Age," between which the Earth is Renovated by Fire, make up the "Age of Ages," which period is called the KINGDOM OF THE SON OF MAN.

At the close of the "Age of Ages" when Christ "shall have put down all rule and all authority and power, for He must reign till He hath put all enemies under his feet," then Christ as the Son of

Man, shall surrender the Kingdom to God, that God may be **ALL IN ALL.** 1 Cor. 15:24-28. This is known as **The Great Abdication.**

There have been many abdications of thrones in the world's history, but none like this. Thrones have been abdicated for various reasons. Some have been forced, others voluntary. Some on account of physical infirmity, or to secure some particular successor. But Christ will not abdicate for any of these reasons. He will abdicate because He has **Finished the Work That Was Given Him to Do as the Son of Man.** He will not surrender His **Human Nature,** but His title "Son of Man" will merge back into that of "Son of God" so that the Divine **Godhead** shall thereafter act in its **Unity,** and God shall be **"ALL IN ALL."**

The Ages of the Ages

As the "Creative Ages" were the "Alpha" Ages, these will be the "Omega" Ages. With the surrender of the "Perfect Kingdom" to the Father, what we speak of as "Time" ceases, and the "Eternal Ages," called the "Ages of the Ages" begin. They correspond to what the Apostle Paul in his Letter to the Ephesians calls the "Ages to Come." Eph. 2:7. And John in the Book of Revelation says that the "Devil" and the "Beast" and the "False Prophet" shall be tormented day and night **forever and ever,** or for the "Aions" of the "Aions," the "Ages of the Ages," Rev. 20:10, and that the "Servants of God" shall reign for the same period. Rev. 22:5.

What those "Ages of Ages" shall reveal of the Plan and Purpose of God we do not know, but if we are His we shall live to know, and possibly take part in their development. What we do know is that we are but in the beginning of things, and as concerning the "Ages," Eternity is still young.

The Epilogue or
Final Testimony and Warnings
Rev. 22:6-21.

"And he said unto me, These sayings are faithful and true; and the Lord God of the Holy Prophets sent His Angel to shew unto His Servants the Things which must **shortly be done.** Behold, I come quickly: blessed is he that keepeth the **sayings of the prophecy of this BOOK.**

"And I John saw these things, and heard them. And when I had heard and seen, I fell down to worship before the feet of the Angel which shewed me these things. Then saith he unto me, See thou do it not: for I am thy Fellowservant, and of the Brethern the Prophets, and of them which keep the sayings of this Book: worship **GOD.**

"And he saith unto me. **Seal not** the sayings of **THE PROPHECY OF THIS BOOK:** for the **TIME IS AT HAND.**

He that is **unjust,** let him be **unjust still:** and he which is **filthy,** let him be **filthy still:** and he that is **righteous,** let him be **righteous still:** and he that is **holy,** let him be **holy still.** And, behold, I come quickly; and my reward is with me, to give every man according as his work shall be. I am **ALPHA** and **OMEGA,** the **Beginning** and the **End,** the **First** and the **Last.**

"Blessed are they that do His Commandments, that they may have right to the **'TREE OF LIFE,'** and may enter in through the gates into the City. For without are **dogs,** and **sorcerers,** and **whoremongers,** and **murderers** and **idolators,** and whosoever **loveth and maketh a lie.**

"I Jesus have sent mine Angel to testify unto you these things in the Churches. I am the **Root** and the **Offspring** of David, and the BRIGHT AND MORNING STAR.

"And the **SPIRIT** (Holy Spirit) and the **BRIDE** (the Church, still on the earth) say **COME.** And let him that is **athirst COME.** And **WHOSOEVER WILL,** let him take of the 'Water of Life' **FREELY.**

"For I testify unto every man that **heareth** the words of the PROPHECY OF THIS BOOK. If any man shall **ADD UNTO THESE THINGS, GOD SHALL ADD UNTO HIM THE PLAGUES THAT ARE WRITTEN IN THIS BOOK:** and if any man shall **TAKE AWAY FROM THE WORDS OF THE BOOK OF THIS PROPHECY, GOD SHALL TAKE AWAY HIS PART OUT OF THE BOOK OF LIFE AND OUT OF THE HOLY CITY, AND FROM THE THINGS WHICH ARE WRITTEN IN THIS BOOK.**

"He which testifieth these things, saith, Surely **I COME QUICKLY. AMEN. EVEN SO, COME LORD JESUS.**

"THE GRACE OF OUR LORD JESUS CHRIST BE WITH YOU ALL. AMEN."

Dispensational Truth

or

God's Plan and Purpose in the Ages

The book contains 34 chapters of descriptive matter and 42 splendid prophetical charts 9x20 inches, 48 one page charts, and 15 cuts. The charts and cuts are interspersed through the descriptive matter. There are 300 columns of reading matter, each column 4½x8½ inches, equivalent to any ordinary book of 450 pages. The charts are unique, simple, clear, uniform in style, and present every phase of "Dispensational Truth." The book is bound in cloth, atlas form, size 11x11 inches, and the large charts spread over two pages.

The book is the result of 30 years' study of "Dispensational Truth". It is sane. Not a "time-setter." Contains no speculative matter. Is not made up of quotations from other writers, but is based solely on the Scriptures from the "Futurist" standpoint. It is of permanent value, and a standard authority on "Dispensational Truth," and is a mine of information on "Prophetic Truth" for the busy pastor, evangelist, Bible teacher and all lovers of the Word.

This work is not an experiment. Is no longer in its elementary form, but has been revised and enlarged and is now in its twelfth edition, is widely circulated over the world, is highly commended by leading prophetical scholars, and is being used in many Bible Schools. The author has been a preacher and teacher of "Dispensational Truth" for 35 years, and has put into printed form the result of his studies, with the hope that they may be a blessing to the world.

TITLES OF THE CHAPTERS

The Prophetic Word—Pre-Millenialism—Mountain Peaks of Prophecy—The Second Coming of Christ—Rightly Dividing the Word—The Present Evil World—The Dispensational Work of Christ—The Dispensational Work of the Holy Spirit—The Jews—The Gentiles—The Church—The King—The Kingdom—The Sprit World—Spiritism—The Resurrections—The Judgments—Satan—Antichrist—The Satanic Trinity—The Four Gospels—The Seven Churches—The Tribulation—Babylon The Great—Renovation of the Earth—The Covenants—The Mysteries—Types and Antitypes—The Feasts of the Lord—The Offerings—The Three Trees to Which Israel is Compared in the Scriptures—The Dispensational Teaching of the Great Pyramid—Scripture Numerics—The Signs of the Times.

TITLES OF THE CHARTS

(Only the Prominent Ones Named)

The Ages as Viewed From Different Standpoints—The Mountain Peaks of Prophecy—The Perspective of Prophecy—The Two Comings—7000 Years of Human History—Rightly Dividing the World—Relation of Jew, Gentile and Church to Each Other—The Times and Seasons—The Creation of the Earth—Six Days of Re-Creation—7 Cosmic Phases of the Earth—Book of Genesis—The World's 7 Great Crises—The Prophetic Days of Scripture—Greater Life and Work of Christ—The Jews—Book of Exodus—The Royal Grant to Abraham—Book of Daniel—Prophetical Chronology—Daniel's Seventy Weeks—Map of Old Roman Empire—The Gentile Nations—The Church—Failure of Christianity—The King—Kingdom of God Versus Kingdom of Heaven—The Kingdom—The Church Versus the Kingdom—Kingdom of Heaven Parables—Book of Matthew—The Millennial Land—Book of Ezekiel—The Spirit World—Threefold Nature of Man—The Resurrections and Judgments—Judgment of Reward—Satan—Antichrist and "Times of the Gentiles"—The Four Gospels—When the New Testament Books Were Written—Book of Revelation—Messages to the 7 Churches—Daniel's Seventieth Week—Daniel and Revelation Compared—The Covenants—The Mysteries—Types and Antitypes—The Feasts of the Lord—The Tabernacle—Book of Leviticus—The Great Pyramid—Christ and the Saints Compared to the Heavenly Bodies—The Weeks of Scripture—The Signs of the Times.

Rightly Dividing the Word

THIS BOOK COMPARES IN VALUE WITH THE BOOK ON "DISPENSA-
TIONAL TRUTH." ITS PURPOSE IS TO "RIGHTLY DIVIDE" THE "FUNDA-
MENTAL DOCTRINES" IN A SERIES OF "CONTRASTS," AS "LAW AND
GRACE," "FAITH AND WORKS," ETC.

The author has made it the work of his ministry to preach the "Fundamentals."
This volume contains the cream and meat of his sermons and Bible lectures. The
book contains twenty-nine chapters and fifty-five charts. The charts are one-page
charts, clear and simple, and suitable for lantern slides, or biopticon, in Bible class
work. The book contains 330 pages, and is bound in cloth.

The Book of Daniel

THE CLOSING AND CROWNING WORK OF THE REV. CLARENCE LARKIN,
WITH A PICTURE OF THE AUTHOR AND A FACSIMILE OF HIS AUTOGRAPH.
The book contains 267 pages.

The Spirit World

THIS BOOK GIVES THE TEACHINGS OF THE HOLY SCRIPTURES AS TO
THE "SPIRIT WORLD." IT CONTAINS 19 CHAPTERS, AND IS ILLUSTRATED
WITH 27 PICTURES AND 17 CHARTS.

It treats of the "Powers of Good and Evil," of the "Underworld," of "Satan,"
of the "Fallen Angels," of "Demonism," of "Soul Sleep," the "Intermediate State,"
the "Resurrections" and "Judgments" and of "Heaven" and "Hell."

The Second Coming of Christ

THIS IS A "BOOKLET" OF 72 PAGES, SIZE 6x9 INCHES, AND IS ILLUS-
TRATED WITH EIGHT FINE CHARTS, 4½x8 INCHES, AND IS BOUND IN A
PAPER COVER.

This "Booklet" was written for those who desire a little treatise on the "Second
Coming" to circulate among their friends and to give to those who know nothing of
the doctrine, or who desire to know more. It gives a history of the doctrine, vividly
describes the two stages of the Coming, and points out the "Signs of the Times."
It is timely, contains no speculative matter, is no "time-setter," is of permanent value
and is a simple, clear, sane and Biblical exposition of the Blessed Hope of the
Lord's Return.

These books for Sale by

REV. CLARENCE LARKIN ESTATE

P. O. Box 334, Glenside, Pa. 19038

U. S. A.